INTERNATIONAL BUSINESS NEGOTIATION

International Business Negotiation

Principles and Practice

Barry Maude

First published 2014 by
PALGRAVE MACMILLAN

Palgrave Macmillan in the UK is an imprint of Macmillan Publishers Limited, registered in England, company number 785998,4 Crinan Street, London, N1 9XW.

Palgrave® and Macmillan® are registered trademarks in the United States, the United Kingdom, Europe and other countries

ISBN: 978–1–137–27051–1

This book is printed on paper suitable for recycling and made from fully managed and sustained forest sources. Logging, pulping and manufacturing processes are expected to conform to the environmental regulations of the country of origin.

A catalogue record for this book is available from the British Library.

A catalog record for this book is available from the Library of Congress.

Printed in Great Britain by Ashford Colour Press Ltd

Contents

v

Part 2   Practice

List of Illustrations

FIGURES

TABLES

Preface

AIMS AND SCOPE OF THE BOOK

Throughout the world, hundreds of thousands of international business deals are negotiated every day using a wide range of communication methods. Many small firms, for instance, conduct their international business negotiations by phone or over the Internet. Today, so long as a firm has access to a website, its business is international. Virtually any individual or firm in any country can participate in business transactions with the company. Today, international business negotiators do not always have to travel to another country in order to negotiate a business deal face to face. Instead, the haggling can be done by email or fax or videoconference or text messaging. Many communication technologies are available to the international business negotiator.

But irrespective of the communication technologies used, successful international business negotiation depends on the *negotiation skills* of the negotiators. These skills are essential for a wide range of activities that include international sales negotiations, international procurement negotiations, outsourcing, establishing international business partnerships, contractual relationships and so on. In all these areas, unskilful or poorly conducted negotiations can create conflict and misunderstandings and lead to the loss of potential customers and overseas business. That is why the ability to successfully plan and conduct international business negotiations is one of the single most important global business skills – and one which involves building bridges between different cultures.

Cultural differences

People from different countries often have strong and conflicting ideas about private investment, profit, the role of government, individual rights, and many other matters that may arise or be referred to during international business negotiations. That is one of the reasons why a company's negotiators need to know how to present their proposals and suggestions in ways that are culturally sensitive and ideologically acceptable to the other side. Sometimes *tact* – developed, for instance, in role plays before negotiations begin – may be all it takes to enable a manager to respond in a culturally acceptable way to the demands and preferences expressed by the other party's negotiating team.

Practical guidelines

Managers need to know the principles they should observe and the actions they should take to become competent negotiators in the international business context. *International Business Negotiation: Principles and Practice* meets this need by translating negotiation theory and research into practical guidelines for people who participate (or will participate in the future) in international business negotiations. It does so by bringing together the main aspects of international business negotiation – both "principles" and "practice" – into a single volume.

Some competing books deal only with business negotiation in general and not with *international* business negotiation. Some books cover two-party negotiation, but neglect to examine multilateral business negotiation. However, *International Business Negotiation: Principles and Practice* offers a comprehensive coverage of the subject, and provides practical guidelines to negotiators in a wide range of international business situations. What makes the book stand out from other texts is that it shows how to prepare for and effectively participate in the *main kinds* of international business negotiation. Specific kinds of negotiation which are covered in the book are

- international buying and selling negotiations,
- strategic alliance negotiations,
- international joint venture (IJV) negotiations,
- negotiations to resolve international business disputes,
- international merger and acquisition (M&A) negotiations.

The book describes the practical experiences of managers and entrepreneurs who have successfully conducted international business negotiations of various kinds in countries around the world. Yet throughout, the author's comments are grounded in relevant research and theories.

Blend of theory and practice

International Business Negotiation: Principles and Practice is an essential guide to negotiating skills required for effectively participating in the main kinds of international business negotiation in which managers become involved. The book identifies both the opportunities and the problems and pitfalls faced by international business negotiators. It examines how the problems can be reduced – by using various self-help actions, for instance, or by a change of negotiating strategy in the middle of a negotiation.

Blending theory and practice, the book refers to relevant theories and research findings, and illustrates key points with numerous examples and cases drawn from real-life negotiations. Drawing on the author's experience of negotiating and implementing consultancy and training assignments in countries around the world, *International Business Negotiation: Principles and Practice* offers practical and realistic guidelines for improving negotiation practice in a wide range of international and cross-cultural contexts.

READERSHIP

International Business Negotiation: Principles and Practice has been written for undergraduate and postgraduate business and management students, and for students in international management courses. *International Business Negotiation: Principles and Practice* is the only book on the subject that many of these readers will need to buy. The book covers all topics that students need to know about from the point of view of examinations and written assignments. Relevant theories and research are discussed.

Students will buy the book because it is a readable, non-simplistic treatment of the subject. The book presents many real-life cases and situations that the reader will readily relate to, and gives practical recommendations for participating effectively in specific kinds of international business negotiation. The book will also be read by practitioners, that is, managers and business people who participate in international business negotiations from time to time.

HOW THE BOOK IS ORGANISED

The book is organised in two parts – Principles and Practice.

Part 1: Principles

The five chapters comprising Part 1 describe what international business negotiation is and why managers need to be effective negotiators. The different components of negotiation process and the impact made by culture on negotiations are described. The many differences between domestic and international business negotiations, and between two-party and multiparty business negotiations are examined. Major issues that managers must address when conducting international business negotiations are identified.

Part 2: Practice

Part 2 presents clear and practical guidelines for effective participation in international business negotiations. Actions that negotiators can take to reach mutually acceptable agreements are described, including choosing appropriate negotiating strategies. The skills that international business negotiators need to acquire to be effective are discussed, such as the skills required to manage the cross-cultural aspects of negotiation. The most important kinds of international business negotiation are described.

Part 1: Principles

1. International Business Negotiation: An Overview
2. Culture and Negotiation
3. Negotiating Power
4. Negotiation Process
5. Multilateral Business Negotiation

Part 2: Practice

6. Negotiator Selection and Training
7. Pre-negotiation Activities
8. Negotiation Strategies
9. International Buying/Selling Negotiations
10. Alliance, IJV and International M&A Negotiations
11. Dispute Resolution

KEY FEATURES OF THE BOOK

Pedagogic method

The book is structured around short, to-the-point introductions to the theory, followed by many real-life mini-cases and situations that the reader will readily relate to. In support of the student, each chapter ends with a list of key points as well as questions for discussion and written assignments. This structure will be appreciated by students and also by lecturers, who will find it easy to design their classes around the book.

Mini-cases and longer case studies

Various difficulties and dilemmas drawn from international business negotiations in real life are presented in the form of mini-cases. Mini-cases are widely used throughout the book since by comparing and discussing several mini-cases – as opposed to a single long case study – students will have an opportunity to achieve a greater understanding of the underlying negotiation process.

A few somewhat longer case studies are also presented, which go into sufficient detail to allow students to draw conclusions about the dynamics and issues involved. Both mini-cases and longer cases are followed by questions for small-group or classroom discussion.

Summary of key points

In support of the student, each chapter ends with a summary of key points made in the chapter.

Questions for discussion and written assignments

Questions for discussion and written assignments are listed at the end of each chapter for use in classroom discussions, or to provide topics for written assignments.

Small group exercises

Working in pairs or small groups, students discuss key questions posed by the text and develop answers that can then be compared with the answers of other groups.

Graphical illustrations

Some of the concepts, theories and processes discussed in the text are also presented in graphical form. To facilitate classroom discussion, graphical illustrations that are used in the text could be presented by means of PowerPoint or overhead transparencies.

Acknowledgements

I owe thanks to many people for their interest, advice and support. In particular, I would like to thank the following: Carlos Fuentes, Paul Head, Shamal Lahouri, Jessica Mathabatha, Sarah Mlundira, Dr Chima Mordi, Tilinao Otilera, the late Dr Jan Schermer, and Dr Yunzhen Yang.

Thanks are also due to the editorial and production departments of Palgrave Macmillan, to library and IT staff at the British Library, Staffordshire University and Keele University and to the Conflict Resolution Centre, Cape Town.

Palgrave Macmillan would like to thank the Marketing Management Association for permission to reproduce Table 7.1.

Part 1
Principles

International Business Negotiation: An Overview

1

INTRODUCTION

International business has expanded rapidly in recent decades and consequently so has the frequency of business negotiations between firms in different countries. International business refers to economic activities across national boundaries, the most important of these activities being trade and foreign investment. Millions of international business deals are negotiated every day using a wide range of communication methods, including face-to-face discussions, phone calls, emails, faxes, letters, videoconferencing and virtual negotiation. Managers negotiating international business deals must be capable of using all these methods skilfully in order to achieve satisfactory outcomes.

International business negotiation is not a monolithic activity. Numerous activities are involved, such as the selling of goods and services; the purchase of raw materials and supplies; distribution activities; licensing and technology transfer agreements; franchise agreements; integrated manufacturing, cross-border mergers and acquisitions; international business alliances and joint ventures. In some negotiations government plays a prominent role as a participant or as a regulator. There are many cases of a government's refusing to approve a draft agreement on grounds of protecting the public welfare or national sovereignty.

The process of negotiation involves cooperative exchanges of information and offers between the parties. As Ghauri (2003) points out, international business negotiation is essentially a process of give and take in which the negotiators make initial offers, but then keep modifying them and making concessions in order to come close to each other and eventually to reach an agreement. Thus a satisfactory negotiated agreement depends on this process of give and take, concessions and trade-offs across issues. Trade-offs are an important part of the negotiation process. When one issue is linked to another issue cooperation is generated by mutual concession.

Weiss (2006) draws attention to important differences between micro-level and macro-level negotiations in international business. Micro-level negotiation involves bargaining between individuals and often consists of simple buying/selling transactions – numerous small-scale buying-selling transactions are carried out every day by individuals who are in business for themselves. Macro-level negotiation, on the other hand, involves bargaining between companies or between a company and a foreign government. Some macro-level negotiations are very large-scale in terms of the values and the number of issues to be resolved, and sometimes the negotiators have to deal with a complex situation that defies an easy solution. For instance, four or five companies may reach an agreement that is acceptable to the negotiators themselves, but before the agreement can come into force it must be assessed and approved within each company.

Another complication facing international business negotiators is that they must weave their way round – or at least be thoroughly aware of – the laws of two or more countries. These laws are often inconsistent. As a result, clauses may have to be inserted in the contract specifying the governing law in case of disputes between the parties, or specifying contingency arbitration arrangements in case of serious disputes arising. The negotiators also have to take into account such details as tariff structures, import regulations, fluctuating exchange rates and numerous other complicating factors. Not surprisingly, in the contracts they draw up, the devil is usually in the detail.

Much negotiation theory has been developed based on game theory and the search for optimal strategies. But approaches based on game theory and other economic models of negotiation falsely assume the rationality of the negotiators as well as that the information is complete and reliable. "Under the assumption of complete information, negotiators are assumed to be omniscient, hyperrational beings who fully know what others value. In so doing, much of the problem is assumed away" (Lax & Sebenius, 1986, 156). Such assumptions ignore the realities of real-life business negotiations, in which psychological factors and the impact of culture on negotiator behaviour are always present. The practice of international business negotiation would be strengthened if more theory-based decision tools were embedded in international business practice. Such tools would enable the negotiators to deal more effectively with the complex problems and issues that confront them.

COMMUNICATION ASPECTS OF NEGOTIATION

Communication technologies

Millions of international business deals are negotiated worldwide every day. They are carried out by managers, business people, financiers, lawyers, engineers and sales and marketing executives, among others. For all of these people, physical distance or the time difference is often an important factor in determining which communication method to use.

Many negotiations are carried out in face-to-face meetings. But, in addition, a wide range of alternative communication methods are used. Studies show, for instance, that managers are becoming adept users of communication technologies – even that they are becoming addicted to them (Munkejord, 2007). Leonardi et al. (2012) argue that using several communication technologies in combination is becoming common practice in organisations. Firms increasingly recognise that they must be capable of negotiating with foreign clients and business partners using a wide range of communication methods. Moreover, immediate responses and short replies to messages received are becoming the norm, fuelling multi-communications behaviour (Watson-Manheim & Belanger, 2007).

Communication technologies frequently used by managers and business people to conduct international business negotiations include

- text messaging,
- instant messaging,
- faxes,
- document sharing,
- letters,
- phone calls,
- emails,
- videoconferencing,
- virtual negotiation.

According to Stephens et al. (2008), company negotiators are not so much choosing between two possible methods to clinch an international business deal as deciding what *combination* of media to use. They may, for instance, decide to use a collaboration tool to communicate to a colleague information which is to be included in a presentation to a client; communicate the same information in an email attachment; and also deliver the relevant documents by hand when passing the colleague's office.

Negotiating by phone

Communication technologies can be powerful negotiating tools in international business, saving time and money. Negotiating by phone saves time and money, but carrying out a cross-border business transaction by phone can be a risky method of negotiating a deal. It is risky because uncertainties and misunderstandings may be triggered by differences in cultural norms. When negotiators from different countries meet face to face, they gain valuable insights into each other's attitudes and priorities from observing nonverbal behaviours. Nonverbal signals are harder to control than verbal messages, and so are a more reliable indicator of feelings and attitudes. But this information is lacking when negotiating by phone.

Negotiating by email, fax or letter

The expansion of global e-commerce has led to an increasing use of email in negotiating international business deals. But emails, like faxes and other impersonal communication methods, can make it difficult to establish trust and mutual understanding with a client or a business prospect in another country, and consequently make it more difficult to reach a satisfactory agreement. While phone calls and videoconferences allow negotiators to respond immediately to each other's arguments and offers, emails, letters and fax messages lack this quality. As a result, communication is blunted and deal-making opportunities may be lost.

Negotiating international business deals by email can be less successful than face-to-face negotiation, largely because of the lack of social context. In face-to-face negotiations, social context cues provide a valuable guide for negotiators about the progress of the negotiation. But an exchange of emails, by contrast, may leave managers in different countries feeling psychologically as well as geographically distant from each other.

When two negotiators are in different countries, each one needs to establish a comfort level with the other person. This can readily be done over the phone or by using Skype – but not when using email to negotiate. When interacting entirely by email, a personal relationship needs be boosted by means of friendly introductory chit-chat which recognises, for instance, the ways in which the two negotiators are similar to each other. Establishing similarity helps to ensure that a human connection is made in the absence of any face-to-face presence.

Face-to-face negotiation: Videoconferencing

Most business people eventually learn, through experience, that the surest way of building sound relationships with foreign counterparts is by means of informal, face-to-face communication. However, traditional face-to-face negotiations are an expensive option when the companies are based in different countries, since heavy travel and accommodation expenses are often incurred by at least one of the negotiating teams.

One of the advantages of videoconferencing is that it allows managers to view the nonverbal behaviours of overseas customers or business partners without having to physically travel to the location.

Virtual negotiation

Virtual negotiations are an efficient way of reaching a negotiated agreement without incurring heavy expenses. They are possible because of advances in communications technology. The negotiators communicate with each other mainly by videoconferences. Between formal sessions the negotiating teams can continue communicating with each other using email, intranet-internet systems, collaborative software, instant messaging and other electronic means.

> In an international management seminar an export sales manager explained how he successfully negotiated a contract with a state-owned company in Asia using computer-based document sharing and conference-call technology to support the bargaining.

Brett et al. (2009) interviewed negotiating teams from a wide range of sectors and found that team members, who were spread across two continents, kept in touch and decided on negotiating strategies by online chat. This helped them decide, for instance, when to reveal new information, when to make concessions and so on. While virtual sessions are usually adequate for dealing with uncomplicated aspects of an international business negotiation, face-to-face meetings improve the chances that the parties will be able to find ways of resolving complex issues that may arise.

As such examples suggest, managers must be capable of negotiating with their foreign counterparts using a wide range of communication methods. Qualities which enable them to do so include flexibility, an international outlook and cross-cultural communication skills.

Face-to-face negotiation

Electronic media are widely used to carry out international business, but most managers eventually learn that the most reliable way to build a good relationship with a foreign counterpart is by means of informal, face-to-face communication. Many opportunities for informal communication occur in the pre-negotiation stage of negotiations, when preliminary relationship-building sets the stage for an atmosphere of trust and openness during the formal negotiations.

Negotiation is essentially an interactive, relational process in which partners form expectations, engage in self-presentation and impression management tactics, and respond to each other's moves (Kumar & Patriotta, 2011). Investing in relationship building before getting down to serious bargaining can make the difference between success and failure in negotiations. For example, to be successful in negotiations with Chinese companies, Western negotiators need to spend time building relationships and winning the trust of Chinese managers and officials. Using Chinese agents and local consultants as culture guides is also helpful.

According to Nadler (2007), managers in negotiation sessions demonstrate their relationship-building ability by such micro-behaviours as

- taking turns speaking in business interactions;
- using nods and other signs of understanding during business conversations;

- unconsciously matching the verbal and nonverbal communication of the conversational partner, including tone of voice, mannerisms, posture and facial expressions.

SCOPE OF INTERNATIONAL BUSINESS NEGOTIATION

International trade and foreign investment

International business refers to economic activities across national boundaries, of which trade and foreign investment are the most important. The expansion of international business requires managers to negotiate constantly with business partners, suppliers and distributors in foreign countries, and with government officials. International business negotiation has been defined as "the deliberate interaction of two or more parties (at least one of them a business entity), originating from different nations, who are attempting to define or redefine the terms of their interdependence in a business matter" (Weiss, 1993, 270). The parties to which Weiss refers are companies and other organisations from different countries which negotiate with each other or with governments.

International business negotiation is a young field – much younger than international business itself. It is a process involving a cooperative exchange of information and give and take in which the parties modify their offers and expectations in order to come close to each other and eventually reach an agreement. It is a process of finding a solution to a common problem.

Wide-ranging activities

International business negotiations deal with numerous issues ranging from the sale of goods and services, to negotiating strategic alliances and joint ventures – all of which require a large number of issues to be negotiated and mutually acceptable solutions to be achieved. Many negotiations involve third parties – agents, consultants, subcontractors and so forth – who must also be involved in some way in negotiations. Governments are often involved. For instance, one of the negotiating parties may be influenced by its government to insist on employment opportunities, or the provision of infrastructure, being included in the agreement.

Some negotiations are relatively easy to plan and conduct – those involving a simple buying/selling agreement, for instance. Others are more complicated. A wide range of issues has to be addressed before a solution is found that is acceptable to the different negotiating teams. Manrai & Manrai (2010) identify the wide scope of specific activities that may be involved, including

- purchase of raw materials and supplies,
- distribution of products,
- advertising and market research activities,
- licensing and technology transfer agreements,

- franchise agreements,
- integrated manufacturing agreements,
- cross-border mergers and acquisitions,
- strategic business alliances and joint ventures,
- international sales of goods and services.

Government involvement

Large-scale, complex negotiations often involve third parties, such as agents, consultants, advisers, subcontractors and governments. Moreover, government plays an important role in some negotiations either as a participant or as a regulator in the background. The participation of government representatives in the discussions can make the negotiation slow and bureaucratic and affect the outcome. Sometimes government insists on last-minute changes being made to the draft agreement resulting, for instance, in employment opportunity or infrastructure development clauses being inserted in the contract. There are also many examples of a government refusing to approve the draft agreement reached by the parties on grounds of protecting the public welfare or national sovereignty.

Typical examples of international business negotiation are

- a European manufacturer and a Chinese state-owned company negotiate to set up a joint venture in China;
- a Japanese multinational enterprise (MNE) negotiates a licensing agreement with a small Korean manufacturer;
- a trading organisation in Russia negotiates a supplier agreement with a Turkish electronics group;
- two governments embark on negotiations to resolve a long-standing trade dispute.

In all these cases, poorly conducted negotiations could create misunderstanding, conflict and the loss of overseas customers and business opportunities. That is why the ability to effectively plan and conduct international business negotiations is increasing recognised as one of the single most important global business skills.

DIFFERENT TYPES OF NEGOTIATION

Domestic versus international negotiations

Some of the factors that lead to success in both domestic and international business negotiations are the same. They include, for instance,

- preparedness of the negotiators;
- negotiating skills of the negotiators;
- quality of information acquired.

But in many other ways international business negotiation differs from domestic negotiation and requires a different set of skills and capabilities – for instance, the ability to deal with complexity. Obvious complicating factors in international business negotiations are language and cultural barriers.

Major differences between domestic and international business negotiation, together with the impact made by these differences on negotiation outcomes, are examined in a later section.

Bilateral and multilateral negotiation

Multilateral negotiations are a common feature of international business, yet negotiation research focuses mainly on bilateral negotiation – the two-party (dyadic) situation. Most textbooks on negotiation are about two-party negotiation. A likely reason for this emphasis is that two-party negotiations are easier to comprehend and write about than multilateral negotiations – as well as being easier to organise and conduct.

Generally speaking, bilateral negotiation consists of tit-for-tat bargaining with a regular exchange of concessions leading to a solution. The two sides either reach an agreement or do not. Multilateral negotiations, on the other hand, involve many parties and usually multiple issues. They are more difficult to understand and describe. They are difficult to organise and conduct unless a carefully thought-out structure and procedures are imposed (e.g. scheduled meetings and timetables, report-back sessions, a nominated or elected chair, and procedures designed to facilitate orderly discussion).

In multilateral negotiations involving, say, four or more parties, consensus may be the only practical way of reaching overall agreement. An important advantage of consensus decision-making is that it encourages cooperative methods of negotiation because no one party can get what they want unless they are willing to allow other parties to achieve at least some of their negotiating goals. In practice, consensus is often considered to have been achieved when a significant number of parties are in favour of a proposal and the rest do not oppose it.

However, consensus-seeking breaks down when parties have irreconcilable and contradictory interests. Sometimes, rather than block an agreement, parties opposed to a component of the final agreement may abstain. At other times, parties opposed may decide to join a coalition of other parties which have reservations about the way the negotiation is going.

Single-issue and multiple-issue negotiations

Some negotiations focus on a single issue. What price, for instance, should be paid for a particular export order? What should be the deadline for completing an information technology (IT) project in a foreign country? Single-issue negotiations such as these are typically characterised by competitive, distributive bargaining in which one side's gain is the other side's loss (Lewicki et al., 2005).

But in many other negotiations, multiple issues have to be addressed and resolved, and generally this is achieved by the negotiators' showing a willingness to adjust their opening positions to enable an agreement to be reached which spans all the issues (Spector, 1994). Progress towards agreement typically occurs when one side makes proposals suggesting changes to the other party's negotiating position while simultaneously making changes to its own. As the example suggests, multiple-issue negotiation is essentially a process of give and take in which the negotiators keep modifying their initial proposals in order to come close to each other and eventually to reach an agreement.

When multiple issues must be resolved, this process of give and take and making concessions is essential if an agreement is to be reached. Trade-offs across issues and adding issues are also used to create joint gain. When one issue is linked to another issue, cooperation is generated by mutual concession. When additional issues are considered, this can increase the amount of total benefit to both sides and lead to an integrative agreement (Pruitt, 1983).

Micro-level and macro-level negotiations

International business negotiation is not a single, monolithic activity. Weiss (2006), for instance, distinguishes between micro-level and macro-level negotiation.

- Micro-level negotiation occurs between individuals, and is often focused on simple buying/selling transactions. Numerous small-scale buying-selling transactions are carried out every day by individuals who are in business for themselves.
- Macro-level negotiation takes place between organisations such as two international companies, or between a company and a foreign government. Some macro-level negotiations are very large in terms of the values and the number of issues dealt with.

An example of a very large macro-level negotiation is Boeing's sale of twenty-seven 787-Dreamliners to Air India in 2006. In the same year, Boeing completed negotiations for a supply contract with Japan's Toray for the carbon fibre needed to produce the aircraft. Yet the Dreamliner negotiation was just one of many thousands of large-scale international business deals negotiated in 2006. Millions of small-scale deals were also negotiated in the same year.

Some macro-level negotiations are not only very large but also extremely complex, requiring prolonged discussions about multiple issues between multiple parties.

Ready & Tessema (2009) describe a massive hydroelectric project in China which required complex preliminary negotiations, followed by full negotiations among the various parties. Major stakeholders included

- international consulting groups;
- regional and national banks;
- construction contractors;
- international and local equipment suppliers;
- provincial and central government departments.

Even after the main negotiations ended and construction of the project began, countless small-scale negotiations continued between various stakeholders. For example, two engineers from different equipment supply companies would regularly meet over a cup of coffee to discuss such matters as the specifications of an alarm system to be installed in one of the generating stations, or the dates for the arrival of some new equipment.

Sometimes in multiparty negotiations, the negotiators have to deal with a complex overall negotiating situation that defies an easy solution. For example, three or four companies may negotiate an agreement that is acceptable to the negotiators themselves. However, before the agreement can come into force, the agreement must be approved within each entity (Nikolaev, 2007).

CHALLENGES OF INTERNATIONAL BUSINESS NEGOTIATION

Cross-cultural aspect

The cross-cultural nature of international business negotiation – its defining characteristic – helps explain why it can be very difficult to reach acceptable agreements. Brett & Okumura (1998) found that in Japanese-US negotiations there was less understanding of the other party's goals and priorities than in same-culture negotiations. An agreement satisfactory to both sides was therefore more difficult to achieve.

International business negotiation differs from domestic negotiation in many important ways and requires a different set of skills and knowledge. That is why international business negotiators need to do more than simply transfer the tactics and techniques they used successfully at home to the international scene. Cultural empathy and trust-building skills are also needed. Negotiators from some parts of the world tend to distrust foreigners, which causes communication barriers to appear in negotiations. According to Fukuyama (1995), the ability to trust others is linked to economic prosperity. In rich countries there is trust because deterrents to fraud and malpractice exist in the form of financial services authorities, compliance officers and contract enforcement mechanisms. Distrust of foreigners on the other hand is a characteristic of many poor countries.

Other complications springing from the cross-cultural nature of international business include the impact made by different legal and political systems, as well as by different negotiating customs and protocols. However, agreeing on a few basic procedures at the start of international business negotiations helps answer many of the initial questions and uncertainties of the participants. Managers attending a negotiation either as a principal or as an agent usually want to know, for instance, which language will be used, who speaks and in what order, and for how long. A few simple agreed-upon procedures are always appreciated by a culturally diverse group of negotiators and advisers. With their varying approaches and expectations, simple rules and procedures help them quickly get down to solving the problem.

Hazards and difficulties

International business negotiation can be a slow and difficult process because the negotiators have to take into account such details as tariff structures, import regulations, fluctuating exchange rates and numerous other details. Failure to do so means that any agreement reached may be inconclusive and short lasting.

Salacuse (2003) identifies other complications faced by managers conducting international business negotiations. For example, there can be the following issues:

- The negotiators must take into account the laws of two or more countries, depending on the number of parties involved in the negotiation. These laws are often inconsistent. As a result, clauses may have to be inserted in the contract specifying the governing law in case of disputes between the parties, and specifying contingency arbitration arrangements in case of serious disputes arising between the parties.
- Force majeure clauses may have to be inserted in contracts allowing for contract cancellation under certain conditions – for example, in the event of international business conditions being disrupted by war or revolution.
- There may be sudden changes in the international business environment triggered, for instance, by the devaluation of a foreign currency or an increase in taxes payable by foreign investors. The result of such changes might be that the prices and payments specified in the contract are likely to result not in a profit but in a heavy loss. Such reversals are a common hazard of international business. In 2011, for instance, Toyota's vehicle sales in China rose at the slowest pace in seven years after the removal of tax breaks dented demand.

Other complications

Other complications arise from cultural differences; language issues; the need to understand the mindset of negotiating opponents; and negotiators' varying attitudes towards time.

Cultural differences

International business negotiators need cultural empathy. This is a valuable attribute because it helps negotiators see the world as their opponent sees it and allows them to anticipate the opponent's negotiating tactics and strategies. Culture also makes an impact in international business negotiations by exposing major ideological differences among participants. Managers from different countries have strong and conflicting ideas about such sensitive issues as human rights, political authority and private and public ownership. In negotiations, therefore, managers need to take care to present their proposals and recommendations in ways that are ideologically acceptable to the other side.

Language issues

International business negotiations are often carried out by people with different first languages. When this is the case, a decision has to be taken about the language in which the negotiation is to be conducted – a decision which creates winners and losers. The winners are native speakers of the language chosen. In Hong Kong, for instance, many international business negotiations are carried out in Cantonese. Cantonese speakers are therefore the winners. Native speakers of other languages are the losers as they may have difficulty presenting their proposals and ideas in what for them is a foreign language. They may also find it difficult to fully understand the arguments and proposals made by other speakers.

Mindsets

Understanding the mindset of the other side is essential for successful negotiation (Kumar, 2004). For instance, understanding the Chinese mindset will enable foreign negotiators to choose appropriate strategies to be used when negotiating with the Chinese. Important components of the Chinese mindset are ambition and self-confidence, stemming from the country's economic success, and such qualities underlie Chinese negotiating behaviour, which combines slow, deliberate decision-making and tough bargaining (Leung & Yeung, 1995). Price reductions of, say, 50 per cent may be demanded before a deal is made.

Attitudes towards time

In time-oriented cultures such as those of Western Europe and North America, meeting times are planned and adhered to. But in cultures with more flexible attitudes towards time, the starting and finishing times of business negotiating sessions sometimes turn out to be approximate. Managers in such cultures start and end sessions at flexible times, do not take lateness personally and take breaks when they seem appropriate (Guirdham, 2005). In such countries social and business matters often appear to Western negotiators to rub against each other in an almost random manner.

Case Study

MINI-CASE: Pace of negotiations

When three senior managers from an Indian manufacturing company make a business trip to the US, they are surprised by how quickly things get done. Business negotiations that would take weeks or months in India, take just a few days to complete.

Other major differences become obvious to the managers. As they point out to their American counterparts, in India many people are usually involved in making important decisions, and business deals take a long time to set up. But US managers seem to make decisions quickly. The Indians get the impression that the US managers do not need to consult their colleagues or even their boss.

Questions:

1. Why is the pacing of business negotiations in the US faster than in India? What cultural factors are involved?
2. If the Indian managers try to introduce US-style business methodths into their own company when they return to India, what problems might ey encounter?

NEGOTIATION PROCESS

Give and take

International business negotiation can be carried out through a simple exchange of emails, or by two managers making a verbal agreement when they meet at a conference. At most other times, negotiation is more formal and complicated. In all cases, however, the negotiation process consists of an exchange of information and proposals between the parties concerned. International business negotiation is essentially a process of give and take in which the parties keep modifying their offers in order to come close to each other and therefore make an agreement more likely (Ghauri, 2003).

Stages of negotiation

Many authors in the field of business agree that both international and domestic business negotiations move through a series of stages. Faure (2000) discerns four distinct stages: preliminary investigation; business proposal; contract negotiation; implementation of the agreement. Graham's (1987) model of negotiation identifies five distinct stages:

- relationship-building,
- information exchange,
- persuasion,
- concessions,
- agreement.

Relationship-building. Collectivist countries put a high value on relationships (Hofstede, 1980), and their negotiating teams usually give much time and effort to building rapport with the other negotiating team before and during negotiations.

Giving time to relationship-building can improve trust between the team and reduce the risk of conflict disrupting negotiations.

Information exchange. This is a crucial stage. Indeed, negotiators from countries such as Japan tend to view the negotiation process as primarily a way to collect information (Hendon and Hendon, 1990). With Japanese firms, preliminary information exchange may last months or years since in Japanese eyes that is the time it takes to build a trusting relationship (Laroche, 2003).

Persuasion. Hamish et al.'s (1977) analysis of UN Security Council speeches identified three major styles of persuasion in disarmament negotiations: *rational* (e.g. Americans), *emotional* (e.g. Syrians), and *ideological* (e.g. Russians). Western business negotiators often use a combination of the rational and the emotional style. For instance, they throw hard facts on the table and use them to persuade the other side to take the desired action. Asian negotiators may see this as an attempt to push them into taking up a negotiating position prematurely.

Concessions. Exchanging concessions is a key feature of negotiation dynamics (Dupont, 1996). In international business negotiations, a common tactic is to start high, then make concessions. The tactic is usually used with the idea of eliciting counter-concessions, thus moving closer to an agreement. Chinese negotiators often use concessions in this way (Chen, 1996). Overbeck et al. (2010) found that managers make more concessions to negotiators who appear to be angry than to negotiators who appear to be happy.

Agreement. For Western negotiators, a signed contract represents the closure of the negotiation, but negotiators from other parts of the world may see things differently. Japanese negotiators, for instance, usually see the goal of negotiation with a foreign company being the establishment of a long-term business relationship (Salacuse, 2003). A written contract is regarded merely as an expression of that relationship.

Visiting negotiating teams usually underestimate the time required to finalise negotiations and reach an agreement with Chinese companies. Chinese negotiators often need to coordinate with layers of hierarchical committees and officials before an agreement is authorised (Pye, 1986).

Outcomes

Specific cultures prefer certain kinds of negotiation outcomes. American negotiators, for instance, generally prefer to convince the other party about the merits of a particular solution and for a contract to be signed at the end of negotiations (Salacuse, 1998). Asian negotiators, by contrast, often prefer an outcome that reinforces relationships and cooperation. The decision-making method adopted by the negotiators at the start of negotiations (e.g. consensus, majority vote) greatly influences the nature and distribution of outcomes.

However, Brett (2001) suggests that, while negotiators from different cultures use different tactics and strategies in business negotiations, the outcomes do not differ much. The outcomes of negotiation are usually assessed in terms of their effects on the *negotiators' interests* (Lukes, 2005).

Case Study

MINI-CASE: An American in Shanghai

The chief executive officer (CEO) of a North American electronic equipment manufacturing company pays a visit to a well-known Chinese manufacturer based in Shanghai to explore the possibility of the two firms forming a business partnership. The Chinese company is very willing to discuss a possible link between the two companies. It is keen to acquire new technology to meet increasingly sophisticated customer demands, which will enable the company to boost its already strong position in the Chinese market, as well as to tap into regional and international markets.

When the American CEO arrives at the Chinese manufacturer's office in Shanghai, he finds that a formal presentation has been arranged for him, the foreign visitor. During the presentation, the Chinese general manager gives a brief introduction to his company. The Chinese interpreter translates what the general manager says word for word. The company is one of China's *second-class enterprises,* the general manager says. On hearing this, the CEO's enthusiasm for a business partnership immediately evaporates. Accordingly, as the presentation ends, the CEO leaves the building without requesting any further discussions.

The next day, the American complains about the Chinese company to a local official who has been acting as his unofficial culture guide. He is taken aback by the CEO's unfavourable comments, and explains that in China a "second-class enterprise" is a *locally owned* major state enterprise.

The official goes on to say that it could be difficult at this stage to arrange a follow-up meeting to discuss a business partnership. The reason is that the Chinese general manager has lost "face" due to the CEO's abrupt departure from the presentation which was specially arranged for him.

Source: Zhao (2000)

Questions:

1. To what extent were the Chinese interpreter and the Chinese general manager responsible for the situation that has arisen?
2. How should the CEO have handled the situation immediately following the Chinese general manager's introduction?
3. What should have been the CEO's response when the Chinese official told him that a follow-up meeting to discuss a business partnership would be "difficult" to arrange?

Comprehensive draft agreement

In theory, the negotiation process involves an exchange of information, identification of a number of options, and a movement (gradual or abrupt) towards an agreement. In practice, however, this kind of systematic process may be overridden. One of the negotiating parties may, for instance, present the other with a comprehensive *draft agreement* to serve as the basis for discussion throughout the negotiation. If the draft is accepted, then one party has in effect set the agenda for the entire negotiation and speeded movement towards the eventual agreement.

As Salacuse (1999) points out, preparing the draft agreement obliges a company's negotiating team to consult with internal and external constituencies in advance of the actual negotiation. These consultations help ensure that when the draft agreement is presented at the start of negotiations, it represents a negotiating position that has already gained widespread acceptance and support.

NEGOTIATION THEORY

Negotiation research

Much research on international business negotiations has focused on the impact made by national cultural differences – especially how culture shapes the negotiating behaviour of negotiators from different cultures and the negotiating strategies typically used. More specifically, researchers have studied culturally

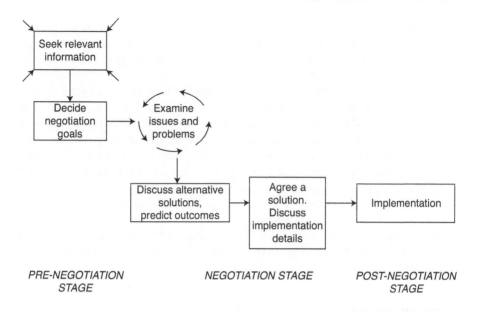

PRE-NEGOTIATION STAGE   **NEGOTIATION STAGE**   **POST-NEGOTIATION STAGE**

Figure 1.1   Using a systematic, problem-solving approach to international business negotiation

Note: Factors that lead to successful outcomes in international business negotiations include the preparedness of the negotiators, the negotiators' negotiating skills, and the quality of information acquired by the parties.

influenced patterns of *information exchange* during negotiations (Adair et al., 2005) and the use of *problem-solving techniques* (Gaham et al., 1988).

Several researchers (e.g. Leung et al., 2005) have shown that the impact of culture on negotiations is context-dependent – a finding which implies that cultural influence is best examined in the context of specific negotiating situations rather than in general terms. To date, relatively little is known about how culture influences the process of international business negotiations.

Lack of a comprehensive theory

Although negotiation theory draws heavily on a wide range of established disciplines (e.g. sociology, economics, social psychology, mathematics and management), a comprehensive theory on international business negotiation does not yet exist (Moor & Weigand, 2004). Perhaps no one theory is capable of fully explicating the processes, strategies and desired outcomes of international business negotiation. As there are several *types* of international business negotiation, each with its own characteristics, not one but several context-specific theories will always be needed.

Another shortcoming: negotiation theory has still not fully caught up with breakthroughs in neuroscience and psychology. Leary et al. (2013, 99) refer to breakthroughs that reveal the positive role of emotion in decision-making, creativity and relationship building – all key factors in reaching agreement. "For example…people with damage to the right hemisphere of the brain (the emotional side) have great difficulty making decisions."

Much of the theory that has been developed has been based on game theory and the search for optimal strategies. Game theory is a well-developed analytical approach to decision-making in negotiations, which determines the outcomes that can be obtained by players acting rationally. But asmany authors have noted,, approaches based on economic models of negotiation falsely assume not only the rationality of the negotiators but also the quasi-perfection of information. Such assumptions ignore the realities of real-life negotiations.

Non-rational factors have a strong influence on negotiator behaviour in many international business negotiations. For instance, psychological and situational factors have been studied by Lewicki et al. (2005) and Brett & Okumura (1998), and been found to strongly influence both negotiator behaviour and negotiation outcomes.

Dual concern model

Early researchers supposed that negotiations begin with a focus on power, with the most powerful party forcing the other to accept his demands. Later studies, however (e.g. Pruitt, 1983), found that successful negotiators rely less on power and more on coordination and cooperation.

Weiss (2006) points out that no model of international business negotiation has gained general acceptance. Many models, however, make a sharp distinction between integrative (cooperative) and distributional (competitive) negotiation. Das & Kumar's (2011) model, based on Pruitt's (1983) dual concern theory, postulates that high joint benefit will arise if the negotiating parties are concerned about both their own outcomes and the other party's outcomes. Das & Kumar (2011) go on to identify four negotiation strategies that are commonly used in negotiations:

- contending
- yielding
- compromising
- problem-solving

The authors emphasise the many advantages of adopting a cooperative, problem-solving strategy in international business negotiations.

Shortage of theory-based applications

The scarcity of *applications* of negotiation theory prompts Brett & Gelfand (2006) to call for more theory-based decision tools to be embedded in international business practice. A range of theory-based tools would, they argue, equip international business negotiators to deal more effectively with the problems and issues that confront them.

Kersten & Cray (1996) point out that the shortage of theory-based applications is partly due to the fact that negotiation theories tend to be descriptive, not prescriptive. This prevents their use, for instance, in computerised support systems. Descriptive models describe what actually happens in negotiations – for instance, by studying the thinking and behaviour of the negotiators in a particular situation. Prescriptive models, by contrast, are normative. They prescribe what negotiators should actually *do* and so lend themselves to applications in various negotiating contexts.

KEY POINTS

1. Throughout the world, millions of international business deals are negotiated every day using "live" face-to-face meetings and other communication methods. These include phone calls, emails, faxes, letters, video conferencing and virtual negotiation. Communication technologies can be powerful negotiating tools, saving time and money, but they must be carefully selected and used with awareness of the risks.

2. Numerous activities are covered in international business negotiations, including such activities as the selling of goods and services; purchase of raw materials and supplies; distribution of products; advertising and market research activities; licensing and technology transfer agreements; franchise agreements; integrated manufacturing agreements; cross-border mergers and acquisitions; and strategic business alliances and joint ventures.

3. Government plays an important role in some international business negotiations either as a participant or as a regulator. Many cases have been documented of a government refusing to approve the draft agreement on grounds of protecting the public welfare or national sovereignty. Direct participation by a government in the negotiation can have the effect of making the proceedings slow and bureaucratic.

4. Macro-level negotiation is carried out between companies, or between a company and a foreign government. Some macro-level negotiations are very large scale in terms of the values and number of issues dealt with. Micro-level negotiation occurs between individuals, and more often than not involves simple buying/selling transactions. Numerous small-scale buying-selling transactions are carried out every day by individuals who are in business for themselves.

5. International business negotiation is essentially a process of give and take, involving cooperative exchanges of information and proposals. The negotiating parties keep modifying their offers and making concessions in order to come close to each other and eventually reach an agreement. In multiple-issue

negotiations, the process of give and take and concession-making is essential if an overall settlement is to be reached. Trade-offs across issues and adding additional issues are commonly used ways to create joint gain.

6. International business negotiators must take into account the laws of two or more countries, depending on the number of parties involved in the negotiation. These laws are often inconsistent. As a result, clauses may have to be inserted in the contract specifying the governing law in case of disputes between the parties, and specifying contingency arbitration arrangements in case of serious disputes arising between the parties. The negotiators also have to take into account such details as tariff structures, import regulations, fluctuating exchange rates and many other details; otherwise, any agreement reached is likely to be unsatisfactory or inconclusive.

7. In multilateral negotiations involving several parties, consensus may be the only practical way of reaching overall agreement. An important advantage of consensus decision-making is that it encourages cooperative negotiation because no one party can get what they want unless they are willing to allow other parties to achieve at least some of their negotiating goals. In practice, consensus is often considered to have been achieved when a significant number of parties are in favour of a proposal and the rest do not oppose it.

8. The various stages of an international business negotiation include relationship-building, information exchange, persuasion, concessions and agreement. Relationship-building is a crucial stage which can make the difference between failure and success in a negotiation. In some countries much time and effort is spent building rapport with negotiating partners at the pre-negotiation stage. Emphasising relationship-building reduces the risk of conflict erupting during the negotiations.

9. Much of the negotiation theory that has been developed has been based on game theory and the search for optimal strategies. However, approaches based on game theory and other economic models of negotiation falsely assume the rationality of the negotiators and the quasi-perfection of information. Such assumptions ignore the realities of real-life negotiations, in which psychological and situational factors, and the impact of culture on negotiator behaviour play an important role.

10. The impact of culture on negotiations is context-dependent, and cultural influence is best examined in the context of specific negotiating situations rather than in general terms. There is a real need for more theory-based decision tools to be embedded in international business practice. Such theory-based tools would better equip negotiators to deal with the actual problems and issues that confront them, including language and legal issues and the many problems stemming from cultural differences.

QUESTIONS FOR DISCUSSION AND WRITTEN ASSIGNMENTS

1. What are the main stages through which international business negotiations tend to move? Explain how each stage affects the negotiators' outcomes.
2. Explain how choosing one language in preference to another as the language in which an international business negotiation is conducted can affect both the interaction and outcome.
3. "International business negotiation is more challenging than domestic business negotiation and requires greater knowledge and skill." True or false?

BIBLIOGRAPHY

Adair, W. L., Weingart, L. & Brett, J. The negotiation dance: time, culture, and Japanese negotiations. *Journal of Applied Psychology*, 92, 2005, 1056–1068.

Brett, J. M. *Negotiating Globally: How to Negotiate Deals, Resolve Disputes, and make Decisions across Cultural Boundaries*. Jossey-Bass, 2001.

Brett, J. M. et al. How to manage your negotiating team. *HBR*, September 2009, 105–109.

Brett, J. & Gelfand, M. A. Cultural analysis of the underlying assumptions of negotiation theory. In L. L. Thompson (ed.) *Negotiation Theory and Research*. Psychology Press, 2006, Hove, 173–201.

Brett, J. M. & Okumura, T. Inter- and intracultural negotiation: U.S. and Japanese negotiators. *Academy of Management Journal*, 41 (5), 1998, 495–510.

Chen, G. O. H. *Negotiating with the Chinese*. Dartmouth, 1996.

Das, T. K. & Kumar, R. Regulatory focus and opportunism in the alliance development process. *Journal of Management*, 37 (3), 2011, 682–708.

Dupont, C. A model of the negotiation process with different strategies. In P. Ghauri & J-C., Usunier (eds) *International Business Negotiations*. Pergamon, 1996.

Faure, G. O. Negotiations to set up joint ventures in China. *International Negotiation*, 5, 2000, 157–189.

Fukuyama, F. Trust: the social virtues and the creation of prosperity, Hamish Hamilton, 1995.

Ghauri, P. & Usunier, J-C. (eds) *International Business Negotiations*. Pergamon, 2nd ed., 2003.

Graham, J. L., Kim, D. K., Lin, C. Y. & Robinson, M. Buyer seller negotiations around the Pacific Rim: differences in fundamental exchange processes. *Journal of Consumer Research*, 15, 1988, 48–54.

Graham, J. L. A theory of interorganisational negotiations. *Research in Marketing*, 9, 1987, 163–183.

Guirdham, M. *Communicating across Cultures at Work*. Palgrave Macmillan, 2nd ed., 2005.

Hamish, E. S., Glenn, D., Witmeyer, D. & Stevenson, K. A. Cultural styles of persuasion. *International Journal of Intercultural Relations*, 1, 1977, 52–66.

Hendon, D. W. & Hendon, R. A. *World-Class Negotiating: Deal-making in the Global Marketplace*. John Wiley, 1990.

Hofstede, G. *Culture's Consequences*. Sage, 1980.

Kersten, G. & Cray, D. Perspectives on representation and analysis of negotiation. *Group Decision and Negotiation*, 5, 1996, 433–468.

Kumar, R. Brahmanical idealism, anarchical individualism, and the dynamics of Indian negotiating behaviour. *International Journal of Cross-cultural Management*, 4 (1), 2004, 39–58.

Kumar, R. & Patriotta, G. Culture and international alliance negotiations: a sensemaking perspective. *International Negotiation*, 16, 2011, 511–533.

Laroche, M. *Managing Cultural Diversity in Technical Professions*. Butterworth-Heinemann, 2003.

Lax, D. & Sebenius, J. K. *The Manager as Negotiator* (Negotiation Theory and Practice in Management), 1986.

Leary,K., Pillemer, J. & Wheeler, M. Negotiating with emotion. *HBR*, 91 (1/2), 2013, 96–103.

Leonardi, P. M., Neeley, T. B. & Gerber, E. M. How managers use multiple media: discrepant events, power, and timing in redundant communication. *Organisation Science*, 23 (1), 2012, 98–117.

Leung, K., Bhagat, R. S., Buchan, N. R., Erez, M. & Gibson, C. B. Culture and international business: recent advances and their implications for future research. *Journal of International Business Studies*, 36, 2005, 357–378.

Leung, T., & Yeung, L. L. Negotiation in the People's Republic of China: results of a survey of small businesses in Hong Kong. *Journal of Small Business Management*, 33 (1), 1995, 70–77.

Lewicki, R., Saunders, D. & Barry, B. *Negotiation*. Irwin/McGraw-Hill, 2005.

Lukes, S. Power and the battle for hearts and minds. *Millenium*, 33 (3), 2005, 477–494.

Manrai, A. & Manrai, A. K. The influence of culture in international business negotiations: a new conceptual framework and managerial implications. *Journal of Transnational Management*, 15, 2010, 69–100.

Moor, A. de & Weigand, H. Business negotiation support: theory and practice. *International Negotiation*, 9 (1), 2004, 31–57.

Munkejord, K. Multiple media use in organisations. . *Journal of Information, Information Technology, and Organizations*, 2, 2007, 95–118.

Nadler, J. Build rapport – and a better deal. *Negotiation*, March 2007.

Nikolaev, A. G. *International Negotiations*. Lexington Books, 2007.

Overbeck, J. R., Neale, M. A. & Govan, C. L. I feel therefore you act: intrapersonal and interpersonal effects of emotion on negotiation as a function of social power. *Organisational Behaviour and Human Decision Processes*, 112, 2010, 126–139.

Pruitt, D. Achieving integrative agreements. In M. H. Bazerman & R. J. Lewicki (eds) *Negotiating in Organizations*. Sage, 1983.

Pye, L. W. The China trade: making the deal. *HBR*, 64, 1986, 79.

RBC perspective. *Organization Science*, 4 (2), 1993, 269–300.

Ready, K. J. & Tessema, M. T. Perceptions and strategies in the negotiation process: a cross cultural examination of U.S. and Malaysia. *International Negotiation*, 14, 2009, 493–517.

Salacuse, J. *The Global Negotiator*. Palgrave Macmillan, 2003.

Salacuse, J. W. Ten ways that culture affects negotiating style: some survey results *Negotiation Journal*, 14 (3), 1998, 221–240.

Salacuse, J. W. Making deals in strange places. In J. W. Breslin & J. X. Z. Rubin (eds) *Negotiation Theory and Practice*. Programme on Negotiation, Harvard Law School, 1999, 251–259.

Spector, P. E. Using self-report questionnaires in OB research. *Journal or Organisational Behaviour*, 15 (5), 1994, 385–392.

Stephens, K. K. et al. Discrete, sequential, and follow-up use of information and communication technology by experienced ICT users. *Management Communication Quarterly*, 22 (2), 2008, 197–231.

Watson-Manheim, M. B. & Belanger, F. Communication media repertoires: dealing with the multiplicity of media choices. *MIS Qly*, 31 (2), 2007, 267–293.

Weiss, S. E. Analysis of complex negotiations in international business: the RBC perspective. *Organisation Science*, 4 (2), 1993, 269–300.

Weiss, S. E. International business negotiation in a globalizing world: reflections on the contributions and future of a (sub)field. *International Negotiation*, 11, 2006, 287–316.

Zhao, Jensen J. The Chinese approach to international business negotiation, *The Journal of Business Communication*, 37 (3), 2000, 209–237.

Culture and Negotiation

2

INTRODUCTION

Negotiators bring to the table numerous culturally derived assumptions about how negotiations should be conducted. As Salacuse (1998) found, such assumptions influence their negotiating behaviour as well as the strategies they use and their desired outcomes. Thus negotiators from "moderate" cultures respond in a measured, cautious way to the other side's offers and proposals (Smith, 2011). Managers from "extremity" cultures, on the other hand, are less cautious and guarded in their responses. Nevertheless, Drake (2001) argues, the *specific roles* played by negotiators make a greater impact than culture on the interaction and outcomes of business negotiations:

Negotiating styles are strongly influenced by culture (Brett, 2001). Indeed, managers can predict the styles likely to be used by foreign business negotiators simply by referring to surveys of national cultural values. Such surveys suggest, for instance, that negotiators from high-femininity cultures such as the Scandinavian countries might be expected to avoid aggressive confrontations and displays of anger, and to adopt a sensible, problem-solving approach to negotiations. Knowledge of the findings of surveys of national cultures is extremely useful for managers who are about to conduct business negotiations in a foreign country because these surveys reveal *central tendencies* – the values, ideas and behaviours that are acceptable in the culture and that foreign business visitors should be aware of and conform to when interacting with local business people.

For international business people, an awareness of national cultural characteristics is important since approaches to business meetings and negotiation that are used successfully in one country may be ineffective in a different country. Thus in the US, *teams* generally outperform sole negotiators in buying/selling negotiations. But in some Asian countries, concern about harmony norms may lead negotiating teams to negotiate less satisfactory outcomes than those achieved by sole negotiators (Gelfand et al., 2013). However, managers need not carry out expensive research on a country-by-country basis in order to learn the negotiating norms of business people from other cultures. There are short-cuts. Country similarity theory is one of them.

But no single study can provide a definitive analysis of the impact made by culture on international business negotiation. That is why Bülow & Kumar (2011) advise students of culture and negotiation to explore the underlying *cultural assumptions* of a given study – as opposed to uncritically accepting its findings, which may turn out to be misleading or only partly true. The findings of many studies are based on data collected in negotiation simulations – which may not be reliable since negotiators often behave differently in "live" and experimental situations. They take fewer risks, for instance, in a real-life business negotiation where a valuable contract is at stake. Numerous studies distinguish between Western individualism and Asian collectivism, but how reliable and accurate is that distinction? As Requejo & Graham (2008) point out, collectivist groups in China and other Asian countries have been shown to exhibit aggressive *individualist traits* in negotiations, including aggressive conversational overlaps and interruptions, threats and rude persistence in asking questions and dangling a better offer in front of the opponent.

Another reason for being cautious about the findings of culture-negotiation studies is that negotiators are influenced by organisational culture as well as national culture. Disentangling the impact made by each kind of culture in a particular business negotiation can be extremely difficult. In Salacuse's (1998) survey, respondents from various countries listed their preferences in such matters as negotiation outcome ("win-win" or "win-lose") and negotiation process ("one leader" or "team"). Respondents' choices were influenced as much by their organisational cultures as by national cultures.

The concept of *cultural distance* is widely used in international business to assess the extent to which the business values and practices in countries differ from one another. As differences increase between the language, laws and business practices of any two countries, business negotiations between negotiators from those countries often become increasingly difficult, with the negotiators failing to understand each other's motivations and intentions. Cultural distance introduces "noise" into negotiations, including misunderstandings, misinterpretations and psychological discomfort. In international mergers and acquisitions (M&A) negotiations, for instance, cultural distance between the parties can lead to inadequate understanding of the foreign market or the local labour situation and ultimately lead to the acquirer paying too much for the acquired company.

CULTURE-NEGOTIATION STUDIES

Macro- and micro-level studies

The influence of culture on business negotiations has been extensively studied (e.g. Chen et al., 2009; Manrai & Manrai, 2010). The cultural background of negotiators has been found to shape their strategies, interaction patterns and desired outcomes in terms of general agreement, contract or business relationships (Salacuse, 1998). Thus, understanding cultural influences on negotiating behaviour and negotiation styles is a crucial skill for international business negotiators.

Bülow & Kumar (2011) note that researchers studying the impact of culture on negotiation have adopted two main perspectives:

- *micro-level* – the behavioural perspective, focusing on negotiators' behaviour;
- *macro-level* – the strategic perspective, focusing on organisational aspects of negotiations.

Researchers who adopt a micro-level perspective focus on the *dynamics of interaction* in negotiations. They examine, for instance, the strategies and dispute resolution methods used by negotiators from different cultures. Such micro-level studies enable managers to predict, with varying degrees of accuracy, the likely negotiating behaviour of negotiators from various countries and to develop appropriate negotiating strategies.

Researchers adopting a macro-level perspective generally study negotiations between organisations based in different countries, or between a company and a foreign government. They often focus on particular aspects of such negotiations and the impact made by these aspects on the negotiation outcomes. For example, Floris et al. (2013) focus on *rhetorical strategies* that were used during an attempted acquisition of Rio Tinto by BHP Billiton.

Helpful analytical frameworks

An example of a micro-level perspective is Brett & Gelfand's (2005) study, which develops a conceptual framework for analysing the negotiation process in a particular negotiation. The framework comprises several key concepts:

- Goals: Are the negotiators motivated to achieve economic goals or social (relational) goals?
- Communication: Do the negotiators use direct communication or indirect communication and avoidance?
- Persuasion: Do the negotiators use rationality or emotions to persuade the other team?

- Information: Do the negotiators use direct information or indirect information sharing?
- Attributions: Do the negotiators make dispositional attributions or situational attributions?

Anecdotal evidence suggests that Brett & Gelfand's (2005) framework helps students of international business negotiation assess the impact made by culture in various negotiating situations.

Another helpful analytical tool is Manrai & Manrai's (2010) conceptual framework. This comprises six key constructs: negotiator's goals, negotiator's inclinations, non-task activities, negotiator's qualifications, negotiation processes and negotiation outcomes.

Practitioner-researcher symbiosis

Studies which examine the effects of culture on negotiation enable managers to predict how foreign negotiators are likely to behave in forthcoming negotiations and the strategies they might use. By being aware of the findings of relevant studies, managers can improve their preparedness and their negotiating performance. Equally, researchers benefit from examining managers' reports of real-life international business negotiations. Practitioners' reports enable researchers to test the validity of their assumptions and theories, and to develop a better understanding of the process of international business negotiation.

Managers should be careful not to uncritically swallow the findings of any particular study about the impact of culture on negotiation. Study findings are sometimes contradictory: some studies arrive at firm conclusions, which are subsequently challenged by other studies. Kumar (2004), for instance, finds that Indian negotiators are stubborn and tend to make few concessions. Requejo & Graham (2008), however, observe that Indian offers are heavily padded and concessions are large. The researchers in each case produce good evidence for their findings, but the findings themselves are contradictory.

In collectivist cultures, relationship is extremely important, with business deals springing from the relationship rather than vice versa. This idea is widely supported by researchers, but in different ways. Ramirez-Marin & Brett (2011), for instance, assume that Latino negotiators, being relationship-oriented, will make low initial demands and try to move negotiations towards integrative agreements. Lewis (2006), by contrast, expects high initial demands from collectivist negotiators followed by large concessions. In Russia, another relationship-oriented culture, negotiators are reportedly cautious about exchanging information in international business negotiations – a tendency which may lead to competitive bargaining and distributive, as opposed to integrative, agreements.

Simulated negotiation studies

Some studies base their findings on data collected in simulated negotiations and other experimental situations. However, uncritically accepting the findings of such studies can be a mistake on the part of negotiators, since they tend to behave differently in "live" and experimental situations. They tend, for instance, to take more risks in simulations than in an actual business negotiation, in which a valued business relationship may be at stake. This disparity between experimental and real-life negotiations reduces the reliability of generalisations about international business negotiations which are based on the findings of negotiation simulations.

Changeable cultural effects

Collectivist negotiators are more likely than individualists to be collaborative and to work towards an integrative agreement (Triandis, 1994). Numerous studies support this general maxim. However, there is evidence to show that when collectivist negotiators are not monitored by their bosses or constituencies, that is, when they are freed from cultural constraints, the effect may be changed or even reversed (Gelfand et al., 2011). In unmonitored situations, negotiators are less accountable for their actions and decisions and, under these conditions, collectivist negotiators sometimes act competitively, while individualist negotiators may become more collaborative.

Yamagishi & Mifune (2008) make substantially the same point. Their results show that typical Japanese patterns of conformity and cooperativeness are greatly reduced when Japanese negotiators do not need to take into account the expectations and evaluations of others. When they are not being observed by other Japanese, Japanese negotiators often become highly competitive. Hashimoto & Yamagishi (2009) found that, although Japanese people are perceived by other Japanese as promoting collaborative, interdependent values, when asked to state their own personal preferences, they often express a strong desire to be independent rather than interdependent. As such examples suggest, the influence of culture on negotiators' behaviour can in certain situations become amplified, reduced or even reversed.

Shifting cultural values

Cultural values and norms are not fixed, and sometimes can change dramatically, as shown by the rapidly shifting nature of business values in the former communist countries of Eastern Europe and the Soviet Union. When Wegener & Liebig (1995) examined how values for justice differed between generations in Germany, they found that in the former East Germany, older people tended towards egalitarian distribution, while younger people chose equity. In West Germany, by contrast, the young tended towards egalitarianism as opposed to equity.

Imprecise terminology

Some of the most commonly used concepts and constructs that are used in studies of culture and negotiation are used imprecisely and are open to various interpretations. Examples are the concepts of collectivism and individualism. Collectivism can be interpreted in a wide variety of ways. For instance, it can be taken to imply in-group favouritism, the importance of the extended family, a collaborative approach to negotiation, an emphasis on relationship building during negotiations, a preference for group decision-making and so on. In the international business context, collectivism is often linked to the importance of connections (*guanxi* or *wasta*). The individualism/collectivism construct has been used by researchers to form an oversimplified East-West dichotomy. The wide range of meanings that "collectivism" carries, shows the imprecision of the collectivism concept.

Understanding cultural influences on international business negotiations is an important skill for negotiators to acquire; however, as Bülow & Kumar (2011) point out, no one study can provide a definitive analysis of the impact of culture on negotiation or provide a single list of dos and don'ts for negotiators. Generalisations based on a particular study sometimes turn out to be inaccurate. The right balance must be found between generalisations and the specifics of particular negotiations. Bülow & Kumar's (2011) advice to students of culture and negotiation is to

- identify the precise research questions behind any particular study;
- explore the researchers' underlying cultural assumptions rather than uncritically accept the findings of the study.

When a business negotiation breaks down, American companies blame the individual, that is, they treat the individual negotiator as the locus of agency and responsibility (Maddux et al., 2011). Japanese negotiators, by contrast, express regret for the breakdown on behalf of their organisation, which is seen to have agency and to be responsible for the breakdown. In this case, two opposing, culturally influenced perceptions exist of the same negotiating event.

How helpful are survey findings?

Surveys of national cultural values capture important differences in the attitudes and behaviours of members of different national cultures, and are therefore pertinent to the study of international business negotiations. However, survey findings have to be interpreted with caution because

- survey respondents comprise only a small proportion of a country's population and may be atypical;
- survey findings describe only the central parts of a tendency and may not capture important characteristics of subcultures or minority groups.

Such limitations complicate the task of understanding the interplay between culture and negotiation within a given cultural grouping. Nevertheless, for managers about to visit a foreign country to participate in business negotiations with local firms, a knowledge of the central tendencies revealed by surveys is extremely useful. Central tendencies reveal behaviours to which negotiators should conform when carrying out negotiations with local organisations.

Often managers and consultants are confronted with values and practices that would be unacceptable at home but that are entirely normal in the foreign country concerned. Examples are child labour in India and China and some African countries, and discrimination against women in some Arab countries. No clear and uncontested code of international business conduct exists to measure the validity of different moral and ethical values produced by different cultures (Guerra & Giner-Sorolla, 2010). Consequently, although surveys of national cultural values provide clues, international business people can never be certain that the way in which they deal with ethical dilemmas encountered abroad is the right way.

Is it right or wrong, for instance, to give a generous tip to a foreign telephone operator to obtain an immediate overseas connection? Is it right or wrong to pay a foreign government official for assistance in securing a lucrative contract? Such payment for services rendered, which might be seen as bribes in the manager's own country, is common practice in some countries, where such payments are not regarded as unethical. Ali (1995) found that in Syria, for instance, it is impossible to get a request processed in any government agency without paying bribes, and that the payment of money for services rendered is considered normal business practice. In Russia, corruption and bribery in business affairs has been widespread since the collapse of the Soviet Union. Kazakov et al. (1997) argue that commissions and bribes have to be tolerated by foreign business executives in Russia who are anxious to close a negotiation and sign a contract.

Such considerations raise the question of whether international business practice is necessarily relative and situational. An expatriate manager working in a Chinese factory dealt with the question in a simplistic way by suppressing personal judgment and conforming to the Chinese company's rules and practices. The strategy worked well at first, but then unravelled. When the manager caught a local employee stealing, he simply followed the rules and handed the employee over to the provincial authorities, who executed him.

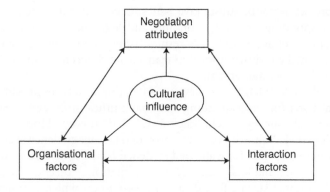

Figure 2.1   Impact of culture on negotiation

Note: In a particular international business negotiation, much of what is explained in terms of
culture is probably a combination of culture, interaction, organisation factors and
negotiator attributes/personality.

INFLUENCE OF CULTURE

Cultural differences

International business negotiators come from cultures that differ in power distance, uncertainty-avoidance, collectivism/individualism and other cultural measures. As a result, they usually have strong and conflicting views about the issues to be discussed, how business negotiations should be conducted, whether decisions should be made by consensus or by majority vote, and the kind of agreement that should be sought.

The existence of cultural differences between negotiators explains why styles and approaches that are used successfully in domestic business negotiations are often ineffective when transferred to an international context. International business negotiations tend to be far more complex than domestic negotiations, with much of the complexity stemming from clashing cultural values and ideologies as well as legal pluralism and monetary factors (Weiss, 2006). Moreover, when people from different cultures interact in business negotiations, the *differences* between them become salient and hinder communication (Stahl et al., 2010).

Influence of national cultures

International business negotiations take place between people from different countries who have absorbed their national cultures' values, beliefs, communicative norms and negotiating styles. Negotiators bring to the table numerous culturally derived assumptions, such as what constitutes "correct" negotiating behaviour, or what kind of agreement negotiators should try to reach.

Negotiators' ideas about substantive issues to be debated in negotiations and about corresponding political, economic and legal matters are also culturally derived (Tinsley et al., 2011). As a result clashing, culturally derived ideas and opinions can make it difficult for two teams from different countries to reach a mutually satisfactory agreement.

Hofstede's (1980) landmark survey of 40 national cultures provided the first theoretical basis for understanding national cultural differences. Since then, other large-scale surveys, including the GLOBE survey (House, 2004) and Schwartz's (1994) Value Survey, have provided further evidence about national cultural differences, and have allowed evidence-based conclusions to be drawn about the impact made by culture in international business negotiations. Hofstede's original survey found *four dimensions* on which national cultures differ, that is, power distance, uncertainty avoidance, masculinity-femininity and individualism-collectivism. A fifth dimension, Confucian Dynamism/ Long-term Orientation, was added after the original study was replicated in China (Hofstede, 1997). This fifth value dimension suggests that Asian cultures tend to be long-term oriented. They emphasise the development of long-term relationships through mutual cooperation and complementary obligations.

These studies cover a large cross-section of countries and geographical regions, and provide strong evidence for the likely cultural positioning of managers who will be involved in a forthcoming negotiation. The studies give valuable clues about how managers from different countries might behave in business negotiations and other social situations. The studies show that the most important differences between negotiators from different countries are not superficial differences, such as when to shake hands or when to bow or when to smile, but stem from deeply held beliefs and values absorbed from their respective cultures. Thus, Metcalf et al. (2007) find that Western negotiators take a logical sequential approach to negotiation. They deal with issues one at a time and reach agreement on each issue separately so that the final negotiated agreement is the sum of the smaller agreements. For Asian managers, on the other hand, negotiation is multifaceted and requires a holistic solution. Negotiations conducted in Cantonese, for instance, have a circular pattern, with no distinct phases and with apparently random contributions by participants. Chinese negotiating style reflects traditional Confucian values. According to Woo & Prud'homme (1999), Chinese negotiators never telegraph their next move through a show of emotion: their level of friendliness or coolness remains the same irrespective of whether negotiations are heading for success or failure.

Hall (1966) identifies cultures as high context or low context. People from low-context (Western) cultures tend to be task focussed, and in international business negotiations they communicate their message explicitly. Individuals from high-context (collectivist) cultures, on the other hand, communicate messages implicitly (e.g. nonverbally) and focus on building relationships.

How managers can use survey findings

Managers can use surveys of national cultural values to predict the behaviour and negotiating styles likely to be used in forthcoming negotiations by foreign counterparts. If, for instance, negotiations are to be held in a high power-distance country such as India, Saudi Arabia or France, they can deduce from survey findings that protocol will probably have to be strictly observed, that formal communication will be expected, and that important decisions taken by negotiators may have to be endorsed by top-level managers or officials. They can predict that negotiators from high-masculinity cultures, such as Russia, may well adopt a blunt, competitive negotiation style and resist compromise; whereas, negotiators from high-femininity cultures, such as the Scandinavian countries, will be likely to avoid aggressive confrontations and displays of anger, and to adopt a sensible, problem-solving approach to dealing with any disputes that arise. Elgstrom (1990) notes that during negotiations about Swedish aid to Tanzania, the Swedish negotiators showed their feminine side by being reluctant to table proposals containing harsh demands and conditions.

Surveys of national cultural values point to the strong collectivist and power-distance orientation of Indonesia, and this information alone gives managers adequate advance warning about the likely negotiating behaviour of Indonesian negotiators in forthcoming negotiations. For instance, the Indonesian negotiators

- will be used to negotiating in a team environment;
- will probably place much emphasis on the authority of the team leader of both sides;
- will be unlikely to challenge the team leaders' opinions, or suggestions concerning procedural matters.

The Indonesian team leader might nevertheless be expected to seek consensus among members of the negotiating team before taking important decisions.

Influence of regional cultures

International business people need to understand how culture affects the way in which negotiations are conducted and business decisions are taken in various countries and in different geographical regions, so that they have some idea of what to expect before setting out, for instance, on a sales tour of the Middle East. One problem is that generalisations about regional cultures are vaguer and easier to challenge than generalisations about national cultures. Nevertheless, generalisations about the characteristics of business people in important economic regions such as the Middle East can be extremely helpful for managers. Hofstede et al. (2010), for instance, find that Arab countries score high on power distance and collectivism dimensions, moderately on masculine, and low on long-term orientation. These scores suggest that Arab negotiators from a range of countries might be expected to respect and follow the wishes of people in authority; to focus on relationship building when conducting business negotiations; and to follow traditional values which, in the eyes of Western negotiators, are very conservative.

Country similarity theory

Some researchers study the characteristics of regions by using data relating to national cultures to draw conclusions about a regional culture. But the concept of regional culture is vaguer and more problematical than the concept of national culture, and is more difficult to handle in terms of predicting possible effects in business negotiations involving, say, Scandinavian and Latino negotiators, or Arabic and Southern African negotiators.

A wide range of national and regional styles and preferences come into play in international business negotiations. Business people and managers who carry out negotiations in many parts of the world need to be aware of the communicative characteristics and preferences of participants from other cultures so that they can adjust their own negotiating style according to the norms of the region or country where negotiations take place. To acquire knowledge of the negotiating preferences and characteristics of other cultures, managers need not carry out exhaustive and expensive research on a country-by-country basis. There are shortcuts. *Country similarity theory,* for instance, explains that when countries are similar to each other in language, per capita incomes, extent of industrialisation, technology, literacy levels and other important features, people from those countries will tend to react in similar ways (in negotiations and elsewhere) to a given argument or appeal (O'Connell, 1997). The countries in a given group, in effect, possess regional characteristics.

The implication is that the negotiating characteristics and preferences of a group of countries in a given geographical area – the Baltic countries, say, or the countries of southern Africa – are likely to be very similar with regard to business negotiations, provided that the countries in the group resemble each other in many other ways. When this is the case, knowledge derived from personal experience of how business negotiations are conducted in one of the countries (in Zimbabwe, for instance) can be applied with a reasonable level of confidence to negotiations held in other countries of the same group (that is, in South Africa, Namibia, Swaziland, Botswana, Malawi and Lesotho).

Influence of organisational cultures

Differences of organisational culture affect the process and interactions of international business negotiation (Epstein, 2004). Organisational culture is the pattern of shared behaviours, values and beliefs that provide a foundation of understanding of the organisational functioning processes and norms which direct employee behaviour. According to Schein (1986), organisational culture is an amalgamation of the national culture and the backgrounds of individuals assembled in the organisational setting, that is, the pattern of shared values and beliefs that provides the norms directing employee behaviour.

International business negotiations are affected as much by differences of organisational culture as by national cultural differences. When Sony acquired Columbia Pictures, for instance, organisational cultural differences between Japanese and American managers created numerous misunderstandings and miscommunications that affected performance (Nakamoto, 2000). Often when a company based in one country merges with another company based in another country, it is the clash of *organisational* cultures that prevents a smooth, effective integration. Thus, the poor performance of Daimler Chrysler is often attributed to the clash of organisational cultures that led to major integration problems.

Negotiators may be as much influenced by their organisational cultures as by their national cultures, and disentangling the impact made by each is extremely difficult. Gelfand et al. (2011), however, produce evidence to show that in international business negotiations, organisational culture and the structure of organisational rewards can, together, provide a situation strong enough to override the effects of national cultures. Brouthers et al. (1955) argue that the chances of successful negotiations are improved when both the national and the organisational cultures of the companies concerned are close rather than distant, and when the firms have good pre-existing relationships and coopera-tive, problem-solving organisational cultures.

In Salacuse's (1998) survey, respondents from various countries listed their preferences in such matters as negotiation outcome ("win-win" or "win-lose"), and negotiation process ("one leader" or "team"). There were striking cultural similarities at the national level, but respondents' choices were also mediated by their organisational and professional cultures. Groups of military personnel, for instance, made similar choices regardless of nationality.

Organisational subcultures

Large organisations contain many subcultures. Subcultures exist at different levels and in different parts of the organisation, for example, in different departments and in different geographical locations. Each of these organisational subcultures develops its own values and practices. Thus, when Elashmawi & Harris (1998) asked engineers from Petronas to list the cultural values of the engineering division, the values that were perceived as important were risk-taking, good project management and keeping abreast of current technology. By contrast, the marketing group at Petronas felt that their functional responsibility required them to focus most of all on maximising revenue and minimising costs.

As the example suggests, the values held by a particular departmental subcul-ture differ – to a greater or lesser extent – from the values of other subcultures in the same firm, as well as from the "official" company values promoted by top management. Overall organisational culture, Schein (1990) argues, is a negotiated outcome of the interaction between the various subcultures.

Cultural empathy

When international business negotiations are complicated by clashing national and organisational cultures, successful outcomes are more likely when the negotiators demonstrate cultural empathy (Erickson & Shultz, 1982). Cultural empathy is a general skill or attitude that helps a person feel as a person from another culture feels. This ability enables negotiators to empathise with the behaviours, feelings and thoughts of negotiators from other cultures, and to make necessary adjustments in their own negotiating behaviour. Kumar (2004) argues that understanding the *mindset* of the other negotiating team, obtained through cultural empathy, is a prerequisite for successful international business negotiation since it enables negotiators to adjust their strategies and offers in order to make them acceptable to the other team.

NEGOTIATING STYLES

Cultural variations

Culture influences the negotiation styles used in international business negotiations (Brett, 2001). American-style negotiation, for instance, reflects American individualism, and is a competitive process of offers and counter-offers aimed at maximising the negotiator's share of outcomes (Kumar & Worm, 2004). Kumar (2004) points to the contending style of many Indian negotiators in which the Indians, members of a hierarchical, high power-distance society, rigidly stick to their positions and expect the other party to concede even though such an approach may lead to impasse.

Negotiating style is strongly influenced by culture. Thus negotiators from high power-distance societies have been found to feel comfortable in formal negotiations where protocols are observed and where most of the discussion that takes place is between the most senior managers on both sides of the table (Metcalf & Bird, 2004). The style adopted by negotiators from low uncertainty-avoidance cultures is to use *factual arguments* to convince their opponents, while negotiators from high uncertainty-avoidance cultures often use *emotional appeals* (Metcalf & Bird, 2004). Salacuse's (1998) survey of 12 cultural groups found that that 91 percent of Chinese and Mexicans and all Brazilians preferred a one-leader negotiating team, whereas only 40 percent of Nigerians and French preferred a one-leader team. A general agreement reached during negotiation was strongly preferred by Japanese negotiators, and least preferred by English negotiators. Japanese managers used much indirect communication in negotiations, while Americans used a very low percentage of such communication. Brazilians showed emotion consistently during negotiations, whereas Germans rarely expressed emotions.

Linear and circular styles

Asian negotiators are culturally predisposed to deal with negotiating issues simultaneously rather than sequentially, placing much less emphasis than Western negotiators do on structure and sequence (Metcalf et al., 2007). Western negotiators, on the other hand, tend to split a negotiation into several smaller tasks – prices, quantities, payment terms, import duties and so forth – and then deal with these smaller tasks separately so that the final negotiated agreement is the sum of the smaller agreements. Ding (1996) observes that Chinese negotiations held in Cantonese tend to have a circular pattern with no distinct phases, and apparently random contributions by the participants. While the negotiators, following culturally derived norms, attend to the bigger picture first, and then discuss smaller issues, Western negotiators usually do the opposite, moving from discussing details to general principles or conclusions.

High-involvement style

According to Aritz & Walker (2010), Russians, Italians, Greeks and Spaniards usually use a high-involvement style in meetings – a style which is often seen as aggressive and pushy by other cultural groups because of frequent interruptions and conversational overlaps. Collectivist cultures generally, and Asian countries in particular, tend to use a high-considerateness style. In a cross-cultural business meeting between Asian and American managers, the Asians' high considerateness style (being considerate of others, taking fewer turns, not imposing one's own opinions) may give priority to the enthusiastic involvement style of the Americans.

Deferential style

Most Asians are concerned to show deference or respect in their interactions with others (Scollon & Scollon, 2001). In business negotiations, this trait is reflected in the deferential style adopted by many Asian negotiators, who tend to defer to and side with high-status, powerful individuals in a negotiation, such as leaders of national delegations, and to avoid disagreeing with them. Even when these powerful individuals fail to contribute to the discussion, their silences are interpreted by the negotiators. As a result, decision-making is left to the powerful.

Scollon & Scollon (2001) make the point that Japanese people are extremely sensitive to differences in social status. In business negotiations between Japanese negotiators, the party with lesser status often averts his eyes during the negotiation in deference to the other party's superior status. Chinese negotiators are equally status conscious and may insist on negotiating only with counterparts of the same or the higher hierarchical level (Woo & Prud'homme, 1999).

"Moderate" and "extremity" styles

Smith (2011) distinguishes between "moderate" and "extremity" cultures. In international business negotiations, Smith (2011) argues, managers from "moderate" cultures express their opinions cautiously, and respond in a measured, cautious way to the other side's offers and proposals. Managers from "extremity" cultures, on the other hand, tend to be far less cautious and guarded in their responses. Extremity cultures include Israel, Venezuela and Saudi Arabia. Examples of moderate cultures are China and Japan.

Other commonly used styles

Shell (2006) identifies other negotiating styles that are widely used in international business negotiations:

Collaborative.
Individuals who enjoy helping others solve tough problems tend to use a collaborative negotiation style. Collaborative negotiators seek to create options that will lead to mutual gain for the parties.

Competitive.
Competitive negotiators have strong instincts for all aspects of negotiation and are often strategic. They often overlook the importance of relationships in negotiations.

Accommodating.
Accommodating negotiators are concerned with building and maintaining business relationships. Accommodators are sensitive to the emotional states and body language of the other party.

Compromising.
Compromising negotiators are, for whatever reason, eager to close the deal. Compromisers may rush the negotiation and make concessions too quickly.

Avoiding.
Managers who are avoiders dislike the negotiation situation. In international business, negotiation avoiders are often perceived as tactful and diplomatic. They tend to defer to others as a way of avoiding confrontation.

How culture influences reactions to proposals

The way in which negotiators react to proposals may also be culturally influenced. For example, Western negotiators generally react positively to proposals that are likely to bring innovation and change. Chinese negotiators, on the other hand, react negatively to such proposals if there is any risk that they might cause job losses or social instability (Chen, 1996).

Decision-making styles

In theory, international business negotiation is a systematic and orderly process leading to rational decisions and a negotiated agreement between people from different countries. But in practice, the process is overridden by the influence of culture. Culture, according to Graham (1996), underlies the logical sequential approach to decision-making adopted by Westerners as much as it does the circular, holistic approach of Asian negotiators. Foster (1992) compares the decision-making styles in negotiations of Japanese and American negotiators. The risk-averse, people-oriented Japanese take a long time to make decisions because in Japan, making a decision involves a large number of people and many in-group meetings before and after negotiations. The time-conscious, individualistic Americans, on the other hand, like to arrive at decisions quickly and at the table.

In high power-distance countries with hierarchical organisational structures, many key decisions are made by top-level managers or officials, such as mayors or governors. When international business negotiations are held in these countries, decisions taken during the negotiations may need to be approved by these high-level executives or officials (Chen, 1996).

As Foster (1992) points out, American negotiators make decisions logically, but are notoriously casual about protocols relating to terms of address, dress, business cards, behaviour at social events and so on. This casualness contrasts with practice in some European countries such as Germany and France where the use of last names and titles, instead of first names, is obligatory. In Japan and China, great importance is attached to the exchange of business cards at the pre-negotiation stage.

> **Case Study**
>
> ### MINI-CASE: The downside of contracts
>
> When a Portuguese packaging company holds face-to-face negotiations in India with an Indian jute exporter, it signs a five-year contract on what it believes at the time to be very favourable terms. However, 12 months into the

contract, the world price of jute has fallen by $12. At this stage, the Portuguese company makes a formal request that the contract be renegotiated. The Indian company's rejection of the request leads to the two sides becoming embroiled in a serious dispute.

In its letter replying to the Portuguese request, the Indian exporter rules out renegotiation and points out that, although it does not regard the small print in supply contracts as sacrosanct, prices agreed by the parties and clearly stated in the contract are much more important. Moreover, the prices stated in the contract are legally binding. The Portuguese company should get better legal advice the next time it negotiates a supply contract with a foreign supplier.

After discussing the letter, the Portuguese see that their options are limited. They now realise that when negotiating the original contract in India, they should have ensured that clauses were inserted specifying actions to be taken in the event of future disputes, together with the dispute resolution procedure that would be used. They are undecided about what their next move should be.

Questions:

1. *What should be the Portuguese company's next move?*
2. *To what extent are cultural factors responsible for the situation that has arisen?*
3. *What options does the Portuguese company have as it continues to negotiate with the Indians?*
4. *What actions should the Portuguese negotiating team have taken when negotiating the original contract to reduce the risks to which they were exposing themselves?*

NEGOTIATING CONTEXT

Culture and context

International business negotiations never take place in a vacuum: they are always situated in a particular social context in which the negotiations are embedded and with which culture interacts. An example of how culture interacts with context is Graham's (1990) description of how a relatively weak negotiating team is influenced by and adjusts to a more powerful host team's culture. However, many studies examine the effects of culture on business negotiations without paying sufficient attention to the contextual aspects. Indeed, Drake (2001) argues that in most contexts, cultural factors are unimportant, compared with the specific roles played by negotiators – buyer, seller, devil's advocate, lead negotiator and so forth – and that in business negotiations, roles affect outcomes more directly. Negotiating behaviour and styles, learned and accepted in a particular country and cultural context, may be unacceptable and ineffective in a different cultural context.

Such considerations help explain why a given approach to business negotiation that is used successfully in a particular national context often turns out to be ineffective when transferred to a different national context. In the US, for instance, teams outperform sole negotiators in buying/selling negotiations (Thompson et al., 1996). However, this team advantage is not observed in some collectivist countries, which have different social norms. Thus Gelfand et al. (2013) accurately predicted the negative effect of teams on negotiation outcomes in Taiwan. The team context in Taiwan would amplify a concern with harmony and would lead Taiwanese negotiating teams to negotiate suboptimal outcomes. That was the prediction, and two simulation studies subsequently showed that Taiwanese teams indeed negotiated less advantageous outcomes than Taiwanese sole negotiators. The implication of the research for Taiwanese and organisations in other collectivist countries is that the organisations need to exercise caution when deciding whether or not to send a team to conduct business negotiations with foreign firms. For Western opponents, facing a Taiwanese sole negotiator may prove more challenging than facing a Taiwanese team.

Cultural distance

Cultural distance is an important contextual factor which influences the interaction and outcomes of international business negotiations. The concept of cultural distance is widely used in international business to assess the extent to which the business values and practices in countries differ from each other. As differences increase between any two countries' language, laws and business practices, communication and cooperation between companies or business people from the countries becomes increasingly difficult since they may fail to understand each other's motivations and intentions (Kumar & Nti, 2004). In international business negotiations, negotiators may even fail to agree on the nature of the situation which they are negotiating. For instance, are they negotiating to maintain a relationship or to agree how profits and responsibilities should be distributed?

The complexity and ambiguity of international business negotiations are greater when there is cultural distance between the parties. Cultural distance is defined as the extent to which the cultural norms in one country are different from those in another country (Kogut & Singh, 1988). Kogut & Singh's index of cultural distance is based on the deviation from each of Hofsted's (1980) national culture scales – power distance, uncertainty avoidance, masculinity/femininity and individualism/collectivism. The index has been used by researchers to examine the impact of national cultural differences on a wide range of international joint venture (IJV) and cross-border acquisition outcomes, for instance, post-acquisition performance, return on equity, sales growth and management turnover.

Cultural distance in IJVs and acquisitions

According to Kogut & Singh (1988), cultural distance increases the probability of a multinational enterprise (MNE) choosing joint ventures over acquisition since cultural distance can reduce an acquisition's performance by increasing the costs of integration. In the context of an international acquisition, cultural distance may lead to the acquirer overpaying for a foreign firm due to inadequate understanding of local and regional markets. In the context of an IJV operation, cultural distance may translate into conflict within the IJV regarding the norms and routines for new product development, organisational design, management styles and other aspects of management that influence the IJV's bottom-line results.

Ideological distance

Ideological distance, a component of cultural distance, can act as a powerful barrier during international business negotiations, especially if the companies are from countries which are distant from each other in many other ways, including language, religion and level of economic development. Negotiating teams need to be aware before negotiations begin of ideological differences which could affect the negotiations, such as different beliefs about basic human rights. Part of the team's preparations for negotiation should include deciding how they will deal with any ideological clashes that may occur and how they will present their proposals in a way that is ideologically acceptable to the other side.

Integration mechanisms

During international merger negotiations, an *integration campaign* aimed at minimising cultural differences between the partners in an IJV or an acquisition often needs to be discussed and agreed. Stahl & Voigt (2008) argue that in the case of international M&A, a well-designed integration process is essential for capturing the anticipated synergies of the merger. Integration efforts may include informal coordination mechanisms such as short-term visits, joint training programmes, and task forces and committees.

SMALL-GROUP EXERCISE: Discussion Questions

Working in small groups, discuss each of the following questions and write down the group's agreed answer. At the end of the exercise, each group may present its answers to the other groups for comment.

1. *"Miscommunications and misunderstandings are inevitable during international business negotiations between negotiators from different countries speaking different languages."* Give your reasons (with specific examples) for agreeing or disagreeing with this statement.
2. What are the most important effects that cultural differences have on international sales negotiations?
3. What practical steps can negotiators take before and during negotiations to reduce the risks of conflict and mutual misunderstanding?

COMMUNICATION MATTERS

Cultural influence

Fisher (1980) compared American, French, Mexican and Japanese negotiators and noted how different culturally derived mannerisms and forms of verbal and nonverbal communication impeded negotiation even before the substantive negotiating issues were addressed.

Communicative behaviours learned and accepted in one culture may be totally unacceptable in another cultural setting. In some countries, it is acceptable to use a spittoon during a negotiation, or to spit in public. The Japanese report discomfort at the aggressive staring of their American negotiation counterparts, but the Americans think that something must be wrong because the Japanese will not look them in the eye (Graham & Sano, 1996). In the US, eye averting is often seen as a sign of caginess or deception.

Graham (1985) studied the communication of negotiators from various countries, and noted that

- *Japanese*: made promises and rarely made threats. They used "no" and "you" infrequently, and avoided facial gazing.
- *Russians*: often maintained silence for long periods during a negotiation. They asked many questions (only the Chinese asked more).
- *Brazil*: used many commands and much facial gazing. They often touched one another on the arm during the negotiation.
- *French*: used an aggressive negotiating style with a high percentage of threats and warnings. They used interruptions and facial gazing.
- *Chinese*: asked many questions. Nearly three-quarters of statements by Chinese negotiators were information-exchange tactics.

"Noise" in negotiations

In international business negotiations, cultural distance affects communication by introducing "noise" – misunderstandings, misinterpretations and psychological discomfort – which causes the parties to be unsure about each other. Does the other side trust them? Can they trust the other side? In the event of conflict arising after the negotiations have concluded, will it be possible to resolve the conflict quickly? In joint venture negotiations, to what extent is there a risk of future opportunistic behaviour by the other, culturally distant party?

The success of international business negotiations depends on negotiators' ability to bridge barriers of distrust springing from cultural differences and to communicate effectively. In many negotiations, differences of language and communication norms, together with incompatible organisational cultures create formidable barriers. When negotiations are held in culturally distant countries, typical problems that arise include

- the inability to understand the local decision-making process;
- the lack of understanding role of the government's role, and the status of business in the local community.

In China, there is often a need for frequent summaries of negotiation proceedings – partly because of the Chinese communication approach, which, to Western negotiators, gives the impression of discussing all issues at once without apparent focus or order (Nisbett, 2003).

Nonverbal communication

Another important aspect of negotiating behaviour that is influenced by culture relates to nonverbal signals. During international business negotiations, negotiators' attitudes and emotions are communicated nonverbally without their conscious awareness. For instance, two managers from different ethnic groups may unconsciously communicate dislike for each other by avoiding eye contact, and by sitting or standing at a great distance from each other. Such nonverbal signals give valuable insights into the negotiators' attitudes and priorities. In the tense atmosphere of a business negotiation posture, facial expression and body tension are harder to control than verbal communication, and so are more reliable indicators of feeling and intention.

Studies show that negotiators may use nonverbal signals to assert their dominance and increase psychological pressure on the opponent. Semnani-Azad & Adair (2011), for instance, describe nonverbal power moves made by Canadian negotiators, who use seemingly inoffensive, relaxed posture as a powerful signal to opponents. The Canadians' apparent relaxed attitude signalled a negotiator who did not have to try very hard and who, because of that, was failing to honour the opponent's face. In a somewhat similar use of nonverbal signals to communicate dominance, Chinese participants in Semnani-Azad & Adair's (2011) study made use of forward-leaning, paper-spreading space occupation.

Such evidence shows that in international business negotiations there is no one way, no common standard, for asserting dominance over the opposing party. There are only culturally influenced variations. A single norm of dominant negotiator behaviour based on cultural consensus cannot be isolated. Bülow & Kumar (2011) make the same point about many other culturally influenced types of negotiator behaviour.

Many nonverbal behaviours are cultural products, and therefore liable to be misunderstood. Silence is a type of nonverbal behaviour that is culturally influenced. Periods of silence make most Western negotiators feel very uncomfortable, for instance. East Asians, on the other hand, have no problem with silence in negotiations – so much so that they tend not to be successful in turn maintenance and may be squeezed out of the discussion when negotiating with Europeans (Clyne, 1994). The Chinese method of apologising by bowing and smiling may be seen by Western negotiators as a sign of insincerity and untrust-worthiness. At the end of a sales negotiation in Brazil, an American manager made an OK sign with his hand by joining thumb and forefinger. His intention was to express satisfaction with a good negotiating session, but in Brazil the gesture is seen as obscene, and an invitation to a follow-up negotiation was not forthcoming.

Choosing an interpreter

When negotiators with different mother tongues discuss an issue using a lingua franca or the first language of one of the parties, misunderstandings may arise and motives may be questioned. The problem can be mitigated by using an interpreter. In international business negotiations, interpreters should ideally have the same cultural background as one of the negotiating teams, together with an excellent knowledge of the other teams' cultural values and prac-tices. This level of experience and understanding will allow the interpreter to communicate a speaker's intended meaning. If, for example, "fair play" has to be translated into Russian, the interpreter should, from his or her knowledge of Russian culture, be able to find a Russian phrase that captures the intended meaning. Professional interpreters should also be capable of clearing up many cross-cultural misunderstandings by providing appropriate explanations, such as "The speaker's facial expression indicates that she thinks the time-frame being proposed is unrealistic."

Salacuse (2003) presents guidelines to help managers using interpreters to negotiate more effectively. For instance, managers should choose their own interpreters. It can be a mistake to rely on the other side's interpreter unless someone on your team understands the language and can check the transla-tion. It is always important to brief the interpreter on the background of the negotiation – the companies involved, the nature of their businesses, the desired outcome of the negotiations and so on. Salacuse advises negotiators to beware of interpreters who try to take control of negotiations or slant them in a partic-ular way. The risk of this happening can be high if the interpreter also works as a middleman, agent or business consultant and is hoping for future business opportunities from the deal.

Need to brief interpreters

Interpreters in international business negotiations need a good understanding of negotiating procedure and vocabulary as well as an understanding commonly used technical terminology for the subject being discussed. They need to be briefed in advance on any specialised vocabulary that may be used. During negotiating sessions, the interpreter should not be expected to work non-stop for long periods, as the strain of prolonged concentration leads to translation errors. Most interpreters find it easier to provide accurate translations when managers speak clearly and slowly and utter only a few phrases before pausing for the translation to be made.

Sometimes a member of one of the negotiating teams offers to act as interpreter, but this arrangement can be risky. When Western consultants were carrying out a sociological survey of villages in a rural area of India, a member of the Brahmin caste who knew the local language offered to act as interpreter.

But the villagers gave answers that they thought the Brahmin wanted to hear. Sometimes the Brahmin put words in the villagers' mouths and supplied answers he thought they should have made.

Such lapses led to numerous inaccuracies, and the consultants were forced to suspend the fieldwork until a professional interpreter could be brought in from the city.

KEY POINTS

1. The cultural background of negotiators influences their negotiating behaviour, strategies and desired outcomes in terms of general agreement, contract or business relationships. Negotiators from low uncertainty-avoidance cultures, for instance, tend to use *factual arguments* to convince their opponents, while negotiators from high uncertainty-avoidance cultures may use *emotional appeals*. Managers from "moderate" cultures respond in a measured, cautious way to the other side's offers and proposals. Managers from "extremity" cultures, on the other hand, tend to be less cautious and guarded in their responses.
2. International business negotiations take place between people from different countries who have absorbed their national cultures' values, beliefs and communicative norms. Negotiators bring to the table culturally derived assumptions about what constitutes correct negotiating behaviour. By consulting surveys of national cultural values, managers can predict the negotiating styles and strategies likely to be used by foreign negotiators. Negotiators from high-femininity cultures, such as the Scandinavian countries, might, for instance, be expected to avoid aggressive confrontations and displays of anger, and to adopt a sensible, problem-solving approach to the negotiations.
3. No one study of culture and negotiation can provide a single list of dos and don'ts for international business negotiators. Sweeping generalisations about culture's impact on negotiation need to be balanced against the specifics of particular negotiations. Students of culture and negotiation should explore the underlying cultural assumptions of a study as opposed to uncritically accepting its findings. Many studies of the impact of culture on negotiation use data collected in simulated negotiations. But negotiators behave differ-

ently in "live" and experimental situations. They tend, for instance, to take fewer risks in an actual business negotiation in which a valuable contract is at stake.

4. Generalisations about *regional cultures* are vaguer and easier to challenge than generalisations about national cultures. Nevertheless, awareness of the characteristics of economic regions can be very helpful for international business negotiators. Arab countries score high on power distance and collectivism dimensions, moderately on masculine, and low on long-term orientation. This suggests that Arab negotiators might be expected to respect and follow the instructions of people in authority, and to focus on relationship building when conducting business negotiations.

5. To acquire knowledge of the negotiating preferences and characteristics of other cultures, managers need not carry out exhaustive and expensive research on a country-by-country basis. There are shortcuts. Country similarity theory, for instance, explains that when countries are similar to each other in language, per capita incomes, extent of industrialisation, technology, literacy levels and other important features, people from those countries will tend to react in similar ways – in negotiations and elsewhere – to a given argument or appeal. (O'Connell, 1997)

6. Negotiators are influenced by organisational culture as well as by national culture. Disentangling the impact made by each kind of culture is difficult. In Salacuse's (1998) survey, respondents from various countries listed their preferences in such matters as negotiation outcome ("win-win" or "win-lose"), and negotiation process ("one leader" or "team"). There were striking cultural similarities at the national level, but respondents' choices were also mediated by their organisational and professional cultures. Groups of military personnel, for instance, made similar choices regardless of nationality.

7. A knowledge of the central tendencies revealed by surveys of national cultures is very useful for managers who are about to visit a foreign country to participate in business negotiations. The central tendencies reveal values, ideas and behaviours that are acceptable in the country concerned and that foreign business visitors should be aware of and conform to during negotiations with local firms and when interacting with local people.

8. Approaches to negotiation that are used successfully in one context and one country often turn out to be ineffective when transferred to a different context and a different country. In the US, for instance, teams outperform sole negotiators in buying/selling negotiations. But the effect of teams on business negotiations differs across cultures. For instance, harmony norms predominate in Taiwan and many other collectivist cultures, and concern with harmony may lead Taiwanese negotiating teams to negotiate less satisfactory outcomes than those achieved by Taiwanese sole negotiators.

9. The concept of cultural distance is widely used in international business to assess the extent to which the business values and practices in countries differ from each other. As differences increase between any two countries' language,

laws and business practices, negotiations between business people from the countries become increasingly difficult. The negotiators may fail to understand each other's motivations and intentions. Cultural distance introduces "noise" into the negotiations – misunderstandings, misinterpretations and psychological discomfort. For example, in international acquisition negotiations, cultural distance between the parties can lead to inadequate understanding of the foreign market and lead to the acquirer paying too much for the target company.

QUESTIONS FOR DISCUSSION AND WRITTEN ASSIGNMENTS

1. "When managers negotiate with people from other cultures, the differences between them become salient." Describe three major differences that impinge on international business negotiations. How do these differences influence the outcomes achieved?
2. "Culture influences the negotiation styles that are used in international business negotiations." Briefly describe the typical negotiation styles of negotiators from

   i. Scandinavian countries
   ii. Latin American countries
   iii. The US
   iv. China
   v. Japan

3. Explain the main differences between high-context and low-context cultures, and the impact made by these differences on business negotiations between teams from high-context and low-context countries.

BIBLIOGRAPHY

Ali, A. J. Cultural discontinuity and Arab management thought. *International Studies of Management and Organisation*, 25 (3), 1995, 7–30.

Aritz, J. & Walker, R. C. Cognitive organization and identity maintenance in multicultural teams: a discourse analysis of decision-making meetings. *Journal of Business Communication*, 47 (1), 2010, 20–41.

Brett, J. M. *Negotiating Globally*. Jossey-Bass, 2001.

Brett, J. & Gelfand, M. A cultural analysis of the underlying assumptions of negotiation theory. In L. L. Thompson (ed.) *Frontiers of Social Psychology: Negotiations*. Psychology Press, 2005, 173–202.

Brouthers, K. D., Brouthers, L. E. & Wilkinson, T. Strategic alliances: choose your partners. *Long Range Planning*, 28 (3), 1955, 18–25.

Bülow, A. M. & Kumar, R. Culture and negotiation. *International Negotiation*, 16 (3), 2011, 349–359.

Chen, G. O. H. *Negotiating with the Chinese*. Dartmouth, 1996.

Chen, Y-R., Leung, K. & Chen, C. C. Bringing national culture to the table: making a difference with cross-cultural differences and perspectives. *The Academy of Management Annals*, 3 (1), 2009, 217–249.

Clyne, M. *Inter-cultural Communication at Work*. Cambridge University Press, 1994.

Ding, D. Exploring Chinese conflict management styles in joint venture in the People's Republic of China. *Management Research News*, 19 (9), 1996, 45–55.

Drake, L. E. The culture-negotiation link. *Human Communication Research*, 27 (3), 2001, 317–349.

Elashmawi, F. & Harris, P. R. *Multicultural Management 2000: Essential Cultural Insights for Global Business Success*. Gulf Publishing, 1998.

Elgstrom, O. Norms, culture, and cognitive patterns in foreign aid negotiations. *Negotiation Journal*, (6), 1990, 147–159.

Epstein, M. J. The drivers of success in post-merger integration. *Organisational Dynamics*, 33, 2004, 174–189.

Erickson, F. & Shultz, J. *The Counsellor as Gatekeeper: Social Interaction in Interviews*. Academic Press, 1982.

Fisher, G. *International Negotiation: A Cross-cultural Perspective*. Intercultural Press, 1980.

Floris, M., Grant, D. & Cutcher, L. Mining the discourse: strategizing during BHP Billiton's attempted acquisition of Rio Tinto. *Journal of Management Studies*, 50 (7), 2013, 1185–1215.

Foster, D. A. *Bargaining across Borders*. McGraw-Hill, 1992.

Gelfand, M. J., Lun, J., Lyons, S. & Shteynberg, G. Descriptive norms as carriers of culture in negotiation. *International Negotiation*, 16 (3), 2011, 361–381.

Gelfand, M. J., Brett, J., Gunia, B. C., Imai, L., Huang, T-J. & Hsu, B-F. Toward a culture-by-context perspective on negotiation: negotiating teams in the United States and Taiwan. *Journal of Applied Psychology*, 98 (3), 2013, 504–513.

Graham, J. The influence of culture on the negotiation process. *Journal of International Business Studies*, 16, 1985, 81–96.

Graham, J. Vis-à-vis international business negotiations. In P. Ghauri & J-C. Usunier (eds) *International Business Negotiations*. Pergamon, 1996, 69–90.

Graham, J. L. An exploratory study of the process of marketing negotiations using a cross-cultural perspective. In R. C. Scarcella, E. S. Andersen & S. D. Krashen (eds) *Developing Communicative Competence in a Second Language*. Heinle and Heinle, 1990, 239–279.

Graham, J. & Sano, Y. Business negotiations between Japanese and Americans. In P. Ghauri & J-C. Usunier (eds) *International Business Negotiations*. Pergamon, 1996, 353–367.

Guerra, V. M. & Giner-Sorolla, R. The community, autonomy, and divinity scale (CADS): a new tool for the cross-cultural study of morality. *Journal of Cross-cultural Psychology*, 41 (1), 2010, 35–50.

Hall, E. T. *The Hidden Dimension*. New York: Doubleday, 1966.

Hashimoto, H. & Yamagishi, T. Self-sustaining mechanism behind Japanese interdependence. Paper presented at the GCOE 3rd International Symposium: Socio-Ecological Approaches to Cultural and Social Psychological Processes. Hokkaido, 2009.

Hofstede, G. *Culture's Consequences: International Differences in Work-related Values*. Sage, 1980.

Hofstede, G. *Cultures and Organisations: Software of the Mind*. McGraw Hill, rev. ed., 1997.

Hofstede, G., Hofstede, G. J., & Minkov, M. *Cultures and Organizations: Software of the Mind*. McGraw-Hill, 3rd ed., 2010.

House, R. J. et al. (eds) *Culture, Leadership and Organisations: The GLOBE Study of 62 Societies*. Sage, 2004.

Kazakov, A. Y. et al. Business ethics and civil society in Russia. *International Studies of Management and Organisation*, 27 (1), 1997, 5–18.

Kogut, B. & Singh, H. The effect of national culture on the choice of entry mode. *Journal of International Business Studies*, 19, 1988, 411–432.

Kumar, R. & Nti, K. O. National cultural values and the evolution of process and outcome discrepancies in international strategic alliances. *Journal of Applied Behavioural Science*, 40, 2004, 344–361.

Kumar, R. & Worm, V. Institutional dynamics and the negotiation process: comparing India and China. *International Journal of Conflict Management*, 15 (3), 2004, 304–334.

Kumar, R. Culture and emotions in intercultural negotiations: an overview. In M. J. Gelfand and J. M. Brett (eds) *The Handbook of Negotiation and Culture*. Stanford University Press, 2004, 95–113.

Lewis, R. *When Cultures Collide*. Nicholas Brealey, 2006.

Maddux, W. W., Kim, P. H., Okumura, T. & Brett, J. M. Cultural differences in the functions and meaning of apologies, *International Negotiation*, 16 (3), 2011, 405–425.

Manrai, L. A. & Manrai, A. K. The influence of culture in international business negotiations: a new conceptual framework and managerial implications. *Journal of Transnational Management*, 15, 2010, 69–100.

Metcalf. L. et al. Cultural influences in negotiations, *International Journal of Cross Cultural Management*, 7 (2), 2007, 163–164.

Metcalf, L. & Bird. A. (2004). Integrating the Hofstede dimensions and twelve aspects of negotiating behavior: a six-country comparison. In Vinken, H. et al. (eds), *Comparing Cultures*. Brill, 2004, 251–269.

Nakamoto, M. When culture masks communication. *Financial Times*, 23 October 2000, 15.

Nisbett, R. E. *The Geography of Thought: How Asians and Westerners Think Differently...and Why*, Free Press, 2003.

O'Connell, J. (ed.) *The Blackwell Encyclopaedic Dictionary of International Management*. Blackwell, 1997.

Ramirez-Marin, J. Y. & Brett, J. M. Relational construal in negotiation: propositions and examples from Latin and Anglo Cultures. *International Negotiation*, 16 (3), 2011, 383–404.

Requejo, W. H. & Graham, J. L. *Global Negotiation: The New Rules*. Palgrave Macmillan, 2008.

Salacuse, J. W. Ten ways that culture affects negotiating style: some survey results. *Negotiation Journal*, 14 (3), 1998, 221–240.

Salacuse, J. W. *The Global Negotiator: Making, Managing and Mending Deals around the World in the Twenty-first Century*. Palgrave Macmillan, 2003.

Schein, E. H. Culture: the missing concept in organisational studies. *Administrative Science Quarterly*, 41 (2), 1986, 229–240.

Schein, E. H. Organisational culture. *American Psychologist*, 45 (2), 1990, 109–119.

Schwartz, S. H. Beyond individualism/collectivism: new cultural dimensions of values. In U. Kim et al. (eds) *Individualism and Collectivism: Theory, Method, and Applications*. Sage, 1994, 85–119.

Scollon, R. & Scollon, S. W. *Intercultural Communication: A Discourse Approach*, 2nd ed. Blackwell, 2nd ed., 2001.

Semnani-Azad, Z. & Adair, W. L. The display of "dominant" nonverbal cues in negotiation: the role of culture and gender. *International Negotiation*, 16 (3), 2011, 451–479.

Shell, R. G. *Bargaining for Advantage*. Penguin Books, 2006.

Smith, P. B. Communication styles as dimensions of national culture. *Journal of Cross-cultural Psychology*, 42 (2), 2011, 216–233.

Stahl, G. K., Maznevski, M., Voigt, A. & Jonsen, K. Unravelling the effects of cultural diversity in teams: A meta-analysis of research on multicultural work groups. *Journal of International Business Studies*, 41, 2010, 371–392.

Stahl, G. K. & Voigt, A. Do cultural differences matter in mergers and acquisitions? A tentative model and meta-analytical examination. *Organisation Science*, 19, 2008, 160–176.

Thompson, L., Peterson, E. & Brodt, S. Team negotiation: an examination of integrative and distributive bargaining. *Journal of Personality and Social Psychology*, 70, 1996, 66–78.

Tinsley, C. H., Turan, N. M., Aslani, S. & Weingart, L. R. The interplay between culturally and situationally based mental models of intercultural dispute resolution: West meets Middle East. *International Negotiation*, 16 (3), 2011, 481–510.

Triandis, H. C. *Culture and Social Behavior*. New York: McGraw-Hill, 1994.

Wegener, B. & Liebig, S. Dominant ideologies and the variation of distributive justice norms: a comparison of East and West Germany, and the United States. In J. R. Kuegel, D. S. Mason and B. Wegener (eds) *Social Justice and Political Change*. De Gruyter, 1995, 239–262.

Weiss, S. E. International business negotiation in a globalizing world: reflections on the contributions and future of a (sub)field. *International Negotiation*, 11, 2006, 287–316.

Woo, H. S. & Prud'homme, C. Cultural characteristics prevalent in the Chinese negotiation process. *European Business Review*, 99 (5), 1999, 313.

Yamagishi, T. & Mifune, N. (2008). Does shared group membership promote altruism? *Rationality and Society*, 20, 2008, 5–30.

Negotiating Power

3

INTRODUCTION

Negotiating power consists of the capabilities negotiators can acquire to give themselves an advantage in international business negotiations and increase the probability of achieving their negotiating goals. Power is a central element of negotiations (Zartman, 1994). Parties with negotiating power have the ability change other parties' behaviour, although a negotiator with negotiating power may choose not to use it. Abuses of negotiating power occur when a company uses its power in negotiations to make unreasonable demands. Because both parties in an international business negotiation have alternatives, negotiating power is necessarily a relative concept. A party's power is high or low relative to the other party. Power equality increases interdependence between the parties. Often in international business negotiations the parties have equal negotiating power, which means that neither can dictate the terms of the agreement: they have to rely on negotiation to reach a satisfactory agreement. A satisfactory agreement is one that allows the parties to protect their interests and achieve at least some of their negotiation goals.

Sources of negotiating power in international business negotiations include capital, technology and established marketing networks – as well as a company's innovative capacity and knowledge. In alliance negotiations, for instance, a company's negotiating power often stems from its *technological and business knowledge* as embedded in patents, trademarks, copyrights and other kinds of intellectual property. For example, over many decades AT&T's possession of numerous patents and trademarks has given the company great negotiating power in international business negotiations (Dupont, 1996). *Local knowledge* also plays an important role, for instance, in negotiations between multinational enterprises (MNEs) and their foreign subsidiaries, or between international joint venture (IJV) partners. Local knowledge includes familiarity with local business practices, legal requirements, local market conditions, relations with government and so forth. (Kamoche & Harvey, 2006).

During an international business negotiation, becoming fixated on a single option ties negotiators' hands and reduces their negotiating power. Managers can increase their negotiating power by preparing several optional packages for the other side to consider. In the fast-changing world of international business, options are needed because they allow the negotiator to be flexible and change strategic direction if necessary. A manager with only one sales package to offer is powerless if the other side rejects the package. The best alternative to a negotiated agreement (BATNA) is an important option because it provides the negotiator's bottom line or reservation price, that is, the minimum amount required for a deal to be acceptable.

In the past, the negotiating power of MNEs vis-à-vis the emerging markets of China, India, Russia and Brazil and South Africa was based largely on an MNEs' financial resources and technological capabilities. But negotiating power that relies on these traditional assets is diminishing in international markets. In China, for instance, the rise of China's own markets is making the Chinese far less dependent on Western MNEs than they were as recently as 20 years ago. In the future, successful business deals with the Chinese will depend on offering the right products and services to the right customers at the right price (Stalk & Michael, 2011).

Hard-power tactics used by negotiators in international business negotiations include crude displays of assets and capability, threats to withhold payments and the setting of unreasonable deadlines. Large, powerful companies sometimes use these tactics when negotiating with organisations in less developed countries. The hard-power tactic of displaying anger in a business negotiation may lead a less powerful negotiator to fear that his or her economic outcomes will be reduced. Negotiators who experience fear and other negative emotions in negotiations in effect lose negotiating power by becoming risk-averse conflict avoiders – and therefore less effective negotiators.

WHAT IS NEGOTIATING POWER?

Concept and definitions

Negotiating power is the relative ability of parties in a negotiation to exert influence over each other because of their size, resources or status. Zartman (1994) defines negotiating power as the ability of one party in a negotiation to cause the other party to change behaviour in a given direction. In international business negotiations, negotiating power gives a party a high degree of control over the interaction and negotiating outcomes. Both tangible and intangible sources of negotiating power are important. Tangible sources of negotiating power include capital, technology, expert knowledge of the subject of negotiation and so on. Intangible sources of negotiating power include innovative ability, creativity, tactical acuity and negotiating skill. According to Lewicki, Saunders & Barry (2009), negotiating power consists of the capabilities negotiators can assemble to give themselves an advantage in a negotiation and increase the probability of achieving their negotiating goals. When negotiating the terms of an IJV, for instance, a company may consciously exploit its technology-based reputation or its control of distribution channels to give itself an advantage and obtain preferential terms.

Stevens (1963) and other early researchers supposed that negotiations of all kinds begin with a focus on power that usually results in the most powerful party forcing the other party or parties to accept its demands. However, later studies have found that successful negotiators rely less on power and more on cooperation and restraint to achieve their negotiating goals. Moreover, in international business negotiations restraint may be shown by negotiators who have much negotiating power but choose not to use it. According to Greenhalgh & Gilkey (1993), female negotiators often choose not to exploit their own or their organisations' negotiating power because they tend to see the negotiation encounter as just one component of a long-term relationship. This perception prompts female negotiators (as well as negotiators from some collectivist countries) to adopt a *problem-solving approach* to negotiation that avoids conflict and leads to mutual gain between the parties. Walters et al. (1998) found that female negotiators are less likely than male negotiators to adopt competitive, hard-bargaining strategies, and are more likely to share information and reach agreements amicably and quickly.

Bargaining

Negotiation can be viewed as a form of problem solving in which the parties see negotiation as a method of jointly finding a solution to a common problem. *Bargaining*, by contrast, is characterised by a competitive spirit in which the parties try competitively to maximise individual gains. A bargainer has a win-lose orientation and a distributive interest. A negotiator has a win-win orientation and an integrative interest.

Whereas the negotiation process includes the full range of interaction among the parties, bargaining is a narrower process that takes place within the frame of negotiation. Thus bargaining can be regarded as a subprocess of negotiation. According to Gulliver (1979), bargaining is limited to the presentation and exchange of specific proposals for the terms of agreement on particular issues. Each party typically identifies bottom-line, opening, and fall-back positions, and concessions are made grudgingly.

Bargaining theory is based on the assumption that decision making in a negotiation can be treated as if it refers to a single issue (e.g. the profits of a cross-border project) and that it can be measured in terms of money (Gulliver, 1979).

Precisely this aspect of bargaining reduces its usefulness as a tool for international business negotiators since international business negotiators usually have to take decisions about *several* complex issues negotiated simultaneously. Many authors, however (e.g. Lax & Sebenius, 1986), regard the distinction between negotiation and bargaining as of little practical value in view of the wide variation in usage. In practice, "negotiating power" and "bargaining power" tend to be used interchangeably.

Abuses of negotiating power

Negotiating power is neither good nor bad; rather, it is the *abuse* of negotiating power that draws criticism. In international business negotiations, powerful and ambitious companies sometimes abuse their bargaining power by making unreasonable demands (Greve et al., 2010). In these negotiations the less powerful party typically responds by making repeated concessions and engaging in other kinds of submissive behaviour. Brett et al. (2009) give the example of managers of large and powerful Chinese organisations negotiating with foreign sales representatives in China and demanding price reductions of as much as 50 percent if a deal is to be finalised. Another example is the MNE which used hard-power tactics to set up an exploitative deal with a small distributor in Jamaica. From the outset of negotiation it was obvious that the MNE, with its vastly greater resources, possessed much greater bargaining power than the local distributor. The MNE's negotiating team went on to use their superior power to make extreme demands as a condition of finalising an agreement.

Dunning (2003) argues that globalisation is continuously increasing the negotiating power of MNEs which are thereby able to take advantage of the weak, uncoordinated regulatory powers of developing countries in Africa, Asia and South America. Regulatory bodies in these countries tend to be weak and ineffective. As a result, Downing argues, the countries are increasingly powerless to control the activities of powerful MNEs operating within their borders.

Greve et al. (2010) note that in IJV negotiations, one of the partners sometimes abuses its negotiating power by threatening to withhold valuable resources from the venture or even to walk away from the table unless its demands for preferential terms are met. Abuses of negotiating power are commonplace in other contexts. Goal-focused posturing, for instance, regularly takes place in the United Nations (UN). Having a veto in the UN Security Council gives some members the right to block resolutions by abstaining from voting – which is roughly equivalent to walking away from the negotiating table if their demands are not met.

Balance of negotiating power

In international business negotiations, negotiating power partly depends on who needs whom the most. If neither party has more negotiating power than their opponent, then neither side can *impose* a deal. Each side's power is limited, that is, neither side can unilaterally decide the outcome without negotiating with the other side. This balance-of-power situation encourages the parties to continue negotiating, thereby increasing the probability of a satisfactory negotiated agreement being reached.

Power-balance fluctuations

Consider the situation of a multinational mining company embarking on negotiations with the government of a developing country about mineral extraction rights in the country. During the initial negotiations, because of its great financial and technological resources which the country needs, the company possesses much greater bargaining power than the government. The government needs the company more than the company needs the government – a situation which gives the company great negotiating power. The company can demonstrate its negotiating power by refusing to invest, or by walking away from the table.

Further down the line, however, the balance of negotiating power may swing. Once the contract has been signed and the company has invested, the company becomes hostage to its own sunk costs. As a result, over the following months and years the negotiating power of the company gradually diminishes. The government, by contrast, gains negotiating power by inviting other multinational companies to negotiate for similar projects in the country. When the government's negotiating power exceeds that of the mining company, that is, when the company needs the government more than the government needs the company, the government may call for renegotiation of the contract in order to improve the terms of the original agreement.

In international business, contract renegotiation often occurs when there has been a decisive shift in the power balance between the parties (Raiffa, 1982). In the past, following several high-profile renegotiations that have occurred, foreign investors have called for penalties to be imposed on the party (usually the host government) which breaks the original contract. Tacit collusion among investing firms sometimes achieves the same end by making it unprofitable for a host government to force renegotiation on any one of them.

Economic and military power

After studying the complicated and extremely protracted negotiations between Turkey, Syria and Iraq about water allocations from the Euphrates and the Tigris Rivers, Daoudy (2009) notes the various forms of negotiating power that were displayed by the parties at different times. Negotiating power was closely related throughout the negotiations to a country's economic and military power. As Turkey possessed the most economic and military resources, it therefore had much greater negotiating power in negotiations than the other parties. This advantage gave Turkey the capacity to set and control the negotiation agenda – and therefore the negotiations.

Syria and Iraq, the less powerful parties, were motivated by the obvious *imbalance* of power to act opportunistically. They did so by making bilateral, short-term agreements in order to achieve at least some of their negotiating goals.

Case Study

MINI-CASE: Power balance?

Sometimes, reaching a negotiated agreement is the only way in which the parties can achieve their goals. That was the case in the 1980s when IBM embarked on negotiations with the Mexican government about establishing production plants in Mexico. Before detailed negotiations began, the two sides had to educate each other, in formal and informal discussions, about computer technology and local conditions respectively. The negotiations themselves were conducted both by means of informal discussions and through a process of formal proposals and responses.

At the time of the initial negotiations, IBM's willingness to contribute resources and technological know-how to the proposed project gave the company great negotiating power. This was matched, however, by the power of the Mexican government whose negotiators were given power to authorise the project – or to turn it down.

The resulting power balance led to protracted and complex negotiations. Numerous actors, ranging from individuals, groups and departments, to organisations and groups of organisations, were involved at various times in the negotiations. Both sides also went through constant internal negotiations.

Eventually, however, a final agreement was reached. A wholly owned IBM operation would produce 603,000 PCs over five years, and transfer new technology within six months of its US debut.

Source: Weiss (1996)

Questions:

1. *Develop an argument to show that in fact an imbalance of negotiating power probably existed between the parties during the negotiations. Identify the factors accounting for the imbalance.*
2. *Under what circumstances might the power balance swing in favour of the government? What might be the immediate and long-term consequences of such a swing?*

Hard power and soft power

Hard power is often used in international business negotiations. It involves the use of threats, payments and other forms of coercion. Hard-power negotiating strategies that are frequently used by international business negotiators include crude displays of assets and capability as well as

- demonstrations of market share, control of distribution channels and so forth;
- threats to withhold payments or approvals;
- unreasonable demands;
- unreasonable deadlines.

In the context of international business, an effective use of hard power was Bill Gates's threat to halt development of Office for Mac unless Apple adopted Microsoft's Web browser. A more benign use of hard power was Sony's bid to attract developers to its video game platform by cutting industry-standard licensing fees in half (Yoffie & Kwak, 2006).

Hard-power strategies can be effective when used as bargaining chips in business negotiations. They are, however, less effective at building trust and a long-term relationship between the parties. Indeed, they can inspire a backlash, driving companies to avoid being dependent on a more powerful partner.

Soft power

Soft power has been described as the behavioural way of achieving one's goals and getting the outcomes one wants through cooperation and attraction, as opposed to coercion (Nye, 2004). Soft power is often used by governments. In international business negotiations, strategies based on uses of soft power rely on leading the other side to want what one wants through incentives and persuasion, rather than through threats and bribes.

An example of the use of soft power is the agreement signed in Algiers following lengthy negotiations between Chinese negotiators and the Algerian government. Under the agreement, the Chinese would finance and build a multimillion dollar mosque in Algiers. Another example of the use of soft power is the new space-age headquarters of the African Union in Addis Ababa, which is being designed and built by the Chinese as a gift to Africa.

International business negotiators often use a combination of hard and soft power in negotiations to achieve their goals, with soft power setting the stage for the more selective use of hard power. The soft power strategy of *sharing information,* for instance, plays a pivotal role in most international business negotiations. Sharing information might involve providing a potential alliance partner with market intelligence or providing a foreign supplier with information about the company's future product plans in order to encourage cooperation.

Case Study

MINI-CASE: Hard-power strategy

In international business negotiations, it is common practice for powerful negotiators to use their bargaining strength to obtain the best possible deal for themselves – to gain the most from an opponent while conceding the least.

An example of how hard negotiating power can be used to obtain highly favourable outcomes for the powerful party is General Electric's "final-offer-first" approach. GE used to frequently employ this approach during negotiations with domestic and foreign labour unions. Firm offers and demands were decided by the company in advance. These were presented very early in the negotiations in a spirit of take it or leave it. GE's great bargaining strength in these negotiations came from very thorough pre-negotiation preparation combined with a policy of direct communication with employees, while at the same time ignoring union officials.

Questions:

1. *To what extent can GE's former "final-offer-first" approach to negotiation be considered an abuse of negotiating power?*
2. *Negotiating power has been described as the ability of a negotiator to follow a distributive, win-lose strategy in a negotiation and achieve a favourable outcome. Formulate a better description of negotiating power in the context of international business negotiation.*

SOURCES OF NEGOTIATING POWER

Varied sources

Several researchers (e.g. Dobrijevic et al., 2011) have identified the main sources of negotiating power in international business negotiations. Awareness and understanding of these varied sources of negotiating power can help managers involved in international business negotiations assess the strengths and weaknesses of their opponents, and predict the negotiating strategies they are likely to use. Sources of negotiating power include

- knowledge
- language
- need
- relationships
- time

Knowledge

Two kinds of knowledge in particular increase a company's negotiating power in international business negotiations:

Business and technological knowledge. Much of a company's knowledge is embedded in patents, trademarks, copyrights and other kinds of intellectual property. For instance, AT&T's numerous patents and trademarks have consistently given the company great negotiating power in international business negotiations.

Local knowledge. Local knowledge plays a key role in negotiations between MNEs and their foreign subsidiaries, and in alliance and IJV negotiations. Ghemawat (2007) argues that local knowledge and the fact that overseas subsidiaries are embedded in local contexts are key success factors for MNEs. Local knowledge includes local business practices, legal requirements, local market conditions, relations with government and so on (Kamoche & Harvey, 2006).

Negotiators who are knowledgeable about the specific subject of a negotiation have considerable negotiating power because they are equipped to answer questions and deal with objections and can therefore influence the other side.

The negotiating power of Western companies in the emerging markets of China, India, Russia, Brazil and South Africa tends to be based on Western companies' technological and business knowledge, although, according to Stalk & Michael (2011), negotiating power based on such assets is diminishing rapidly. In China, for instance, the rise of China's own markets is making the Chinese far less dependent on Western companies than they were even two decades ago. Increasingly, successful business deals with companies in the emerging economies of Asia and South America are going to depend on offering the right products and services to the right customers at the right price.

Tacit knowledge

Technical experts working on, say, a product development team often share the same expert and tacit knowledge. Tacit knowledge acquired through a manager's experience of international business and other situations is a key asset in many international business contexts. But tacit knowledge is personal and held inside the manager's head. It is difficult to put into words and difficult to demonstrate in a negotiation. According to Brown & Duguid (2001), tacit knowledge is best studied and understood at the level of communities of practice within an organisation or a network of organisations.

Language

Language is a potent source of negotiating power in international business negotiations. When the negotiators have different mother tongues, a working language may have to be chosen for the negotiation. The choice of a working language creates winners and losers. Non-native speakers of the language that is chosen are the losers since they may have difficulty presenting ideas and proposals in what for them is a foreign language. They may have to resort to interpreters during negotiating sessions and to translation for documents. Fortunately, translation is becoming easier and more affordable with the emergence of sophisticated translation software.

Mäkelä et al. (2006) identify a "clustering" phenomenon of firms, for example, subsidiaries of an MNE, with close linguistic and cultural affinity. In the case of MNE subsidiary companies, the firms communicate, cooperate and share knowledge with each other. By contrast, subsidiaries with major linguistic and cultural differences may fail to communicate knowledge to each other unless headquarters insists on their making a greater effort.

In international business negotiations, managers from firms in countries with close linguistic and cultural affinity – Spain and Portugal, for instance, or Namibia and South Africa – can usually communicate and negotiate effectively with each other. There is little or no loss of negotiating power in negotiations as a result of cultural and linguistic difference. This is not the case, however, when the negotiating firms are based in countries with great linguistic and cultural differences, such as Australia and Russia or Korea and Iceland.

Many companies such as those based in countries of the former Soviet Union face major challenges, including inadequate negotiating power, as they attempt to operate globally. A major reason is that their managers have to conduct negotiations in a language – typically English – which is not their mother tongue. The problem can be reduced by training managers in these and other non-English speaking countries to use *basic business English* – as opposed to standard, grammatically correct English – thus equipping them to participate in business negotiations in many parts of the world. As Charles (2007) points out, the frame of reference of basic business English is provided by the globalised business community, whose members have many values in common, such as doing profitable business.

Need

In both international and domestic business negotiations, the relative power of the parties generally depends on who needs whom the most. Thus, when Dobrijevic et al. (2011) interviewed 31 negotiators, they found that they regarded *need* as the most relied-on source of power in any given negotiating situation. The greater the need of one of the parties, the greater the power of the negotiator who was able to supply that need. If, for instance, a company has a unique product which an overseas buyer really needs, this gives the company negotiating power over the buyer.

In negotiations between an MNE and a manufacturing company in a developing country, sources of bargaining power for the MNE might be its potential for market penetration, combined with the manufacturing company's reliance on the MNE for financial resources and technical expertise.

Relationships

Relationships are an important source of bargaining power. In the context of international business, the content, duration and importance of relationship-building behaviours differ across cultures (Hodgson et al., 2000). Negotiators from the collectivist countries of South America, Asia and Africa, for instance, generally attach great importance to the relationship-building stage of international business negotiations. Managers participating in international business negotiations in these countries should therefore regard time spent in small talk before and during negotiations not as time wasted but as an opportunity for relationship building.

Building interorganisational and interpersonal relationships is, according to Leung & Yeung (1995), a prerequisite for successful negotiations with the Chinese. In China, relationships with foreign firms are regarded as valuable social capital. Staber (2006) has produced evidence to show that Chinese managers tend to place more value on the relationship with the opposing party than on the written contract.

Whereas Western negotiators usually want to get down to business as soon as possible, Chinese negotiators will not seriously consider a business deal with foreigners who do not display the all-important behavioural traits of friendship and trust (Breth & Kaiping, 1988). Japanese negotiators see the main goal of negotiations with a foreign company as being to establish a long-term relationship – and any written contract is merely an expression of that relationship (Salacuse, 2003). Preliminary information-exchange with Japanese companies may take many months because, in Japanese eyes, that is the time it takes to build a trusting relationship with a foreign firm (Laroche, 2003).

In international business negotiations, deal-focused and time-conscious Western negotiators often fail to invest time and effort in building rapport with the other team. Instead, they tend to over-rely on their knowledge and experience to see them through. Sebenius (2002, 81) distinguishes between deal-focused and relationship-focused cultures. "In deal-focused cultures, relationships grow out of deals; in relationship-focused cultures, deals arise from already developed relationships." Kumar et al. (2005) point to the important role of informal communication in building a relationship with negotiating opponents from diverse cultural backgrounds. Informal communication in early contacts between the parties (e.g. during pre-negotiation social events) smooths the flow of discussion in later formal negotiations.

Time

Hall (1976) identifies two predominant patterns of time schedule behaviours in the world. In *monochronic* societies, people engage in one activity at a time and tend to follow time schedules. But persons in *polychronic* societies engage in multiple activities simultaneously and view time schedules as flexible. Monochronic managers will typically cut a negotiating session short to stay on schedule, whereas polychronic managers will continue to negotiate until they feel that everything has been covered. Western countries such as the US, Germany, France and the Scandinavian countries are monochronic. Arabian, Japanese and Latin American cultures are polychronic (Manrai & Manrai, 2010).

In international business negotiations, the party with the least time constraint often has the greater bargaining power. Negotiators who are under constant pressure from head office to finalise negotiations may resort to making unnecessary concessions or unwise trade-offs in order to speed progress towards an agreement. An international procurement manager for a Dutch retail chain came under unexpected time pressure after receiving a phone call from head office telling him to quickly conclude negotiations he was holding in India with a garment manufacturer. Later the procurement manager attended a management seminar at which he made the point that the time pressure applied by head office while he was in India had reduced his bargaining power by making it impossible for him to find alternative suppliers.

When Foster (1992) compared the negotiating styles of Japanese and American negotiators, the time-conscious Americans wanted to arrive at decisions very quickly with no time wasted. The risk-averse Japanese, on the other hand, took a very long time to make decisions. For the Japanese it was necessary to carry out numerous internal consultations. The effort paid off, however, because the decisions reached were sound and efficiently implemented.

Such marked variations in negotiators' attitudes to time help explain why international business negotiations generally take much longer to complete than domestic negotiations (Herbig & Kramer, 1991). For instance, negotiations between American and Japanese negotiators were about six times longer than single-culture negotiations in Japan or the US. Usunier (1996) advises Western negotiators negotiating with firms in polychronic countries to plan softly, introduce time slack, allow for delays and not to tell the other side when they are leaving because the date may need to be changed.

POWER OF OPTIONS

Alternative packages

Sometimes a negotiating team goes into an international business negotiation with only a single, carefully worked out and carefully priced option to offer. The result of this approach is that the team loses much negotiating power if the option fails to meet the other side's needs and is rejected. To avoid such situations, Fisher et al. (1991) believe that negotiators should generate as many options as possible so that the parties are not hemmed in by a particular alternative presented early in the negotiation.

Options give negotiators bargaining power. In cross-border buying/selling negotiations, for instance, a buyer who has several *alternative suppliers* to fall back on derives bargaining power from that simple fact. In the same way, an export sales manager who knows that two or three willing buyers are only a phone call away has great bargaining power which he or she can exploit in negotiations with potential buyers merely by hinting that he or she has a Plan B. This helps to explain why, for many negotiators, developing a number of different options or alternative packages is an essential pre-negotiation task. Unless several alternative packages are generated, Trotman et al. (2005) argue, opening offers will dominate the discussion and reduce the value of the settlement.

Examples of alternative packages that might be prepared for an important cross-border sales negotiation are

- two or three alternative terms of payment;
- various percentages for sharing advertising and promotion expenses;
- packages with and without free installation;
- packages with and without extended warranty;
- alternative reservation prices.

How many options?

Generating a large number of options requires resources and can be a costly process. The process can be simplified by listing the pros and cons of each option before negotiations begin – a procedure that should help the team decide which is the *preferred option* and what should be said about it. Often the preferred option is the first one presented and discussed when formal negotiations begin. In routine, low-value negotiations only two options, a preferred package and a fall-back option, should give the team sufficient flexibility to arrive at a satisfactory agreement.

According to Medvec & Galinsky (2005), negotiators from countries which are high in uncertainty-avoidance often feel overwhelmed if presented with too many options and, as a result, may postpone making a decision. Thus when a negotiator is faced with an opponent from a high uncertainty-avoidance country such as Venezuela or Greece, the number of options to be presented to the other side might be limited to two or three.

Metge (2001) describes the Maori approach to handling options during negotiations. Typically, a Maori negotiating team pools all the relevant information it possesses. It then identifies a range of different options and discusses the advantages, disadvantages and likely consequences of each of them. As the discussion goes on, individuals group themselves in support of two or three favoured options. But when it becomes obvious that one particular option commands majority support, the holders of minority views let go of them and assent to the majority view. The final decision is unanimous.

Role of options

Olekalns et al. (2004) found that optional packages are often presented and become the focus of discussion at a relatively late stage in negotiations. About two-thirds of the way through the discussions, negotiators stop acting competitively, adopt a problem-solving mode and begin to discuss and compare old and new options. During this late stage they also set about building trust and a good relationship with the other team.

In complex, protracted negotiations, presenting new alternatives to the package already on the table revitalises the negotiation process and prevents deadlock. The new options provide the negotiators with additional measuring rods for evaluating the value of the negotiated agreement.

Assessing options

In an international business negotiation, a quick and easy way of assessing options which are on the table is in terms of their cost, feasibility and impact:

Cost. What would be the long-term and short-term costs of adopting each of the options?

Feasibility. How feasible is each option in terms of availability, reliability of supply and so forth?

Impact. Would the option have a positive or negative impact on the current situation in terms of stakeholder reaction, impact on work force and so forth?

Relatively sophisticated techniques may be needed to evaluate more complex options. Examples of complex options that may be debated during an international business negotiation are various profit-distribution options for an international joint venture and various technology transfer packages. A technique that can be applied to the evaluation of complex options such as these is contained in multi-attribute value theory (MAVT). According to Keeney & Raiffa (1976), MAVT provides negotiators with a means of making an overall assessment of options or packages with multiple attributes. When applied to a particular option, the method allows compensation of weak performance of one criterion by strong performance of another criterion. It then aggregates the option's performance across all the criteria to form an overall assessment. The second stage of the assessment is to compare the aggregate scores of the various options, with the aim of producing a preference order of the various options, based on the negotiator's value judgements.

"Away-from-table" options

An important source of negotiating power is not having to rely on negotiation to achieve a good outcome (Fisher et al., 1991). Managers negotiate in order to set up international business deals, but there are many possible alternatives to negotiation as a way of clinching a deal. For example, there are many potential buyers in various locations around the world for an export shipment of high-quality hosiery. If a sales manager is conducting negotiations with a particular overseas distributor, the manager gains negotiating power simply by realising that the overseas distributor is not the only possible buyer. Actions taken "away from the table" by the sales manager can greatly affect the outcome. The sales manager can, for instance, search for another buyer or a better price on the Internet while continuing to conduct face-to-face negotiations with the distributor. Such "away-from-table" actions can decisively influence both the interaction and the outcomes of the negotiation.

The BATNA option

Decades of research show that negotiating power hinges on a structural element of negotiation, that is, the strength of a negotiator's BATNA (Gunia et al., 2013). A strong BATNA increases a negotiating team's power by making the team less dependent on a particular negotiation to meet its needs. In international business negotiations, negotiators can effectively ignore offers which are inferior to their BATNA. A strong BATNA gives the team the power to push for better terms, as well as the power to walk away if the counterpart demurs. Such considerations help explain why BATNAs are strong predictors of negotiation outcomes.

Fisher et al.'s (1991) checklist of principles designed to help negotiators improve their negotiating power includes the principle "Know your BATNA." The BATNA is, in effect, a negotiator's bottom line or reservation price, that is, the minimum amount required for a deal to be acceptable. Being clear about the BATNA gives a manager negotiating power by increasing his or her goal clarity at the negotiating table. Based on the BATNA, the manager knows which offers are worth pursuing and which should be rejected.

Consider the case of the German sales manager who hoped to sell a shipment of previous-generation machine tools to a potential buyer in Egypt: The sales manager has already obtained a written offer from a scrap merchant in Germany to buy the machine tools for $30,000. The sales manager's BATNA is therefore $30,000 since that is the amount he could get for the machine tools even if negotiations with the Egyptian firm are unsuccessful.

In this case, the BATNA increases the sales manager's bargaining power by enabling him to make demands and extract concessions from the Egyptian company. More important, simply having a BATNA protects the sales manager from accepting unfavourable terms and gives him the freedom to walk away from the table if negotiations are leading nowhere. The case illustrates how not having to rely on negotiation to achieve the desired outcome is an important source of negotiating power.

Actions recommended by Fisher et al. (1991) for determining the BATNA are the following:

1. Develop a list of actions to take in case negotiation does not produce an acceptable agreement.
2. Convert the more promising ideas from the list into practical options.
3. Select the best option.

The advice seems to be very clear-cut, but in practice finding the BATNA can be extremely difficult, especially when many interdependent uncertainties are involved. Typical uncertainties relate to timing, availability of finance, work force or government reactions, price and so on. Such uncertainties affect many international business transactions – and related BATNA decisions. In complex, high-stake business negotiations, a technical adviser sometimes has to be called in to find the company's BATNA and convert it into a reservation price.

EMOTION IN NEGOTIATION

Impact of positive and negative emotions

Allred et al. (1996) found that negotiators who experienced anger were less accurate in assessing their counterparts' interests and achieved lower joint outcomes in contrast to negotiators who experienced a lesser degree of anger. The implication is that when negative feelings are dominant in business negotiations, the negotiation process may fail to generate integrative outcomes or may end in failure. By contrast, negotiators who express positive emotions acquire a measure of negotiating power and are more imaginative about proposing solutions that lead to satisfactory joint payoffs (Thompson, 1998).

Negative emotions influence the interaction and often the outcomes of international business negotiations. They are often caused by negotiators' concerns about failing to make progress towards achieving their goals, and they vary in their frequency, duration and intensity (Oatley & Johnson-Laird, 1995). Negative feelings which are often displayed in international business negotiations include sadness, anger, fear and a wish to escape (flight), and such negative *feelings* may be transformed into negative *behaviour*, such as contemptuously rejecting an offer which is well above the negotiator's BATNA. Kumar (1999) gives the example of negotiations between American and Japanese trade delegations in which the Americans became frustrated by the slow progress of the talks and began to express their negative feelings by negative behaviour, such as aggressive staring and sarcastic verbal comments.

This behaviour by the Americans evoked an escape response from the Japanese which they expressed by avoiding eye contact and by prolonged periods of silence – behaviour which was not easy for the Americans to decode. This only increased the Americans' frustration and led them to indulge in more overtly aggressive behaviour. At this point the leader of the Japanese delegation suggested a coffee break.

Negotiators who experience negative emotions are less likely to respond in a positive way to proposals made in good faith by their counterparts. Moreover, they are more likely to remember information which is negative in tone.

Positive role of emotion in negotiations

While emotion in negotiation can have the effect of reducing a negotiator's power to control events and steer the proceedings to a satisfactory outcome, in some cases emotion can play a more positive role. For instance, *feelings of concern* for the other party and the other party's outcomes may encourage negotiators to keep moving towards an agreement by compromising, exchanging concessions, making trade-offs and so on. Even negative emotions expressed in international business negotiations can have positive consequences. For instance, a manager's obvious disappointment about failing to successfully negotiate a supply contract may make the other party feel guilty as a result of the manager's disappointment. Disappointment is a supplication emotion, a call for help. Lelieveld et al. (2012) suggest that guilty feelings about the other person's disappointment may lead to concessions being made to make amends. Similarly, when a negotiator displays anger, the other participants may feel that they themselves are responsible and make concessions to restore harmony (Filipowicz et al., 2011).

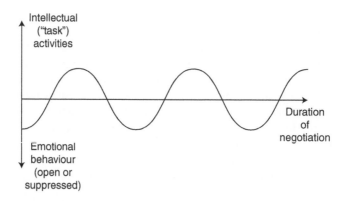

Figure 3.1   Intellectual and emotional activities in negotiations

Note: Negotiating sessions oscillate between intellectual and emotional activity. The pressures of decision making (an intellectual activity) arouse emotions in negotiators.

Non-rational behaviour

Much negotiation theory is based on economic or mathematical models of negotiation. These models have been widely criticised for being unrealistic since factors other than rationality have a greater influence on negotiator behaviour. Such factors include

- the impact made on negotiations by a negotiator's personality or disposition;
- the impact made on negotiators' behaviour by cultural values and norms;
- psychological traits, such as a negotiator's tendency to avoid risk or conflict.

Emotional, non-rational behaviour which may be expressed in international business negotiations can affect both the interaction and the outcomes. Displays of anger, for instance, may be an early warning sign of negative consequences at a later stage (Sinaceur & Tiedens, 2006). A contemptuous rejection by a powerful opponent of an offer made in good faith may lead a negotiating team to fear that their economic outcomes will be reduced. Negotiators who experience fear of this kind may become risk averse and conflict avoiders. Lelieveld et al. (2012) make the point that fear of negative consequences may lead negotiators to make unnecessary concessions in order to avoid further conflict.

Stress and anxiety

Leary et al. (2013) interviewed experienced negotiators and found that *anxiety* is a common emotion experienced by negotiators. The negotiating power of anxious negotiators is undermined since anxious negotiators have lower expectations than nonanxious negotiators, make lower first offers, respond more quickly to offers and leave the table sooner.

Many negotiators experience stress and anxiety in negotiations. Gudykunst (1995) found that in negotiations and other group situations, stress and anxiety lead to misinterpretations, misunderstandings and other kinds of communication failure. Scollon & Scollon (2001, 153) point out that psychologists specialising in the treatment of stress have indicated that the narrow emphasis by Americans on information and control in negotiation is part of what has been called the Type-A behaviour syndrome: "This syndrome, which is closely associated with heart disease, has been observed to emphasise an excessive attention to numbers, quantities, and direct communication on the one hand, and to downplay or minimise human relationships on the other."

According to Leary et al. (2013), negotiating is stressful for managers due to

- *Lack of control.* The managers are negotiating to achieve something they cannot achieve unilaterally.
- *Lack of feedback.* Feedback on negotiators' performance is absent.

- *Unpredictability.* In negotiations there are numerous unknowns – a potent source of stress. It is not known whether the negotiation will have a successful outcome.

Cultural influence

Some emotional displays in international business negotiations are the product of culture. American negotiators, for instance, will angrily confront opponents if they think that confrontation is needed to resolve an issue (Keidel, 1996). In China, by contrast, displaying negative emotions during negotiations is frowned upon and can lead to loss of face for Chinese. According to Shenkar and Ronen (1987), Chinese negotiators display emotional restraint and politeness throughout a negotiation so that interpersonal harmony is maintained. Kumar (1999) makes the point that Confucian-based negotiators may settle for sub-optimal agreements since agreement helps the negotiators achieve their face-related goals.

Western negotiators are more likely to display anger and other negative emotions than are negotiators from Asian cultures, who tend to hide their feelings in business negotiations (Prestwich, 2007). However, the other side's perceived intransigence can cause tension and anger even among Asian negotiators. One Chinese participant in US-Chinese negotiations told researchers: "The other team stood tight on the issue of delivery charges. They just wouldn't budge, and this made us mad."

International business negotiations which involve negotiators from different racial groups often generate tensions severe enough to reduce the negotiators'

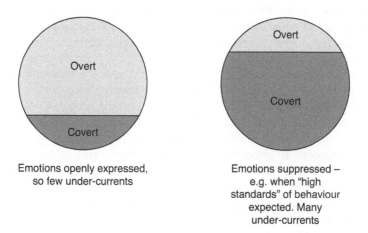

Emotions openly expressed, so few under-currents

Emotions suppressed – e.g. when "high standards" of behaviour expected. Many under-currents

Figure 3.2   Open and suppressed emotions in international business negotiations

Note: Emotions are present in all negotiations, but, partly depending on the cultural origin of the negotiator, are suppressed or openly expressed. When suppressed they can be difficult to deal with as the cause of noncooperation by the negotiator is unknown.

problem-solving ability and therefore the likelihood of reaching a satisfactory agreement (Davidson & Greenhalgh, 1999). Physiological symptoms of tension include high blood pressure, racing pulse, tense muscles, heavy breathing, sweaty palms, shaky legs, an upset stomach and even disrupted vision (Adler et al., 1998).

KEY POINTS

1. Negotiating power is the ability of one party in a negotiation to cause the other party to change behaviour in a given direction (Zartman, 1994). This ability may stem from the powerful party's size and resources as well as from its negotiation strategies. Tangible sources of negotiating power include capital, technology and knowledge. Intangible sources include creativity, a reputation for trustworthy behaviour and negotiators' skills of logical analysis and quantitative assessment.

2. A company's technological and business knowledge – an important source of negotiating power – is usually embedded in patents, trademarks, copyrights and other kinds of intellectual property. AT&T's numerous patents, trademarks and copyrights have given the company great bargaining power over several decades. *Local knowledge* plays a key role in negotiations between MNEs and their foreign subsidiaries. Local knowledge includes local business practices and legal requirements, local market conditions and relations with government.

3. Abuses of negotiating power occur when a company uses its power in negotiations to make unreasonable demands. The less powerful party typically responds through submissive behaviours such as repeatedly making concessions. Large, powerful companies which are negotiating with foreign sales representatives sometimes demand huge price reductions if a deal is to be finalised. But in many international business negotiations, the parties have equal negotiating power. Neither can dictate the terms of the agreement. Instead they have to rely on negotiation to reach a mutually acceptable agreement. Some negotiators rely less on power and more on cooperation to achieve their goals.

4. Soft power, often used by governments, is the behavioural way of obtaining the outcomes desired by an organisation through cooperation and attraction as opposed to deadlines, threats and other forms of coercion. Negotiators who use soft-power tactics rely on persuasion to lead others in the desired direction. Hard power in negotiations may involve threats to withhold payments and crude displays of assets and capabilities. Many successful negotiators will use both hard-power and soft-power tactics to help them achieve their negotiation goals.

5. Developing a number of different options or alternative packages is an important pre-negotiation task. Unless several alternative packages are generated, initial offers will dominate negotiating sessions and reduce the value of the settlement. Options give bargaining power to negotiators. In cross-border

buying/selling negotiations, a buyer who has several alternative suppliers to fall back on derives bargaining power from that simple fact. If a team has only a single carefully priced option to offer, and the offer is rejected, the team's negotiating power is greatly reduced.

6. Relationships are an important source of bargaining power. The importance of relationship-building behaviours differs across cultures. Negotiators from many collectivist countries attach great importance to building a good business relationship with the other negotiating party. Successful negotiating outcomes may depend on it. In negotiations with Chinese companies, for instance, success in building good interorganisational and interpersonal relationships greatly increases the likelihood that a mutually satisfactory agreement will be reached.

7. In international business negotiations, actions that negotiators take "away from the table" can greatly affect the negotiated outcomes. While continuing to conduct face-to-face negotiations with a potential foreign buyer, for instance, a sales team might simultaneously search for other possible buyers or a better price on the Internet. Such activities can greatly influence the interactions and outcomes of the negotiation.

8. The BATNA is in effect the minimum amount required for a deal to be acceptable. Being clear about the BATNA gives a manager negotiating power by increasing his or her goal clarity, allowing him or her to know which offers are worth pursuing and which should be rejected. Finding the BATNA can be very difficult when many interdependent uncertainties are involved. A technical adviser may have to be called in to find the BATNA and convert it into a reservation price.

9. Negative emotions influence the interaction and often the outcomes of international business negotiations. They are often caused by negotiators' concerns about the negotiations failing to make progress, and they vary in frequency, duration and intensity. Negative feelings that are displayed in international business negotiations include sadness, anger, fear and a wish to escape (flight). Conflict erupts when negative feelings which have built up in a negotiation are transformed into negative behaviour.

10. Displays of anger by a powerful opponent or a contemptuous rejection of an offer made in good faith may lead a negotiating team to fear that their economic outcomes will be reduced. Negotiators who experience fear of this kind in effect lose negotiating power, and they may become risk averse and conflict avoiders. Fear of negative consequences may lead them to make unnecessary concessions to avoid further conflict.

QUESTIONS FOR DISCUSSION AND WRITTEN ASSIGNMENTS

1. Explain the difference between hard-power and soft-power negotiating strategies in the context of international business negotiations. What are the pros and cons of using hard-power strategies?

2. Various types of knowledge are a source of negotiating power in alliance and international joint venture negotiations. Identify the different types of knowledge and explain why each type gives negotiating power to a negotiating team.
3. "Successful negotiating outcomes derive from negotiators' ability to build a strong relationship between the parties." Develop two arguments, one supporting the statement, and the other opposing it.
4. Explain how the choice of working language for an international business negotiation creates winners and losers.

BIBLIOGRAPHY

Adler, R. S., Rosen, B. & Silverstein, E. M. Emotions in negotiation: how to manage fear and anger. *Negotiation Journal*, 14, 1998, 161–179.

Allred, K., Mallozzi, F. J., Matsui, F. & Raia, C. P. Anger and compassion in negotiation. Working Paper, 1996.

Breth, R. & Kaiping, J. Negotiating the contract. In R. Breth & J. Kaiping (eds) *A business guide to China*. Victoria College Press, 1988.

Brett, J. M. et al. How to manage your negotiating team. *HBR*, 87 (9), 2009, 105–109.

Brown, J. S. & Duguid, P. Knowledge and organisation: a social-practice perspective. *Organisation Science*, 12, 2001, 198–213.

Charles, M. Language matters in global communication. *Journal of Business Communication*, 44 (3), 2007, 260–282.

Daoudy, M. Asymmetric power: negotiating water in the Euphrates and Tigris. *International Negotiation*, 14, 2009, 361–391.

Davidson, M. N. & Greenhalgh, L. The role of emotion in negotiation: the impact of anger and race. In R. J. Bies, R. Lewicki & B. H. Sheppard (eds) *Research in Negotiation in Organizations*. Vol. 7, JAI Press, 1999, 3–26.

Dobrijevic, G., Stanisic, M. & Masic, B. Sources of negotiation power: an exploratory study. *South African Journal of Business Management*, 42 (2), 2011, 35–41.

Dunning, J. H. (ed.) *Making Globalisation Good: The Moral Challenge of Global Capitalism*. OUP, 2003.

Dupont, C. A model of the negotiation process with different strategies. *International Business Negotiations* 1, 1996, 39.

Filipowicz, A., Barsade, S. & Melwani, S. Understanding emotional transitions: the interpersonal consequences of changing emotions in negotiation. *Journal of Personality and Social Psychology*, 101, 2011, 541–556.

Fisher, R., Ury, W. & Patton, B. *Getting to Yes: Negotiating Agreement without Giving In*. Penguin Books, 2nd ed., 1991.

Foster, D. A. *Bargaining Across Borders: How to Negotiate Business Successfully Anywhere in the World*. McGraw-Hill, 1992.

Ghemawat, P. Managing differences: the central challenge of global strategy. *Harvard Business Review*, 85 (3), 2007, 58–68.

Greenhalgh, L. & Gilkey, R. W. Our game, your rules: developing effective negotiating approaches. In R. Lewicki, J. A. Litterer, D. M. Saunders & J. W. Minton (eds) *Negotiation: Readings, Exercises, and Cases*. Irwin, 1993, 414–423.

Greve, H. R., Baum, J. A. C., Mitsuhashi, H. & Rowley, T. J. Built to last but falling apart: cohesion, friction, and withdrawal from interfirm alliances. *Academy of Management Journal*, 53 (2), 2010, 302–322.

Gudykunst, W. B. Anxiety/uncertainty management (AUM) theory: current status. In R. L. Wiseman (ed.) *Intercultural Communication Theory*. Sage, 1995, 8–58.

Gulliver, P. *Disputes and Negotiations: A Cross-Cultural Perspective*. Academic Press, 1979.

Gunia, B. C. et al. The remarkable robustness of the first-offer effect: across culture, power, and issues. *Personality and Social Psychology Bulletin*, 39 (12), 2013, 1547–1558.

Hall, E. T. *Beyond Culture*. Anchor Books, 1976.

Herbig, P. & Kramer, M. Do's and don'ts of cross-cultural negotiations. *Industrial Marketing Management*, 21, 1992, 287–298.

Hodgson, J. D., Sano, Y. & Graham, J. L. *Doing Business with New Japan*. Rowman and Littlefield, 2000.

Kamoche, K. & Harvey, M. Knowledge diffusion in the African context. *Thunderbird International Business Review*, 48 (2), 2006, 157–181.

Keeney, R. & Raiffa, H. *Decisions with Multiple Objectives*. Wiley, 1976.

Keidel, L. *Conflict or Connection: Interpersonal Relationships in Cross-cultural Settings*. EMIS, 1996.

Kumar, R. Communicative conflict in intercultural negotiations: the case of American and Japanese business negotiations. *International Negotiation*, 4, 1999, 63–78.

Kumar, R. A script theoretical analysis of international negotiating behaviour. In R. J. Bies, R. J. Lewicki & B. H. Sheppard (eds) *Research in Negotiation in Organizations*, Vol. 7, JAI Press, 1999, 285–311.

Kumar, R., Rufin, C. & Rangan, U. Negotiating complexity and legitimacy in independent power development. *Journal of World Business*, 40 (3), 2005, 302–320.

Laroche, L. *Managing Cultural Diversity in Technical Professions*. Butterworth-Heinemann, 2003.

Leary, K., Pillemer, J. & Wheeler, M. Negotiating with emotion. *HBR*, 91 (1/2) 2013, 96–103.

Lelieveld, G-J. et al. Why anger and disappointment affect others' bargaining behaviour differently. *Personality and Social Psychology Bulletin*, 38 (9), 2012, 1209–1221.

Leung, T. & Yeung, L. L. Negotiation in the People's Republic of Gbina: results of a survey of small businesses in Hong Kong. *Journal of Small Business Management*, 33 (1), 1995, 70–77.

Lewicki, R., Saunders, D. M. & Barry, B. *Negotiation*. McGraw-Hill/Irwin, 6th ed., 2009.

Mäkelä, K., Kalla, H. K. & Piekkari, R. Interpersonal knowledge sharing within multinationals: Homophily as a driver for clustering. In K. Mäkelä (ed.) *Essays on Interpersonal Level Knowledge Sharing within the Multinational Corporation* (Helsinki School of Economics A-277). HSE Print, 2006.

Manrai, L. A. & Manrai, A. K. The influence of culture in international business negotiations: a new conceptual framework and managerial implications. *Journal of Transnational Management*, 15, 2010, 69–100.

Medvec, V. H. & Galinsky, A. D. Putting more on the table: how making multiple offers can increase the final value of the deal. *Negotiation*, April 2005, 3–5.

Metge, J. *Korero Tahi: Talking Together*. Aukland University Press, 2001.

Nadler, J. Build rapport – and a better deal. *Negotiation*, March 2007, 9–11.

Nye, J. *Soft Power: The Means to Success in World Politics. Public Affairs*, 2004.

Oatley, K. & Johnson-Laird, P. N. The communicative theory of emotions: empirical tests, mental models, and implications for social interaction. In L. L. Martin & A. Tesser (eds) *Goals and Affect*. Erlbaum, 1995.

Olekalns, M., Brett, J. M. & Weingart, L. R. Phases, transitions and interruptions: modelling processes in multi-party negotiations. *International Journal of Conflict Management*, 14, 2004, 191–212.

Prestwich, R. Cross-cultural negotiating: a Japanese-American case study from higher education. *International Negotiation*, 12, 2007, 29–55.

Pruitt, D. G. *Bargaining Behaviour*. Academic Press, 1981.

Raiffa, H. *The Art and Science of Negotiation*. Harvard University Press, 1982.

Salacuse, J. W. *The Global Negotiator: Making, Managing and Mending Deals around the World in the Twenty-first Century*. Palgrave Macmillan, 2003.

Schein, E. *Process Consultation: Its Role in Organisational Development*. Addison Wesley, 1969.

Scollon, R. & Scollon, S. W. *Intercultural Communication: A Discourse Approach*. Blackwell, 2nd ed., 2001.

Sebenius, J. K. The hidden challenge of cross-border negotiations. *HBR*, 80 (3), 2002, 76–85.

Shenkar, O. & Ronen, S. The cultural context of negotiations: the implications of Chinese interpersonal norms. *The Journal of Applied Behavioral Science*, 23 (2), 1987, 263–275.

Sinaceur, M. & Tiedens, L. Get mad and get more than even: when and why anger expression is effective in negotiation. *Journal of Experimental Social Psychology*, 42, 2006, 314–322.

Staber, U. Social capital processes in cross-cultural management. *International Journal of Cross Cultural Management*, 6 (2), 2006, 189–203.

Stalk, G. & Michael, D. What the West doesn't get about China. *Harvard Business Review*, 89 (6), 2011, 25–27.

Stevens, S. M. *Strategy and Collective Bargaining Negotiation*. McGraw-Hill, 1963.

Thompson, L. *The Mind and Heart of the Negotiator*. Prentice Hall, 1998.

Trotman, K. T., Wright, A. M. & Wright, S. Auditor negotiations: an examination of the efficacy of intervention methods. *The Accounting Review*, 80 (1), 2005, 349–367.

Usunier, J-C. The role of time in international business negotiations. In P. Ghauri & J-C. Usunier (eds) *International Business Negotiations*. Pergamon, 1996, 153–172.

Walters, A., Stuhlmacher, A. & Meyer, L. Gender and negotiator competitiveness: a meta-analysis. *Organizational Behaviour and Human Decision Processes*, 76, 1998, 1–29.

Weiss, S. The IBM-Mexico microcomputer investment negotiations. In P. Ghauri & J-C. Usunier (eds) *International Business Negotiations*. Pergamon, 1996, 305–334.

Zartman, I. W. *International Multilateral Negotiation*. Jossey-Bass, 1994.

Yoffie, D. B. and Kwak, M. With friends like these: the art of managing complementors. *HBR*, 84 (9), 2006, 88–98.

Zartman, I. W. & Rubin, J. Z. (eds) *Power & Negotiation*. University of Michigan Press, 2000.

Negotiation Process 4

INTRODUCTION

International business negotiation is a process of give and take between parties from different countries in which the parties keep modifying their offers in order to come close to each other and make an agreement more likely (Ghauri, 1996). The process includes communication between the parties, information exchange, persuasion efforts and usually a pattern of mutual concessions and tradeoffs. Innumerable international business transactions are carried out every day which require only a few simple procedures to execute, for instance, an exchange of emails. More sophisticated procedures are needed for large-scale, complex negotiations. Too much procedure, however, can inhibit the discussion and lead to sub-optimal agreements being made. Only a few studies have investigated the negotiation processes involved in the various kinds of international business negotiation – international joint venture (IJV) negotiations, for instance – and few have studied the impact made by cultural differences on international business negotiations (Das & Kumar, 2011).

Negotiation structure, which evolves through a natural process over the course of a negotiation or series of negotiations, can be strategically guided to improve the parties' outcomes (Sebenius, 1992). By manipulating important elements of structure – parties, issues and interests – the Zone of Possible Agreement (ZOPA) can be expanded, and a negotiated agreement therefore made more likely. Western negotiators tend to bargain about issues one at a time, while collectivist negotiators often prefer to consider groups of issues together. *Adding issues* to a negotiation often leads to tradeoffs being made which open the way to more favourable outcomes for both parties. *Outcomes* are the results of negotiation that are highly salient to the parties involved (Balakrishnan & Patton, 2006). In international business negotiations, the key outcomes are usually economic outcomes (e.g. profits) and levels of satisfaction with aspects of the negotiation itself (e.g. time taken to reach agreement).

For Western-based firms, international business is contractual in nature. For these firms, contracts reduce risk and promote cooperation. *Control-oriented contracts* cut the risk of opportunistic behaviour by international business partners, but leave little room for discretion and trust development. *Coordination-oriented contracts*, in contrast, provide communication channels and mechanisms for resolving disputes.

Contingent contracts function like bets. The terms in the contract hinge on the uncertain outcome of a future event. Negotiators who form different conclusions about, say, the risk of future currency fluctuations may opt to draw up a contingent contract stating that the price to be paid, say, for an export shipment of furniture will be contingent on the currency's actual rate at the time of settlement.

Many authors assume that "negotiation process" refers to the *internal dynamics* of a negotiation in which proposals and offers are made and modified by the parties. But the assumption ignores the part played by *external* dynamics. In international business there are many cases of a negotiation being influenced and constrained by separate but related *external* negotiations. If, for instance, two subsidiaries of an multinational enterprise (MNE) operating in a foreign country hold separate negotiations with the host government about tax breaks, each negotiation will be influenced by the discussions and decisions made in the other negotiation (Crump, 2007). Similarly, multilateral trade negotiations may influence bilateral trade negotiations conducted at lower, regional or national levels.

Increasingly, managers use two or more communication technologies in combination as part of the negotiation process (Leonardi et al., 2012). They may, for instance, use document sharing to communicate relevant information to the other party. The same information is then sent as an email attachment, and a final check is made by phone to ensure that the information has been received and understood. Negotiators try to further their own interests, both tangible (e.g. profits, orders) and intangible (e.g. social approval, reputation, self-esteem). Take-it-or-leave-it offers by a negotiating opponent may be rejected if they threaten a negotiator's self-esteem.

CONCEPT AND DEFINITIONS

Sequence of stages

Negotiation process consists of a sequence of stages (Das & Teng, 2002). The process may be fuzzy as the stages may overlap, be of different duration, and may develop over time. In the context of international business, negotiation process involves constant tension and eventual balance between integrative and distributive outcomes – between trying to achieve competitive goals and searching for joint gains.

A key stage of the negotiation process is the agreement stage. In some cases a negotiated agreement is achieved although it covers up serious disagreements between the parties with vague and ambiguous phrases, but such agreements often lead to conflict further down the line (Brett & Crotty, 2008). When the disputes are serious, they may have to be resolved by resorting to expensive dispute resolution procedures.

Mutual concessions and tradeoffs

International business negotiation is defined as the deliberate interaction of two or more parties from different countries, at least one of them a business entity, which are attempting to define or redefine the terms of their interdependence in a business matter (Weiss, 1993, 270). Brett & Crotty (2008) see international business negotiation as a process by which people with conflicting interests determine how they are going to allocate resources or work together. The process itself consists of communication between the parties, information exchange, persuasion attempts, and a pattern of mutual concessions and trade-offs. Interactions between the parties lead, in most cases, to a final negotiated agreement. To have a successful outcome, the process requires give and take by both sides.

The give and take process consists of negotiators making initial offers and demands, and then adjusting them if doing so will make them acceptable to the other side and agreement more likely. Exchanging information and proposals can be carried out using the Internet, in face-to-face meetings, by telephone, by fax, through a simple exchange of emails, or even through informal *verbal agreements* made, for instance, when two managers bump into each other in an airport lounge. The wide-ranging nature of international business negotiation adds weight to Ghauri's (1996) view that business negotiation is essentially a form of problem-solving in which the parties view the negotiation as a joint process and a way of finding a solution to a common problem.

Cultural preferences affect international business process and the way in which negotiators deal with the issues. Western negotiators, for instance, prefer to bargain about issues one at a time, whereas negotiators from collectivist countries often prefer to consider groups of issues together (Schuster & Copeland, 1999). A few international business negotiations focus on a single issue, such as the price to be paid for a single export shipment, or the starting and finishing dates of an international development project. Single-issue negotiations such as these are usually characterised by competitive, distributive bargaining in which one side's gain is the other side's loss.

Internal and external dynamics

Many authors explain the negotiation process by referring to the *internal dynamics* of a negotiation, including the power of the different parties, their negotiation strategies, the pattern of interrelated concessions and tradeoffs, and the various negotiation stages that lead to an agreement. Lewicki et al. (1999), for instance, see negotiation as a dynamic process in which proposals and offers are made and modified by the negotiating parties over the course of the negotiation. Changes that the parties make in their original negotiating positions usually make it possible for agreement eventually to be reached. These changes in negotiating position, the researchers imply, are brought about by *internal* factors.

But in international business negotiations, changes in negotiating position are often brought about by *external* factors. For instance, an international business negotiation may be strongly influenced by a separate negotiation which involves some or all of the same parties and the same negotiating issues, for instance, the issue of legal constraints on remitting profits from a given foreign country (Crump, 2007). In such a case, the interaction and outcomes of each negotiation will be influenced and constrained by the issues discussed and decisions taken in the other, separate negotiation.

In international business there are many cases of one negotiation influencing or determining the process and outcomes of a related negotiation. For example, multilateral trade negotiations with global implications such as the World Trade Organization (WTO) Doha round, are superordinate to international trade negotiations conducted at lower levels. As a result, the WTO negotiations greatly influence and have a cascading impact on lower-level regional and bilateral negotiations. The example recalls Putnam's (1988) description of the dynamics of two-level games. Two-level negotiation games are played at both lower and higher levels, with higher-level (superordinate) games setting some of the rules for games played at lower levels.

Negotiating positions – the stands taken by each party on the various issues to be negotiated – can be influenced by both internal and external factors. Negotiating positions differ from negotiating interests. Negotiating interests are what each side feels is really important to them. Negotiators learn about each other's interests by careful listening during negotiating sessions and pre-negotiation social events. The information gained provides clues about offers and proposals likely to be attractive to the other party. When negotiators who are involved in an international business negotiation focus on understanding *interests* – their own and the other party's – rather than the *positions* of the parties, the result is likely to be joint problem-solving, not adversarial positioning.

Case Study

MINI-CASE: Scope of services

A European consulting firm bids to carry out a nationwide vocational education and training study in an Asian country and is subsequently invited to attend negotiations with the appropriate government agency. Inviting bidders to conduct negotiations on price before the award of a contract is confirmed is common practice in the case of international agencies and with the international aid departments of some national governments.

At one point in the subsequent negotiation, strong concerns are expressed by the government team about the proposed starting and finishing dates for the study, and about the consultant's fees and expenses as set out in the financial proposal. Government negotiators also strongly criticise the imprecise nature of the scope of services to be provided by the consultant as set out in the consultant's proposal document.

However, the disputes are resolved when the consultant provides further information which is much more detailed than the information contained in the firm's proposal document. The new information specifies the schedule of activities to be undertaken and the methods to be used by the consultant for collecting and analysing data. Precise details are also given of report-back mechanisms to be established by the consultant, with the aim of ensuring that the government has all the information needed for effectively monitoring and supervising the project.

This additional information clarifies the situation and satisfies the government agency. As a result, the consultants' team feels that it will be able to work within the terms and conditions stated in the draft contract.

Question:

1. *In addition to providing the additional, higher-quality information, what other actions could the consultants' team take during the course of the negotiation to resolve the conflict and ensure that its plans for carrying out the project are approved?*

ELEMENTS OF NEGOTIATION PROCESS

Many authors (e.g. Lewicki et al., 2005) regard the negotiation process as a combination of various interrelated elements, including

- communication;
- information exchanges;
- concessions and tradeoffs;
- persuasion attempts; and
- agreement and associated outcomes.

Communication

Physical distance and time difference are important factors in determining which communication methods a manager should use when negotiating with foreign business partners. Many international business negotiations are carried out in face-to-face meetings, but phone calls, emails and faxes are also widely used, and managers increasingly rely on communication technologies for conducting negotiations (Leonardi et al., 2012). Indeed, the use of several communication technologies *in combination* is becoming common practice (Stephens et al., 2008). For example, a manager might use document sharing to communicate pertinent information to a negotiating opponent before sending the same information as an email attachment, and finally check by phone that the information has been received and understood.

Communication technologies can be powerful tools in conducting international business, saving time and money. They enable managers to participate in negotiations with foreign customers or business partners without having to physically travel to the location. But although video conferencing and other electronic methods are adequate for dealing with routine or uncomplicated aspects of negotiation, face-to-face meetings are often needed to resolve more complex issues.

Information

Information exchange is a key component of the international business negotiation process, and the quality of information is an important factor that helps steer negotiators towards a satisfactory agreement. Information exchange often involves assessments of the likely impact of various options that are on the table, although the calculus of outcome benefits is so complex that only crude estimates can be given.

How much of the information provided by a negotiation opponent be taken at face value? Lewicki et al.'s (2005) answer is that a negotiator who believes all the information provided by the other side risks being manipulated if this party should behave dishonestly. Conversely, a negotiator who tells the other side the complete, honest truth about his or her interests and positions risks being outmanoeuvred in negotiating sessions and will probably never reach a settlement that is better than his or her minimum acceptable level.

In international business negotiations, asking direct questions about costs, order books, financial data, employee skills and other relevant information is normal practice for negotiators from Western Europe and North America (Schuster & Copeland, 1999). However, when facing negotiators from high-context cultures in Asia or the Middle East, Western negotiators may have to use more indirect methods to gain information since direct questioning is thought to be rude and insulting.

Japanese managers view the entire negotiation process as primarily a way to collect information (Laroche, 2003). With Japanese firms, preliminary

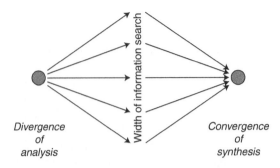

Figure 4.1   Information and solutions

Note: Information is a key component of the negotiation process. The wider the information search, the more accurate the solution.

information exchange may last months or years since in Japanese eyes that is the time it takes to build a trusting relationship.

Concessions

Concessions can be regarded as a sign of goodwill or a sign of weakness. The first case often leads to reciprocation and matching concessions from the other team. The exchange of concessions is a key feature of the international business negotiation process since, when a negotiator makes a concession, it often prompts the other side to reciprocate, thus moving the negotiators closer to an agreement. Bazerman & Neale (1992) point out that collaborative negotiators tend to make larger and more frequent concessions as a demonstration of goodwill, with the result that they obtain larger concessions from the other team and end up with a better agreements for themselves.

A concession signals a reluctance to risk conflict. Thus when negotiation stalls, concession-making is one of the best tools to keep both sides talking. A small concession – immediate delivery, for instance, or the provision of free training for the other company's technical staff – can stabilise a difficult negotiation and keep the discussion moving towards an agreement. A big concession by one of the parties may stimulate the other to table a proposal for an overall agreement.

According to Chen (1996), Chinese negotiators are trained to use concessions tactically. They tend to start high, but then make concessions with the aim of encouraging counter-concessions. Many Western negotiators use short-term tactical concessions, whereas Japanese negotiators often make late concessions as a lead-in to the final agreement (Schuster & Copeland, 1999). In multi-party negotiations, the pattern of concessions is necessarily more complicated. Interdependence of the parties means that an exchange of concessions usually involves more than just two parties. In a three-party negotiation, for instance, if A makes a concession to B, B may need to make a concession to C, who in turn needs to make a concession to A for the tradeoff to be complete.

Tradeoffs

Making tradeoffs means making sacrifices on some issues in order to make gains on others. An export sales manager, for instance, might agree to a lower price in return for a quick settlement or payment in hard currency. Tradeoffs across issues are frequently used by negotiators to create joint gain and make an integrative agreement possible. Joint gains are possible when each party attaches different levels of importance to the various issues being negotiated.

In two-party negotiations, tradeoffs are between issues that are of high value to one party and low value to the other. In *multiparty* business negotiations, making tradeoffs is the usual method used by managers to bring about agreement (Kuulaa & Stam, 2008). Each of the multiple parties sacrifices some objectives to secure others. If none of the parties is prepared to do so, the result is stalemate.

Some managers prefer to deal with issue bundles during an international business negotiation. For instance, they may negotiate price, delivery and after-sales service in a single bundle. They do so because issue bundling saves time and offers scope for creative tradeoffs.

Persuasion

Persuasion attempts are made in international business negotiations to overcome resistance to proposals. The kind of persuasion used may be influenced by the negotiator's cultural background. According to Metcalf & Bird (2004), negotiators from low uncertainty-avoidance cultures tend to use rational and fact-based persuasion attempts, while negotiators from high uncertainty-avoidance cultures use emotional appeals. *Rational persuasion* uses logical arguments and typically makes reference to labour costs, market data, availability of relevant skills, profitability, tax breaks and so forth. *Emotional persuasion* typically relies on appeals to patriotism, duty, relationships and so on. In practice, international business negotiators use both rational arguments and emotional persuasion in order to achieve their negotiating goals.

Western negotiators sometimes throw hard facts on the table at the start of business negotiations and use them to persuade the other side to take the desired action. Their assumption is that hard facts convince. Such an approach can, however, backfire. Chinese negotiators, for instance, would see this approach as a crude attempt to force them to take up a position prematurely and become involved in avoidable conflict (Chen, 1996).

Agreement

For Western negotiators, a signed agreement or contract represents closure of the negotiation, but negotiators from some parts of the world see things differently. Japanese negotiators, for instance, usually see the purpose of negotiating with a foreign company as the establishment of a long-term business relationship with the company concerned (Salacuse, 2003).

In some Asian and Latin American countries, a written agreement is seen mainly as an expression of the business relationship that has already been built up. Foreign negotiating teams often underestimate the amount of time required to make a formal agreement with Chinese companies since, as Pye (1986) points out, Chinese negotiators often need to coordinate with layers of hierarchical committees and officials before an agreement is authorised.

Outcomes

Negotiation outcomes are the results of negotiation that are highly salient to the parties involved (Balakrishnan & Patton, 2006). In international business negotiations, typical outcomes are

- economic outcomes (e.g. profits);
- relationships built with other parties; and
- satisfaction with the negotiation itself (e.g. its efficiency).

Outcomes are usually assessed in terms of their effects on the negotiators' *interests*. Surprises after the contract has been signed may leave the agreement nominally workable, but with radically changed outcomes from those anticipated by the parties.

The greater the complexity of an international business negotiation, the less likely it is that the outcomes will be well defined (Kumar & Patriotta, 2011). The firms may arrive at an agreement without fully understanding the implications of what they have agreed to. When that is the case, the outcomes will be particularly difficult to measure.

Assessing outcomes

One way of assessing the overall success of a negotiation is to calculate the *joint gains*. Joint gains are a measure of the entire pool of resources created by the negotiators, as opposed to calculating how well one party did. The joint gains in buying/selling negotiations, for instance, might be estimated by calculating the net value of the deal for both the buyer and the seller. Olekalns & Smith (2000) argue that joint gains go hand in hand with the parties' sharing information about their negotiating goals, interests and priorities.

Assessing the outcomes of an international business negotiation for just one of the parties is a much simpler task than making an overall assessment. In many cases, the party's *profits* (immediate, short-term and long-term) are the key measures of success, followed by the party's *level of satisfaction* with the negotiation, for instance, regarding the extent to which the negotiation led to an improved business relationship with the other party. Weiss (2006) argues that in international business negotiations, process and outcomes are intertwined and recurring, not a single iteration.

According to Brett (2001), negotiating strategies used by the negotiators have a limited effect on outcomes. Although the negotiators in international business negotiations come from diverse cultures and use different, culturally influenced negotiating strategies and tactics, the outcomes do not differ much.

PROCEDURAL ASPECTS

Simple procedures

International business negotiation is a process by which people with conflicting interests determine how they are going to allocate resources or work together (Brett & Crotty, 2008). Even when the parties are separated by thousands of miles and negotiate only by telephone or videoconference, a basic level of procedure is needed to guide the parties towards a mutually acceptable agreement. In face-to-face negotiations, for instance, a basic level of procedure answers many of the initial questions and uncertainties of participants, such as what language will be used, who will speak and in what order, and how decisions will be made.

Many international business deals are very simple commercial transactions which require only the simplest of procedures, such as an exchange of emails, to execute. Simple procedures, however, are incapable of resolving problems that arise in more complex negotiating situations. Nikolaev (2007) gives the example of multiparty negotiations in which negotiating teams reach a straightforward agreement that is acceptable to the teams themselves. But before the agreement can come into force it must be approved within each of the companies concerned – a requirement that can mean extremely long delays or impasse.

More sophisticated procedures

Complex international business negotiations require sophisticated procedures. Suchman & Cahill (1996), for instance, explain the successful negotiation of deals in Silicon Valley by referring to the sophisticated procedural framework that provided orientation and coordination for the diverse scientists, consultants, lawyers and venture capitalists drawn into specific ventures from many parts of the world.

Negotiations between IBM and the Mexican government about establishing production plants in Mexico involved multiple issues and numerous actors, ranging from individuals to departments and divisions. Careful planning and sophisticated procedural arrangements were needed to ensure that the right issues were addressed by the right people at the right time. Weiss (1996) points out that the two sides had to negotiate *informally* by means of informal communication and numerous informal discussions with each other, as well as *formally* through a pattern of formal proposals and responses.

When negotiations are very wide-ranging and complex, sophisticated procedures and programming are needed to ensure that all the issues are addressed at the appropriate time. A huge hydroelectric project in China, for instance, partly funded by the Asian Development Bank, required complex coordinated negotiations and discussions among numerous parties and stakeholders. These included international and national banks, international construction contractors, equipment suppliers, consulting groups, and provincial and central government departments.

But international business negotiators sometimes have to deal with a complex overall negotiating situation which even sophisticated negotiation process may be incapable of resolving. For instance, negotiating teams from different countries may reach an agreement that can come into force only after approval by the negotiators' top managers – approval which the managers may refuse to give. The example suggests the need for negotiators to develop *constituent involvement strategies* which will involve constituents such as headquarters management more closely in the negotiation process. Constituents may be unwilling to accept agreements that have been negotiated without the constituents themselves having been involved in the negotiating process.

Creative procedures

In international business negotiations, creative procedures can sometimes overcome blockages. Creative procedure characterised negotiations in Chile between a US manufacturer and a Chilean firm. The parties disagreed about numerous important issues including prices, terms of payment and warranty details of a technology transfer deal. Heated disagreements in negotiating sessions repeatedly disrupted attempts to draw up a draft contract. But eventually the parties found a way round the problem.

Whenever a major conflict erupted, the negotiating teams worked separately on the issue in empty offices. Then, when formal negotiations resumed, each team presented its proposals for overcoming the conflict. By the teams' using this creative procedure, the conflict was resolved.

Conflict-management procedures

Conflict is an inherent part of international business negotiation. According to Salacuse (2010), negotiation is a process by which two or more parties, with some apparent conflict, seek to advance their individual interests through agreement on some future action. Appropriate procedures are necessary to prevent conflict disrupting the negotiation, particularly when highly controversial issues are being debated. Having to observe formal procedures – having to address all comments to the chair, for instance – can take much of the heat out of the debate and reduce the level of conflict.

Most negotiators welcome a degree of formal procedure because it means that they do not have to exert themselves to obtain a fair hearing. Moreover, the behaviour of other participants becomes more predictable and is more easily contained. Too much formal procedure, however, inhibits the discussion and leads to sub-optimal decisions being made. Thus an essential skill required for chairing international business negotiations is the ability to judge *how much* procedure a particular negotiation requires. Procedure should act as a catalyst, creating order and solutions out of conflict and uncertainty. If it fails in this function, then it becomes a time-wasting ritual.

STRUCTURE OF NEGOTIATIONS

Components of structure

One way of analysing complex international business negotiations is to focus on the structure and the impact made by each component of the structure on negotiation outcomes. The structure of a given negotiation – number of parties, number of issues, which countries are represented, value of potential outcomes and so on – is likely to be determined by extraneous causes which are functional or dysfunctional for the negotiation (Zartman, 1991). Once the different components of the structure are determined, they provide a means of explaining the outcomes while, at the same time, providing possibilities for manipulating the outcomes.

According to Caputo (2012), the three fundamental components of structure are

- the number of issues;
- the number of parties; and
- the interests of the parties.

The Fiat-Chrysler alliance negotiations of 2009 were analysed by Caputo, who focused on these three basic components of structure. As a result, the researcher was able to map and analyse structural changes that took place in the course of the negotiations.

Manipulating structure

Sebenius (1992) points to the *natural evolution* of structure that occurs in the course of a lengthy international business negotiation, and argues that this natural change process can be strategically guided by the actions taken by the negotiating parties. By manipulating the different elements of structure, for example, parties, issues and interests, negotiators are able to greatly influence negotiation outcomes. For instance,

- manipulating negotiation structure by bringing more parties into an international business negotiation can be a successful strategy, provided that the parties have interests that might influence the negotiation in a positive way;
- dropping a party from a negotiation can be a way of removing an obstacle to a satisfactory agreement; and
- *adding issues* to a negotiation can lead to tradeoffs being made which open the way to integrative agreements and improved outcomes.

By manipulating the elements of negotiation structure in such ways, the ZOPA can be expanded and a negotiated agreement therefore made more likely.

Zone of Possible Agreement (ZOPA)

The ZOPA in a negotiation is the zone of overlap between the parties in which an agreement can be made. An understanding of the ZOPA and how it can be expanded is, according to Lewicki et al. (1999), critical for successful negotiations.

In an international business negotiation, in order to determine whether a potential ZOPA exists, the parties must explore each other's *interests*. Interests are what each party feels is really important. That is why Fisher & Ury (1991) advise negotiators to focus on interests, not positions, during a negotiation. When negotiators focus on understanding each other's interests, this usually leads to joint problem-solving as opposed to competitive posturing. The parties seek ways of creating joint gains by tradeoffs among issues that they value differently.

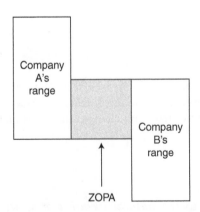

Figure 4.2   Zone of Possible Agreement

Note: Manipulating elements of the negotiation structure can lead to an extension of the ZOPA, thus making an agreement more likely.

STAGES OF NEGOTIATION

Two- and three-stage models

Most authors agree that international business negotiations pass through a series of stages. Lewicki et al.'s (1992) *2-stage model* of negotiation consists of the parties establishing a framework of broad objectives and principles in the first stage. The second stage involves detailed discussion of key issues, concessions, tradeoffs and the packaging of specific issues in order to construct a settlement acceptable to both sides.

Natlandsmyr & Rognes (1995) compared international business negotiations involving Norwegian and Mexican negotiators. They found that Norwegian negotiations had several distinct stages, including an initial *distributive stage*, an *integrative phase* and a final *adjustment phase*. Mexican negotiations, on the other hand, had no distinct stages, indicating a holistic approach to negotiation.

Das & Teng (2002) note that international joint venture negotiations evolve through the stages of *formation, operation, and outcome*. Negotiations between the prospective partners are the norm not only for the initial formation stage but also for the later stages. After the IJV becomes operational, it is faced with management control, cost allocation and other issues which have to be negotiated between the partners.

Four-stage models

Adair & Brett's (2005) results, derived from studying negotiating dyads from ten countries, provide empirical support for a four-stage model consisting of (a) relational positioning, (b) problem identification, (c) solution generation and (d) agreement.

Adair & Brett conclude that negotiators from diverse cultures share a view of the negotiation process that leads them through similar behavioural sequences and through similar stages – the four stages of their model. For instance, negotiators from all cultures tend to increase the number of reciprocal offers made during the agreement stage.

Faure (2000) also identifies four different stages in international business negotiation – preliminary investigation, business proposal, agreement/contract negotiation and implementation of the agreement.

Five-stage model

Graham's (1987) 5-stage model consists of five distinct stages: (a) relationship building, (b) information exchange, (c) persuasion, (d) concessions and (e) agreement.

Graham notes that the negotiated agreement often turns out to be a summation of smaller agreements that have been made throughout the negotiation.

Six-stage model

Acuff's (1997) model of negotiation consists of six stages: (a) fact-finding, (b) resistance, (c) reformulation of strategies, (d) hard bargaining and decision-making, (e) agreement and (f) follow-up. In each stage, the negotiators' behaviour varies according to the subject of negotiation, the country in which the negotiation takes place, negotiators' goals, and other contextual factors.

Each of Acuff's (1997) six stages can readily be identified in the following summarised account of a negotiation between a Dutch retailer and a Taiwanese supplier of domestic electronic equipment:

> Before negotiations begin the retailer collects information about specifications, performance, quality and prices of goods offered by the supplier. During a subsequent face-to-face meeting in Taiwan, the retailer questions the supplier's prices and delivery dates and goes on to demand concessions on both issues. The supplier's response is to produce facts, figures and arguments to justify his prices.

> Later, not wishing the negotiation to fail, the supplier rethinks his negotiation strategy and improves his offers. When the improved offers are also rejected, both parties are forced to examine their motivations to conclude a deal. Hard bargaining recommences about price and delivery dates. During this stage concessions are made to win a reciprocal concession from the other party.

> Efforts are made to find a solution, including creative financing. As a result of such efforts agreement is eventually reached and a contract is signed. After returning to the Netherlands, the retailer follows up by phone and email to build a base for future sales.

NEGOTIATING THE CONTRACT

Cultural preferences

For most Western-based firms international business is contractual in nature. Typically, they view a contract as an essential means of reducing risk, facilitating cooperation and promoting good governance because it sets out the rights and obligations of the negotiating parties. When negotiating an IJV, for instance, a comprehensive contract mitigates the risk of opportunistic and disruptive behaviour by the partners during the lifetime of the venture (Lumineau & Malhotra, 2011).

Negotiators from Western countries tend to see a binding contract as the most important outcome of an international business negotiation, but negotiators from other parts of the world perceive things differently. Faure (2000) makes the point that a contract of just a few pages is quite acceptable to Chinese negotiators, whereas Western negotiators may insist on a document running to 100 or more pages, including technical annexes, which will be negotiated word for word and defended clause by clause.

In some Asian countries, merely suggesting that a contract should be drawn up signals distrust of the foreign firm's intentions. As Salacuse (2003) points out, Japanese negotiators usually see the main outcome of negotiating with a foreign company as the establishment of a long-term business relationship with the company, and any written agreement is seen as an expression of that relationship. If the foreign company subsequently insists on both sides keeping strictly to the terms of the contract, the Japanese are likely to perceive such a stance as an expression of distrust that is damaging to the relationship. The Japanese dislike the Western tradition of legalism and prefer to leave contractual areas vague, with general principles being expressed rather than detailed provisions (Prestwich, 2007). According to Usunier (1996), Chinese, Japanese and Korean negotiators see the contract as an organic document which can change as conditions evolve.

Constructing an appropriate contract is such an important feature of international business negotiation that some firms believe that contract-construction should be treated as a separate phase of negotiations, with whole negotiating sessions devoted to the activity. Fortunately, software packages are available (e.g. diCarta) which help negotiators draft an appropriate contract in an efficient and professional manner. Moor & Weigand (2004) suggest that the contract might be negotiated in a series of steps, starting with a general statement and continuing with various levels of detail.

Chinese perception of contracts

For Chen (2008), signing a contract at the conclusion of business negotiations with the Chinese indicates the beginning of real negotiations. Chinese negotiators may perceive that by signing a contract with them, the negotiator considers him- or herself as their friend, who has the responsibility to help his or her friends when they are in trouble in the future. That is why Chinese negotiators prefer contracts based on broad principles and general policies without too much precise detail. Staber (2006) notes that Chinese firms place more value on building relationships – social capital – than on written legal contracts, and believe that any contract problems that arise can be solved through mutual cooperation or renegotiation.

Under China's Uniform Contract Law, contracts can be in written, oral or other forms. Written forms include emails, electronic data exchanges, faxes and letters (Zhao, 2000). Chinese negotiators are taught to use both Chinese and English as the official contract languages in international business negotiations.

Control or coordination contracts?

Lumineau & Malhotra (2011) distinguish between contracts aimed at exerting control and those aimed at facilitating cooperation and coordination:

> *Control-oriented contracts* reduce the risk of exploitative or opportunistic behaviour by international business partners. However, such contracts may also trigger resentment and reduce goodwill so that there is less likelihood of a business relationship surviving a serious dispute. Control-oriented contracts leave little room for discretion, crowd out trust development and inhibit cooperativeness.
>
> *Coordination-oriented contracts,* on the other hand, provide communication channels and mechanisms for resolving future disputes, thereby reducing the risk of serious and protracted misunderstandings and increasing the likelihood of continued collaboration between the parties after a dispute.

The implication is that if the parties anticipate possible future conflict when involved in negotiations to establish a strategic alliance, for instance, a contract structure should be chosen that encourages the development of trust between the parties, that is, a coordination-oriented contract.

Contingent contracts

The National Reconnaissance Office in the US awarded Boeing a five-year contract to build two different complex satellite systems, but six years later and billions of dollars over budget, the contract was torn up because Boeing had failed to deliver. As the example illustrates, great care must be taken when drawing up contracts for complicated, risky undertakings because it is only after the parties have signed and started to implement contracts that major problems emerge.

Protecting their firms against uncertainty and risk is what impels some negotiators to draw up contingent contracts. Contingent contracts function like bets as the terms in the contract hinge on the uncertain outcome of a future event. Many opportunities for using contingent contracts exist in international business (Loewenstein et al., 2003). For instance, two parties involved in an international business deal may differ in their attitude towards the risk of future currency fluctuations. But this difference can serve as a basis for joint gain if the parties agree that the price to be paid will be contingent on the currency's actual rate at the time of settlement.

Lax & Sebenius (1986) describe a situation in which a city and an international firm which are building an electricity plant disagree over the price of electricity – a situation that could easily lead to impasse in the negotiations. At the root of the disagreement lie the parties' differing forecasts about the price of oil, a crucial fuel for the plant. This leads the parties to work out a contingent contract. The price of electricity to be charged to the city will be contingent on future oil prices.

PRACTICAL EXERCISE: Questions for discussion

Working in small groups, discuss each of the following questions. At the end of the exercise, make a brief presentation of the group's answers to the other groups for comment.

1. *What are the different components of negotiation process?*
2. *What are negotiation outcomes? What criteria should be used to assess the outcomes of a cross-border business negotiation?*
3. *Explain the difference between negotiating and bargaining (with examples of each) in the context of international business negotiation.*
4. *Explain how negotiating interests differ from negotiating positions. What are the advantages of knowing the negotiating interests of the other side in an international business negotiation?*
5. *What are the different stages of a) a typical IJV negotiation? b) a typical international buying/selling negotiation?*
6. *From the perspective of an international business negotiator, what are the advantages and disadvantages of the following types of contracts:*

   i. *control-oriented contracts?*
   ii. *coordination-oriented contracts?*
   iii. *contingent contracts?*

Single-text approach

Some international business negotiations begin with one party presenting a draft agreement or contract to the other side for consideration. If the other side accepts the draft without comment, it means in effect that one party has unilaterally set the agenda for the entire negotiation. More often, the other side studies the draft contract, makes changes and returns it to the originator who, in turn, makes changes. This ping-pong process goes on until a final text acceptable to the parties emerges.

A single text produced by this method is normal in multilateral negotiations. Typically, a mediator moves among the negotiating parties, drawing from each of them points they wish to be included in the final text. This practical method may allow an agreement to be developed with which all parties can live. One advantage of the single-text process is that it may prompt a company's negotiating team to consult with constituencies, such as professional bodies or senior executives at company headquarters. These internal consultations increase the probability that the final negotiated agreement will be widely supported at the implementation stage.

Reducing the risks

International business can be more complicated than business carried out in one country, and it usually carries more risks. Variables such as language barriers, different cultures and different values and norms come into play, and in negotiations increase the difficulty of negotiating a satisfactory agreement. Complicating factors such as import regulations, export controls, tariff barriers, fluctuating exchange rates and many other aspects of international business dealings have to be addressed when drawing up a written agreement or contract, and such snares can lead to errors and omissions.

Risk assessment is a self-protection activity which is essential in most international business negotiations. Before starting negotiations to make a cross-border acquisition, for instance, the acquiring firm should ensure that a thorough risk analysis is carried out, together with a careful analysis of relevant geopolitical and other factors. A comprehensive risk assessment should identify major risk factors, such as government interference, the risk of future currency fluctuations affecting the price to be paid, and negative employee attitudes which could lead to poor performance in the acquired company.

Cultural intelligence helps international business negotiators deal effectively with negotiating situations characterised by cultural diversity and many of the uncertainties that go with business deals negotiated in foreign countries. Managers negotiating international business deals need to protect themselves against the hazards. It is sometimes necessary, for instance, to ensure that a force majeure clause is inserted in the contract allowing for contract cancellation under certain conditions, e.g. in the event of international business conditions being disrupted by war or revolution.

KEY POINTS

1. International business negotiation is a process of give and take between parties from different countries in which the parties keep modifying their offers in order to come close to each other and make an agreement more likely. The process consists of communication between the parties, information exchange, persuasion attempts, and a pattern of mutual concessions and tradeoffs. A full range of interactions between the parties leads to the emergence of a final negotiated agreement.
2. Managers increasingly use several communication technologies in combination to carry out international business negotiations. Document sharing, for instance, may be used to communicate pertinent information to the other

side. The same information is sent as an email attachment, with a final check by phone to ensure that the information has been received and understood. Physical distance and time difference are important factors for a manager to consider when deciding which communication methods to use when negotiating with a foreign company.

3. Exchanging information in international business negotiations creates issues of trust and honesty. A negotiator who believes all the information provided by the other party risks being manipulated and exploited if this party should behave dishonestly. Moreover, a negotiator who candidly tells the other side about his or her negotiating interests and positions will probably never reach a settlement that is better than his or her minimum acceptable level.

4. Negotiation includes the full range of interaction among the parties. In international business negotiations, negotiators usually have to take decisions about several complex issues negotiated simultaneously. *Bargaining*, by contrast, is limited to the presentation and exchange of specific proposals on particular issues. Bargaining theory is based on the assumption that decision-making in negotiations can be treated as if it refers to a single issue, such as net profits or labour costs or a project completion date. However, the distinction between negotiation and bargaining has little practical value since the two terms are used interchangeably.

5. A natural evolution of negotiation structure occurs during a negotiation. This can be strategically guided by manipulating the different elements of structure – that is, parties, issues and interests. Adding issues to a negotiation may lead to tradeoffs being made which open the way to integrative agreements. By manipulating issues and the other elements of structure the ZOPA can be expanded, and a negotiated agreement therefore made more likely.

6. If two subsidiaries of an MNE operating in a foreign country hold separate negotiations with the host government about tax breaks, for instance, each negotiation will be influenced and constrained by decisions reached in the other negotiation. Multilateral trade negotiations such as the WTO Doha round are superordinate to trade negotiations at lower levels, and therefore greatly influence and constrain regional and bilateral negotiations. Few studies have investigated the negotiation processes or the impact of national cultural differences on international alliance negotiations.

7. Many opportunities for using contingent contracts exist in international business. The terms in a contingent contract hinge on the uncertain outcome of a future event. Negotiators who form different conclusions about the risk of future currency fluctuations might decide to draw up a contingent contract. This would state that the price to be paid is contingent upon the currency's actual rate at the time of settlement.

8. *Control-oriented contracts* reduce the risk of opportunistic behaviour by foreign business partners, but leave little room for discretion and trust devel-

opment. Thus the chances of a business relationship surviving a serious dispute are small. *Coordination-oriented contracts* provide communication mechanisms for resolving disputes, thus reducing the risk of misunderstandings disrupting cooperation between the parties.

9. Outcomes are the results of negotiation that are highly salient to the parties involved (Balakrishnan & Patton, 2006). Usually they are assessed in terms of their effects on the negotiators' interests. Important outcomes in most international business negotiations include *economic outcomes* (e.g. profits), and *levels of satisfaction* with the whole negotiation, including the agreement and relationships established with other parties.

QUESTIONS FOR DISCUSSION AND WRITTEN ASSIGNMENTS

1. The negotiation process entails exchanging information and proposals. Identify other important components of the negotiation process in international business negotiations, explain their function and importance, and give examples.
2. Explain how the creative use of tradeoffs can create joint gain and lead to an integrative agreement in an international business negotiation. What is the mechanism involved?
3. "The pattern of tradeoffs is far more complicated in multiparty negotiations than in two-party negotiations?" Giving specific examples, explain why this is the case.
4. Explain how an international business negotiation can be influenced and constrained by one or more separate but related negotiations.

BIBLIOGRAPHY

Acuff, F. L. *How to Negotiate Anything with Anyone Anywhere around the World.* American Management Association, 1997.

Adair, W. L. & Brett, J. M. The negotiation dance: time, culture, and behavioural sequences in negotiation. *Organization Science*, 16 (1), 2005, 33–51.

Balakrishnan, P. V. & Patton, C. *Negotiation Agenda Strategies for Bargaining with Buying Teams.* Pennsylvania State University, 2006.

Bazerman, M. H. & Neale, M. A. *Negotiating Rationally.* Free Press, 1992.

Brett, J. M. *Negotiating Globally.* Jossey-Bass, 2001.

Brett, J. M. & Crotty, S. Culture and negotiation. In P. B. Smith, M. F. Peterson & D. C. Thomas (eds) *The Handbook of Cross-cultural Management Research.* Sage, 2008, 269–283.

Caputo, A. Integrative agreements in multilateral negotiations: the case of Fiat and Chrysler. *International Journal of Business and Social Science*, 3 (12), 2012, 167–180.

Chen, G. O. H. *Negotiating with the Chinese*. Dartmouth, 1996.

Chen, M. Negotiating a supply contract in China. *Thunderbird International Business Review*, 50 (4), 2008, 271–281.

Crump, L. A temporal model of negotiation linkage dynamics. *Negotiation Journal*, 23 (2), 2007, 117–153.

Das, T. K. & Kumar, R. Regulatory focus and opportunism in the alliance development process. *Journal of Management*, 37 (3), 2011, 682–708.

Das, T. K. & Teng, B. Managing risks in strategic alliances. *Academy of Management Executive*, 13, 1999, 50–62.

Dupont, C. & Faure, G-O. The negotiation process. In V. A. Kremenyuk (ed.) *International Negotiation: Analysis, Approaches, Issues*. Jossey-Bass, 1991, 40–57.

Faure, G-O. Negotiations to set up joint ventures in China. *International Negotiation*, 5, 2000, 157–189.

Fisher, R., Ury, W. & Patton, B. *Getting to Yes*, Penguin, 2nd ed., 1991.

Ghauri, P. N. Introduction. In Ghauri, P. N. & Usunier, J. C. (eds) *International Business Negotiations*. Pergamon, 1996, 3–20.

Ghauri, P. The role of atmosphere in negotiations. In P. Ghauri & J-C. Usunier (eds) *International Business Negotiations*. Pergamon, 1996, 173–184.

Graham, J. L. Cross-cultural marketing negotiations: a laboratory experiment. *Marketing Science*, 4, 1985, 130–146.

Graham. J. L. A theory of interorganisational negotiations. *Research in Marketing*, 9, 1987, 163–183.

Kumar, R. & Patriotta, G. Culture and international alliance negotiations: a sensemaking perspective. *International Negotiation*, 16, 2011, 511–533.

Kuulaa, M. & Stam, A. A win-win method for multi-party negotiation support. *International Transactions in Operational Research*, 15, 2008, 717–737.

Laroche, L. *Managing Cultural Diversity in Technical Professions*. Butterworth-Heinemann, 2003.

Lax, D. A. & Sebenius, J. K. *The Manager as Negotiator: Bargaining for Cooperation and Competitive Gain*. Free Press, 1986.

Leonardi, P. M., Neeley, T. B. & Gerber, E. M. How managers use multiple media: discrepant events, power, and timing in redundant communication. *Organisation Science*, 23 (1), 2012, 98–117.

Lewicki, R., Saunders, D. & Barry, B. *Negotiation*. Irwin/McGraw-Hill, 2005.

Lewicki, R. J., Minton, J. & Saunders, D. Zone of potential agreement. *Negotiation*. Irwin/McGraw-Hill, 3rd ed., 1999.

Lewicki, R. J., Weiss, S. E. & Lewin, D. Models of conflict, negotiation and third party intervention: a review and synthesis. *Journal of Organizational Behavior*, 13, 1992, 209–252.

Lukes. Power and the battle for hearts and minds. *Millenium*, 33 (3), 2005, 477–494.

Lumineau, F. & Malhotra, D. Trust and collaboration in the aftermath of conflict: the effects of contract structure. *Academy of Management Journal*, 54 (5), 2011, 981–998.

Metcalf, L. E. & Bird, A. Integrating the Hofstede dimensions and twelve aspects of negotiating behavior: a six-country comparison. In H. Vinken, J. Soeters & P. Esters (eds) *Comparing Cultures: Dimensions of Culture in a Comparative Perspective*. Brill, 2004, 251–269.

Moor, A. de & Weigand, H. Business negotiation support: theory and practice. *International Negotiation*, 9 (1), 2004, 31–57.

Natlandsmyr, J. H. & Rognes, R. Culture, behaviour, and negotiation outcomes. *International Journal of Conflict Management*, 6 (1), 1995, 5–29.

Nikolaev, A. G. *International Negotiations*. Lexington Books, 2007.

Olekalns, M. & Smith, P. L. Understanding optimal outcomes: the role of strategy sequences in competitive negotiations. *Human Communication Research*, 26 (4), 2000, 527–557.

Prestwich, R. Cross-cultural negotiating: a Japanese-American case study from higher education. *International Negotiation*, 12, 2007, 29–55.

Putnam, R. D. Diplomacy and domestic politics: the logic of two-level games. *International Organization*, 42 (3), 1988, 427–460.

Pye, L. W. The China trade: making the deal. *HBR*, 64, 1986, 79–84.

Salacuse, J. *The Global Negotiator*. Palgrave Macmillan, 2003.

Salacuse, J. Teaching international business negotiation: reflections on three decades of experience. *International Negotiation*, 15, 2010, 187–228.

Schuster, C. P. & Copeland, M. J. Global business exchanges: similarities and differences around the world. *Journal of International Marketing*, 7 (2), 1999, 63–80.

Sebenius, J. K. Negotiation analysis: a characterization and review. *Management Science*, 38 (1), 1992, 18–38.

Staber, U. Social capital processes in cross-cultural management. *International Journal of Cross Cultural Management*, 6 (2), 2006, 189–203.

Stephens, K. K. et al. Discrete, sequential, and follow-up use of information and communication technology by experienced ICT users. *Management Communication Quarterly*, 22 (2), 2008, 197–231.

Suchman, M. C. & Cahill, M. L. The hired gun as facilitator: lawyers and the suppression of business disputes in Silicon Valley. *Law & Social Inquiry*, 21 (3), 1996, 679–712.

Usunier, J-C. Cultural aspects of international business negotiations. In P. N. Ghauri & J-C. Usunier (eds) *International Business Negotiations*. Pergamon, 1996, 93–118.

Weiss, S. E. Analysis of complex negotiations in international business: the RBC perspective. Organization Science, 4 (2), 1993, 269–300.

Weiss, S. The IBM-Mexico microcomputer investment negotiations. In P. Ghauri & J-C. Usunier (eds) *International Business Negotiations*. Pergamon, 1996, 305–334.

Weiss, S. E. International business negotiation in a globalizing world: reflections on the contributions and future of a (sub)field. *International Negotiation*, 11, 2006, 287–316.

Zartman, I. W. The structure of negotiation. In V. A. Kremenyuk (ed.) *International Negotiation: Analysis, Approaches, Issue.* Jossey-Bass, 1991, 65–77.

Zhao, J. J. The Chinese approach to international business negotiation. *The Journal of Business Communication*, 37 (3), 2000, 209–237.

Multilateral Business Negotiation $\quad$ 5

INTRODUCTION

Multilateral business negotiation, which involves negotiation between three or more parties, is a common feature of international business. The negotiators may be firms, government departments, multinational enterprises (MNEs) negotiating with government agencies, trade unions and professional bodies, environmental protection agencies, local communities or the general public. Many multilateral business negotiations involve both governments and firms, as shown by the 2010 and 2011 negotiations for bank and country bailouts in Europe. Multilateral business negotiations are held continuously in the European Union (EU), and are central to its functioning. Most international business negotiations concern only two parties, while multilateral business negotiations involve three or more parties. Thus all multilateral negotiations are multiparty. In multilateral business negotiations the most influential parties are generally large and successful firms with much experience of negotiation (Money, 1998).

Even companies which do not participate in international business negotiations can be affected by their decisions. For example, companies have to observe international standards, which are decided in multilateral negotiations between governments, international organisations and professional bodies. Airbus, for instance, manufactures planes with wings from Britain, fuselages from Germany, cockpits from France and tailpieces from Spain. When Airbus negotiates with its many partners and suppliers, any agreements reached in the negotiations must conform to international aviation and safety standards which have been agreed upon in multilateral negotiations. The same obligation applies when it conducts bilateral or multilateral negotiations with any of its many subcontractors and suppliers worldwide.

Companies which participate in multilateral business negotiations often underestimate the difficulty of reaching an agreement. In two-party negotiations, only two negotiating partners have to work out the agreement, but in a multilateral negotiation with, say, five parties, five sets of interests have to be considered simultaneously before a solution can emerge that will work for all parties. "Parties" in multiparty business negotiations can be principals or agents. If principals are unqualified or unwilling to negotiate on their own behalf, lawyers, agents or other third parties are often called in to advise them or to negotiate on their behalf.

The complexity of multiparty business negotiations stems from such factors as cultural differences, communication difficulties among negotiators from diverse cultures and legal and regulatory pluralism. Differing interests and clashing values and ideologies among the multiple parties make a satisfactory outcome difficult to achieve. When several companies are hoping to set up an international joint venture, this may translate into multilateral negotiations which last several years (Faure, 2000). In this case, many issues have to be negotiated at many levels. The greater the number of parties participating in a negotiation, the greater the chance of disputes and blockages occurring, and to manage the resulting complexity, a simple structure and procedures are needed as well as appropriate negotiating techniques (Zartman, 2003). Techniques used in multiparty negotiations to overcome blockages include tradeoffs, planned and structured information exchanges and clear voting rules. Voting methods used in multiparty business negotiations range from top-down decision-making to consensus decision-making methods at the other end of the spectrum. Majority-vote methods come somewhere in between.

Influential individuals in multiparty negotiations tend to be extroverted personalities, persons who share a common culture and language with many of the other participants, and persons who adopt a collaborative, problem-solving approach in negotiations. These individuals typically manoeuvre themselves into central positions of influence to try to influence the outcome. They may, for instance, join a *temporary coalition* to sway a decision on a particular issue. Joining a coalition enables negotiators to combine forces and negotiate with stronger parties in a collective, organised manner. Weak parties which join a coalition avoid destructive competition with each other, and gain negotiating strength by pooling their resources. An important advantage of coalitions for non-coalition members is that it enables them to negotiate, in effect, with one party rather than many, thus saving time and lowering costs.

Many conflicting interests and issues have to be addressed in multilateral business negotiations, and the result can be contentious and very lengthy negotiations. To save valuable time, a draft contract is sometimes prepared by one of the parties that resolves all negotiating issues. If the draft contract is accepted by the other parties, it provides a framework for the negotiation. Heated disputes sometimes disrupt multilateral negotiations, and mediation may have to be used to resolve the conflict. The advantage of using mediation is that the conflicting parties gain a better understanding of what caused the conflict and what options they have for dealing with similar problems in the future. In cultures such as Japan that are highly formal and that also seek to avoid conflict, third parties are sometimes called into business negotiations to play a mediator role (Crump & Glendon, 2003).

NEGOTIATION RESEARCH

Two-party emphasis

Global business leads to numerous multilateral negotiations, such as the multilateral or linked bilateral negotiations that take place when a carmaker plans a new assembly plant abroad. Such negotiations involve talks held by multiple parties about multiple issues, and require careful planning and a complicated process leading to a final agreement. Multiparty and multiple-issue negotiation is necessarily based on a process of give and take in which the negotiators keep modifying their initial proposals in order to come close to each other and eventually to reach an agreement (Ghauri, 1996).

Multilateral negotiations are a common feature of international business, yet negotiation research concentrates on the two-party (dyadic) situation (Weiss, 2006). Underlying researchers' interest in two-party business negotiations is the fact that two-party negotiations are relatively easy to plan and study even when the two parties concerned are from culturally distant countries. The two sides either reach an agreement or not. The process is easy to follow and understand. For instance, there is usually a clear pattern of tit-for-tat bargaining based on the reciprocity principle, leading to concessions and tradeoffs and a final agreement. But such a clear and coherent process is rarely the case in multilateral business negotiations. For instance, concessions offered to one party may have a detrimental effect on the other parties, with the result that concessions may not bring the negotiators any closer to a satisfactory agreement, that is, an agreement acceptable to all parties.

When several companies from several different countries negotiate to establish a joint venture or an international alliance, the multilateral negotiations – and linked bilateral negotiations – may last several years (Faure, 2000). Many complex issues have to be negotiated at many levels. Sometimes a full team of engineers, financial experts, lawyers, sales people and interpreters is involved in the negotiations, shuttling between the headquarters of the various companies involved. Weiss (2006) argues that researchers should focus on these and other facts of real-life business negotiation, instead of emphasising such aspects as the culturally motivated behaviour of negotiators.

Very few studies have been made of how satisfactory outcomes are achieved in multilateral business negotiations. But many studies have been made of how national cultural differences shape the strategies used in *bilateral* business negotiations. Studies have focused attention on, among other things, the pattern of information exchange in bilateral negotiations (Adair et al., 2007) and the use of problem-solving strategies (Gaham et al., 1988). Little, however, is known about how culture influences the negotiating processes of *multilateral* business negotiation, even though understanding cultural influence on multilateral business negotiations is a critical skill for managers to acquire. Weiss (2006, 307) argues that researchers should be "more persistent in their pursuit of data from real IB negotiations. We need to get closer to the real phenomenon." According to Greenhalgh (1987), more longitudinal studies of real-life negotiations are needed which analyse a negotiation as a facet of the long-term relationship between the parties.

Multiparty negotiations are much more complicated than two-party negotiations, and are therefore much more difficult to describe and analyse. That helps to explain why, as Devine (1990) notes, most accounts of multilateral business negotiations consist of case studies. Typically, such case studies describe a complicated multilateral negotiation and the lessons to be learned from it. Money (1998) suggests that, for future research, negotiation simulations might be used in preference to case studies in order to collect data on the effects of social networks during international multilateral negotiations. Data might be collected to show, for instance, the nature and strength of coalitions in multilateral negotiations, and the part played by directive leadership. A difficulty associated with this approach is that students participating in simulations come to the negotiation with very little experience to shape their approach. Consequently, they do not always respond in the same way as an experienced negotiator to the pressures of the negotiation process. This raises the question of whether data coming from simulations and simple game-like experiments can be generalised to multilateral, multi-issue negotiations in real-life settings.

MANAGING COMPLEXITY

Wide range of issues and interests

Multilateral business negotiation, a common feature of international business, is a highly complex process, involving many firms, covering numerous issues and taking place over long periods of time. While many international business negotiations involve just two parties, multiparty negotiations include at least three parties and sometimes far more than that. A set of multiparty negotiations, for instance, involving more than 100 parties (governments) led to the World Trade Organization's (WTO) being established in 1994. Typically, in international trade negotiations each round is dominated by bargaining and exchanges of concessions through a complex pattern of multilateral and bilateral negotiations. Creating appropriate structure to achieve order and direction out of all the complexity is a prime activity of the chairperson elected by the parties for that purpose. In multiparty negotiations, the social dynamics and complexity of the negotiations are dramatically increased, and an agreement acceptable to all parties can take a long time to take shape. In Northern Ireland, an agreement acceptable to all parties took decades to emerge.

Negotiations involving multiple parties have to deal with multiple interests and issues far more frequently than do two-party negotiations. This feature of multilateral negotiations greatly complicates the negotiation process. The wide range of interests and issues to be considered makes an integrative agreement which benefits all parties difficult to achieve. The disruptive impact made by clashing interests and values is magnified in multiparty business negotiations. In a two-party business negotiation, only two sides have to reach an agreement, but in multilateral business negotiations an acceptable overall agreement can be extremely difficult to achieve, and many concessions and compromises must be made by the parties. Alternatively, the negotiators may have to be satisfied with a partial agreement covering only a few of the major issues.

In multilateral business negotiations, there is also a greater chance of clashing cultural values and ideologies, and differing expectations about the outcomes, which can slow progress towards an agreement. In some countries in South America, Asia and other parts of the developing world, signing a contract does not necessarily conclude a multiparty negotiation; it merely signifies the intention of the parties to work together (Schuster & Copeland, 1999).

Simple structure and procedures

Other aspects of multilateral business negotiations that slow progress towards an agreement are

- the many parties often have unequal negotiating power;
- many complex and sometimes divisive issues have to be addressed;
- conflict over contentious issues may erupt and polarise the parties.

Such characteristics help explain why a question that lies at the heart of the multiparty negotiation process is how to manage the complexity. The answer, according to Zartman (2003), is by means of *simple structure and procedures*. Unless some simple structure is imposed, such as scheduled meetings with a chair and simple procedures to facilitate orderly discussion, multiparty business negotiations can quickly become chaotic. Simple procedures, clear voting rules and negotiating techniques such as packaging and tradeoffs, help the negotiators keep moving towards a negotiated agreement.

Managing multiple issues

In international business negotiations, more parties mean more complications. The complexity of information processing and interpersonal dynamics in multilateral negotiations increases exponentially with the number of people at the table (Kern et al., 2005). In two-party negotiations, when negotiators are haggling over just one issue such as the price of a computer installation or the date for starting an international development project, one party's win is the other's party's loss. The situation is clear-cut. But in multiparty negotiations, a range of difficult issues is brought to the table. For example, when negotiations take place between companies from several different countries to establish an international joint venture (IJV), many difficult and potentially contentious issues have to be negotiated, such as

- the resource contributions which each of the companies will make to the IJV;
- how profits will be distributed;
- how operating expenses will be allocated;
- how board appointments and senior management positions will be decided.

As negotiations proceed, in order to reach an agreement acceptable to all parties, the negotiators have to focus more and more on identifying the *common interests* of the parties and the mutually beneficial outcomes that are possible.

Lewicki et al.'s (1992) framework/detail approach to managing multiple issues requires the parties first to agree on some broad objectives and principles – the framework – and only then to discuss the details. The framework phase enables a start to be made to the negotiations. The detail phase permits the debate and packaging of specific issues so that a settlement acceptable to all sides can be achieved.

Use of subgroups

Very complicated problems can sometimes be solved in multilateral business negotiations by using appropriate procedures. For instance, subgroups, consisting of technical experts nominated or elected by the various parties, may

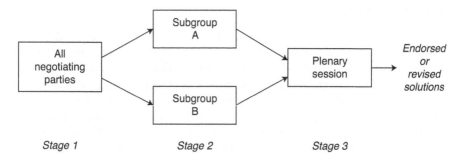

Figure 5.1   Use of subgroups in multiparty negotiations

Note: In multiparty negotiations subgroups of technical experts are often set up. Such subgroups deal efficiently with complex technical and legal issues.

be set up during the negotiations, as shown in Figure 5.1. Subgroups deal efficiently with complicated negotiating issues, and so enable overall progress to be made. Each subgroup will investigate a particular issue – or a single aspect of the issue – and consider various options for dealing with it. In many cases, the recommendations of the subgroup are presented to a plenary session of all the parties for their endorsement or revision.

Willingness to adjust

Lewicki et al. (1999) argue that negotiators who are dealing with multiple issues have to be willing to adjust their opening negotiating positions and align their own interests with those of the other parties in order to enable overall agreement to be reached. An example of how the alignment process actually happens in multiparty business negotiations is when each side proposes changes to the other parties' negotiating positions while simultaneously making changes to its own. This process, which involves give and take, flexibility and willingness by each party to adjust its negotiating stance, is often necessary if an agreement is to be reached in a multiparty business negotiation.

Issue bundles

Another way of managing multiple issues is by negotiating *issue bundles*, as opposed to the traditional approach adopted by bilateral negotiators of negotiating each issue separately. An important advantage of issue bundling is that it is a time-saving method. For example, cost, delivery and after-sales service may be negotiated in a single bundle. Time is saved, although sometimes at the cost of sub-optimal outcomes. For instance, in buying/selling negotiations, separate negotiations are ruled out with another manufacturer offering competitive terms for just a single component of the issue bundle.

Clear voting rules

Meunier (2000) argues that the EU's effectiveness as an international trade negotiator is due to clear voting rules. When the Council of Ministers decrees that negotiating teams representing different EU regional groupings must take decisions by majority vote, as opposed to unanimous vote, those resisting change in each grouping can be outvoted. Thus, agreement between the multiple parties is much more likely. However, agreement in international multilateral business negotiations frequently has to be reached by unanimous vote or consensus. In this context, a unanimous vote means that most parties are in favour, and the rest do not oppose. Parties who do not agree can abstain without blocking an agreement.

In multilateral negotiations, Western firms often give the leader of the firm's negotiating team authority to make decisions after consulting other members of the team. Firms from countries with a strong power-distance orientation usually confer decision-making authority in negotiations on the most senior manager in the negotiating team (Gray, 2010). Companies from collectivist countries, on the other hand, may have a large negotiating team, yet it may not be clear who has the authority to make decisions.

PARTIES IN MULTILATERAL BUSINESS NEGOTIATIONS

Principals and agents

"Parties" in multilateral and bilateral business negotiations can be principals (e.g. companies, governments), representatives, agents, advisers, coalitions of parties, arbitrators and mediators (Crump & Glendon, 2003). In specialised negotiations, principals are sometimes unqualified to negotiate on their own behalf. Lawyers, agents or other third parties are needed to provide principals with the expert negotiation guidance needed for success. Intellectual property negotiations, international commercial property deals, and cross-border merger or acquisition negotiations are examples of business negotiations in which expert guidance is often needed by the parties.

In some multilateral business negotiations the principal is not an individual but an organisational committee, for example, the board or an executive committee, which makes decisions for the company but which may nevertheless lack unity. In this case, the principal will find it difficult to participate in a multilateral, multi-issue business negotiation in a coherent and consistent manner, and may have to appoint an agent or representative to negotiate on the principal's behalf.

According to agency theory (Eisenhardt, 1989), conflict is likely to arise both in international and domestic business negotiations between the best interests of the principal (typically a company) and the best interests of the principal's agent/representative (typically a consultant or lawyer working for a fee). A common example of an agent or representative not acting in the best interests of the company is when the agent accepts a low price or unfavourable terms of payment in order to finalise negotiations and be free to move on to another assignment. In agency theory literature, the term "agent" refers to the manager (agent or representative of the company). In *negotiation literature*, however, an agent is an outside expert who is hired to represent the company's interest, and this is the meaning of the term that is used here.

As Mnookin & Susskind (1999) observe, principals and agents have different motives, interests and standards, and sometimes they have different goals and ethical norms. During multiparty business negotiations, for instance, the agent's main concern may be to accomplish a deal quickly for the reasons stated above, even a deal which is not in the principal's best interests. Avoiding impasse by making an over-generous concession, for instance, can be in the best interests of the agent (since outside agents are usually paid a fee for their efforts), but not in the best interests of the principal.

The situation is one of potential conflict because principal and agent have different interests and asymmetric information. Usually the agent has more information about the topic of negotiation and the local situation. It is difficult for the principal to ensure that the agent is always acting in the company's best interests, especially when the negotiation is taking place in another country. When this is the case, it would be costly and impractical for the company to attempt to observe and assess the agent's behaviour. Bebchuk & Fried (2004) refer to the deviation from the principal's interest by the agent as "agency costs."

In complex multilateral negotiations, instructions from principals may be imprecise and uncertain, making it difficult for the agent to structure the concessions and tradeoffs needed to reach agreement. As a result, the agent is forced to rely on behaviour learned from previous experience. Anecdotal evidence suggests that agents are less willing to yield than principals. They have a tougher outlook, and also a more distant relationship with the other negotiating parties.

Influential parties

Money (1998) presents evidence to show that the most influential *organisations* in multilateral business negotiations, whether domestic or international, are large firms with high levels of trade activity and much previous experience of various kinds of negotiation. The most influential *individuals* in multilateral negotiations tend to be

- extroverted personalities;
- persons who share a common culture and language with many of the other participants;
- persons who adopt a collaborative, problem-solving approach in the negotiations.

These influential individuals typically manoeuvre themselves into central positions of influence in a complex multiparty negotiation to try to bring about the outcome they think is necessary. They may, for instance, join a *temporary coalition* in order to sway a decision on a particular issue, such as management fees or the starting and finishing dates for an international construction project.

Money (1998) finds that in multiparty negotiations, Asians and negotiators from other collectivist cultures tend to form alliances with other parties more frequently than do participants from individualist cultures. Negotiators from high uncertainty-avoidance cultures, on the other hand, may join coalitions because they are afraid to be on the losing side. Irrespective of their cultural backgrounds, Sjostedt (1993) argues, individuals in multiparty negotiations tend to select a specialised role from a limited list, which includes

- *leaders*, who organise and influence fellow negotiators to obtain the outcomes they want;

- *conductors*, who organise, but more quietly, from a neutral position;
- *defenders*, who are single-issue participants, intent on promoting a particular issue or interest;
- *brakers*, who repeatedly object and block agreement over various issues;
- *cruisers*, who have no axe to grind and often become followers of leaders or conductors.

Parties' strategic orientations

Negotiation researchers have long recognised that the negotiators in two-party negotiations have a dominant strategic orientation, usually a competitive or cooperative orientation (De Dreu et al., 2000). The competitive/contending orientation of Indian negotiators, for instance, prompts them to stick to their position and expect the other party to concede – a strategy that can lead to impasse (Kumar, 2004).

The dominant orientation finding has been extended to multiparty negotiations. Olekalns et al. (2003) collected and analysed data from 36 four-person groups and found that most groups begin negotiations with a distributive (competitive) phase, but end cooperatively with an integrative phase. These findings are broadly supported by O'Connor & Adams's (1999) analyses of negotiation scripts, showing that individuals expect the initial phase of a negotiation to centre on positioning and posturing, and later stages to focus on deal-making.

Olekalns et al.'s (2003) findings lead them to conclude that distributive (competitive) behaviour which precedes integrative (cooperative) behaviour is normative in both multiparty and two-party negotiations. Thus multiparty negotiators, like two-party negotiators, tend to be both competitive and cooperative in the same negotiation. The way in which this tendency plays out in multiparty negotiations is that negotiating teams often open with a contending posture, perhaps because they believe that opening cooperatively would signal a strong motive to reach agreement and so be interpreted as a sign of weakness.

FEATURES OF MULTILATERAL BUSINESS NEGOTIATION

Purposes

Multilateral business negotiations are a common feature of international business, and are an important means of resolving conflict about business issues among companies which are based in different countries. The negotiators may be firms in a global industry, government departments from different countries, companies involved in an international trade dispute, or MNEs negotiating with government agencies, for instance, for mineral extraction rights or tax concessions. Many multilateral business negotiations involve both governments and firms – banks, for instance. This was the case with negotiations in 2010 and 2011 for the bank and country bailouts in Europe. Multilateral business negotiations are held continuously in the EU, and are an important means of resolving conflict about trade and business matters among the member states.

Whereas most business negotiations concern only two primary parties, multilateral business negotiations involve three or more parties. Thus all multilateral negotiations are also multiparty negotiations.

Lengthy negotiations

Companies embarking on multilateral negotiations often underestimate the complexity and difficulty of reaching an agreement. In Northern Ireland, an overall agreement took decades to emerge. Negotiations about climate change among the 192 member states of the United Nations (UN) have tended to fall apart due to a clash between various factions about how to reduce greenhouse gas emissions. Negotiations leading to the creation and maintenance of the international space station were very difficult and protracted because complicated agreements had to be negotiated between governments and organisations from 14 different countries. Even the choice of location for a research and development (R&D) consortium's central headquarters involved lengthy, drawn-out difficult negotiations between members of the consortium (Browning et al., 1995).

When very large groups or even entire communities are involved in negotiations, public participation mechanisms may need to be created to provide the means for the multiple parties to make their voices heard in the negotiations. Examples of such mechanisms are advisory committees, public hearings, focus groups and opinion polls.

Choice of negotiation methods

Wong & Fang (2010) describe two ways in which firms carry out multilateral buying/selling negotiations:

- *Negotiate concurrently* with all the parties. When automated systems are used, concurrent negotiation requires much less time to carry out than sequential negotiation. On the other hand, coordinating and analysing the multiple responses can be extremely difficult and time-consuming.
- *Negotiate sequentially* with all the parties regarding, say, the price and timing of a proposed business transaction. Sequential bargaining allows the parties to alternate offer and counteroffer, round by round, and to make concessions until an agreement is reached.

Iterative method

Kuulaa & Stam's (2008) iterative method for advancing a multilateral negotiation towards an optimal agreement involves each party's starting the negotiation process with some inferior outcome or solution (e.g. the party's best alternative to a negotiated agreement [BATNA]) which offers ample opportunity for joint gain. The BATNA solution for a given party is the best that can be achieved if the negotiations fail. Each party has a different BATNA; therefore, each party begins the negotiation with a different initial solution.

At each iteration, the parties move closer to the optimum solution (Pareto optimal). A solution is Pareto optimal if no other feasible solution exists such that any of the parties can improve their status without negatively affecting at least one other party. In practice, the optimal solution can only be calculated by using computers because of the multiple parties involved and the multiple issues that have to be negotiated. The method is similar in general approach to other methods which are based on comparisons of different proposed solutions at each iteration.

Single negotiating text

Multiple parties and the wide range of conflicting interests and issues that have to be considered in multilateral business negotiations can make an integrative, cooperative agreement extremely difficult to achieve. An effective way of reducing the excessive amount of time required to reach an integrative agreement is for one of the parties to prepare an opening package – a complete draft contract – that resolves all negotiating issues. Provided that this draft contract is accepted by the other parties as the basis for discussion, it provides a framework for the entire multilateral negotiation process.

An alternative approach is for the parties to build up an agreement, issue by issue, throughout the negotiation, but this approach is much more difficult and time demanding. Presenting a single negotiating text to several different negotiating teams facilitates orderly discussion and enables the negotiators to move more quickly towards an agreement acceptable to all parties. Raiffa (1982) argues that without a single negotiating text, many multi-issue negotiations would be too diffuse to be effective.

Binding agreements

International agreements and protocols affecting virtually all categories of international business are made by multilateral negotiations involving governments and international organisations every year. Companies throughout the world are affected because they need to conform to the standards agreed in the negotiations. Some multilateral agreements in international business are very complicated to negotiate, but very powerful once all parties have signed the agreement.

The Doha round of trade agreements signed by all 149 members of the WTO is an outstanding example of a powerful agreement. It ensures that all parties, including relatively weak firms with little influence, are treated equally.

IMPACT OF COALITIONS

Why coalitions?

In multilateral business negotiations, both negotiation dynamics and the process can be extremely complex. For example, when five or six firms from different countries are trying to negotiate an agreement regarding the acquisition and valuation of collective goods, keeping track of the effects of any bilateral agreements reached by the parties with various international suppliers can be extremely difficult. *Miscommunication* is another effect of complexity and cultural diversity in multilateral business negotiations. According to Winham (1977), up to 50 percent of attempts to offer concessions are not perceived as concessions by intended recipients – an effect which points up the importance of coalitions in multilateral negotiations.

The most successful parties in multilateral negotiations are often those who align themselves with other players, who form coalitions of parties with broadly similar interests and goals (Crump & Zartman, 2003). In complex multilateral business negotiations, coalitions make the negotiation process more manageable by reducing the number of positions and interests that have to be considered and debated. Although there may be a dozen different packages and a dozen proposed solutions on the table at the start of negotiations, by the time coalitions have formed, these may have fused to two or three. The formation of negotiating coalitions in effect structurally transforms a complex multilateral business negotiation into a much simpler bilateral negotiation.

The formation of one or more coalitions effectively leads to a more efficient negotiation process that benefits everyone involved, including the negotiating companies and other stakeholders who may be affected by the outcomes of a multilateral business negotiation. Coalitions bring advantage not only to members of the coalition but also to those sitting on the other side of the table. An important advantage of coalitions for non-coalition members is the chance to negotiate, in effect, with one party rather than many, thus saving time and lowering costs. Another advantage for non-members is that coalition members feel pressure to give priority to common interests over conflicting ones, thus reducing time wasting in negotiating sessions.

Benefits

International business negotiators intent on achieving good negotiation outcomes are motivated to form temporary coalitions with other negotiators and to develop common negotiation strategies. Once embedded in a coalition, they continue to be influential if they are perceived to be indispensable for the coalition's success.

Negotiators who are in coalitions have a negotiating advantage, since joining a coalition enables them to join forces with other, possibly stronger, parties and negotiate in a collective, organised manner. Weak parties join a coalition to avoid destructive competition with each other, and gain negotiating strength by pooling their resources. Faced with the complexities and uncertainties of multilateral negotiations, companies which form negotiating coalitions are essentially adopting a "Don't go it alone" strategy. Forming a coalition can be an attractive alternative to retaining expert advisers to advise and, in effect, negotiate on the companies' behalf.

Thanks to their membership in a temporary coalition with the US in WTO negotiations, Chile and Singapore both hit above their weight. According to Crump (2011), sharing an agenda with coalition partners created synergies that helped them be effective in the negotiations and achieve their negotiation goals. Money (1998) finds that negotiators from collectivist cultures and uncertainty-avoidance cultures are particularly likely to try to build coalitions during multilateral business negotiations.

Multilateral business negotiations become bilateral encounters or bloc-to-bloc negotiations when negotiators form cross-cutting coalitions that piece together agreements regarding various negotiating issues. However, not all members of a bloc will identify fully with coalition proposals. This dual structure is reflected in shifting coalitions and alliances that often form in the course of lengthy and complex multilateral negotiations. The more threatening non-members of the coalition become, as indicated by their hard-bargaining tactics, the more cohesive the in-group bloc, the coalition, becomes (Druckman, 1991).

Issue-based coalitions

Coalition analysis is a widely used approach for understanding multilateral business negotiations. The predominant view of its proponents, as stated by Zartman (2002), is that a temporary, issue-focused coalition of firms has the effect of bringing in many of the parties which are participating in a multilateral business negotiation behind a package of tradeoffs. This is especially the case for issue-focused coalitions, that is, those formed for a particular purpose, such as gaining a particular concession or winning a vote on a particular issue. Cullen et al. (2000) draw attention to the unstable nature of issue-focused coalitions, pointing out that such coalitions form around a particular issue, and then disband once the issue is resolved. More stable coalitions, which last through an entire negotiation, are often based on their members' pre-existing business relationships.

In multilateral and multinational negotiations, the forming of coalitions is a key facilitating factor. Touval (1989) notes how, in a Law of the Sea Conference, a coalition between a group of emerging markets and a group of landlocked countries was able to greatly influence the outcome.

How coalitions form

The formation of coalitions before and during multilateral business negotiations is a gradual process. Zartman (2003) studied the process and noted that coalition formation begins with the parties bargaining over conditions of pairing, then clustering, and then coalescing into a large coalition. The process involves frequent concessions and tradeoffs as parties move among issue clusters. Concessions are exchanged to align the various parties' positions with each other.

However, not all attempts to form coalitions are successful. Using a computer-mediated coalition game, Beest et al. (2008) found that *communicating anger* during coalition talks is a mistake. Other participants form negative impressions of parties which express anger and may subsequently exclude them from a coalition agreement.

In international multilateral business negotiations, negotiating power can be equated with the ability of parties to protect and advance their own interests. By building coalitions with people who have complementary interests, negotiators can build their power base and advance and protect their interests. Minority coalitions may form simply to gain influence, exert pressure or attain some intermediate objective (Dupont, 1994).

Case Study

MINI-CASE: Structure, times and deadlines

Working in small groups, study the following case and answer the questions. The group's answers may be presented to the other groups for their comments.

A German construction consortium negotiates with a Brazilian firm over a two-week period to finalise plans for a joint road construction programme in Brazil. The negotiating team, which represents three German companies, draws up a lengthy draft contract with numerous technical annexes and presents it to the Brazilian team. The consortium's lead negotiator suggests that this draft contract could serve as the basis for the negotiation. The draft contract is a very businesslike document. Clauses in the contract deal in detail with the various phases of the construction programme and the responsibilities of the parties, with set dates and deadlines and delay penalties.

The Brazilian negotiators request a break from negotiations to give them time to study the document in detail. When, two hours later, the negotiations resume, the Brazilian team rejects the draft contract as impractical.

The German negotiating team is genuinely surprised because they regard a detailed and precise contract as essential for planning and implementing any large construction project. The Germans make the assumption that the *timing* of the construction and the *sequence* of construction activities will go according to the schedule mapped out in the contract. From the viewpoint of all three members of the German consortium, large-scale construction projects require a synchronisation process based on precise times and deadlines, incentives and penalties. Any delays, for instance, should be subject to late penalties.

But the Brazilian negotiating team sees things differently. For them, the relationship of the parties, not a signed contract, will be the most important outcome of the negotiations. The Brazilians' lead negotiator makes the point that the company knows from many previous large-scale construction projects in which it has been involved that numerous implementation problems will be bound to arise. But it also knows that solutions will be found provided that a good relationship has been established between the international partners.

From the Brazilians' viewpoint, the ability of the parties to formulate a precise, implementable plan is something of an illusion. The Brazilians' chief negotiator insists that, based on his company's experience of international projects, precise synchronisation during implementation will be almost impossible. For one thing, attitudes towards time and punctuality are not shared by German and Brazilian firms.

The fact that such divergent approaches have sprung up between the two companies at this early stage of the negotiations makes the consortium's negotiating team worry that synchronising the multiple, interrelated activities of the project will be extremely difficult to carry out in an efficient and cost-effective way. A member of the German team, a civil engineer, is worried that basic attitudes towards planning and organisation and contractual liability are simply not shared with the Brazilian company. As a consequence, numerous expensive delays and hold-ups will be bound to occur, and what should have been a healthy profit for his company from the project could be converted into a loss. Worse still, the reputation of all three German companies will be damaged.

At this stage, the three German companies hold internal discussions to decide whether or not the consortium should withdraw from the negotiations.

Questions:

1. *To what extent are cultural factors responsible for the parties' very different attitudes towards (a) time and planning schedules, (b) contracts, (c) business relationships?*
2. *If negotiations continue, what changes of structure and content might make the German draft contract more acceptable to the Brazilian team?*
3. *Should the German consortium withdraw from the negotiations?*

BLOCKAGES IN MULTIPARTY NEGOTIATIONS

Factors causing blockages

In addition to pursuing their own specific negotiating goals, negotiators often use the negotiation process to protect the interests of their constituencies, such as trade organisations, professional bodies, a government department or a division of their organisation. Meunier (2000) points out that a high degree of pressure by constituencies, in the form of requests or instructions or information campaigns, often ties the negotiators' hands and makes the conclusion of an agreement which is acceptable to all parties less likely. However, negotiators' skill in communication with constituencies can influence them to change their aspiration levels, and can lead to a higher agreement rate because a greater range of agreements will be viewed by them as satisfactory or at least acceptable (Bazerman & Neale, 1983).

Weiss (2006) and other researchers have identified a number of other important factors in addition to pressures from constituencies which cause blockages and prevent agreement from being reached in multilateral international business negotiations. The factors include

- cultural differences between negotiators, including differences in business norms;
- linguistic difficulties;
- ideological diversity;
- legal and regulatory pluralism;
- monetary factors.

Approaches used by practitioners to overcome these problems include structured information exchanges, tradeoffs and clear voting rules.

Structured information exchanges

The greater the number of parties in an international business negotiation, the greater the risk of blockages and deadlock due to conflicting interests and positions. As many as 100 managers and officials may participate in an international trade negotiation, and accordingly the information exchange and information technology (IT) aspects of the negotiation must be very carefully planned and managed.

The organisers of a multiparty negotiation need to ensure that the necessary exchanges of information among the parties take place in an efficient and timely manner, for instance, in a carefully planned series of bilateral discussions. Sebenius (1984) notes that large-scale multilateral trade negotiations typically link the negotiators so that any party can talk to any other party in either private or public discussion.

Most multilateral business negotiations follow an agenda which has been agreed by the parties at the pre-negotiation stage, as part of the crucial process of getting the negotiators to the table. At the pre-negotiation stage, the negotiating teams set the negotiation agenda, manage their internal negotiations, and make the necessary arrangements for structured information exchanges. The process of building interest-based coalitions with other parties is also likely to begin at the pre-negotiation stage to ensure that negotiations do not end in impasse.

Tradeoffs

Tradeoffs are the usual method for bringing about agreements and overcoming blockages in multiparty business negotiations. Each of the multiple parties sacrifices some objectives to secure others. If none is prepared to do so, the result is stalemate. In addition to tradeoffs, the related technique of issue packaging can help negotiators move towards agreement (Kuulaa & Stam, 2008).

In two-party negotiations, tradeoffs are between issues that are of high value to one party and of low value to the other. The situation is clear-cut. But the pattern of tradeoffs is more complex in multiparty negotiations. Interdependence between the parties means that tradeoffs involve more than two members. In a three-party negotiation, for instance, if A makes a concession to B, B may need to make a concession to C, who will, in turn, make a concession to A in order for the tradeoff to be complete. Where more than three parties are involved, the pattern of tradeoffs is much more complicated.

Clear voting rules

As the number of parties involved in an international business negotiation increases, the more difficult it becomes to resolve disputes by unstructured haggling. In multiparty business negotiations, clear voting rules are needed to keep the discussion moving towards agreement. Meunier (2000) argues that the EU's effectiveness as an international business negotiator is largely due to the clear voting rules imposed by the EU Council of Ministers. The rules influence the outcomes. When EU negotiators are given unambiguous instructions to use *unanimous voting*, for instance, the impact on outcomes is great because negotiators in different regional groupings cannot obtain more than what the region's most conservative or recalcitrant member state is willing to concede. When, on the other hand, the EU negotiating team follows *majority vote* rules, conservative or recalcitrant EU member states can be outvoted. Consequently a more favourable agreement is likely from the point of view of the other participants in the negotiations.

In international business negotiations, voting methods range from top-down decision-making to consensus decision-making methods at the other end of the spectrum. Majority-vote methods fall somewhere in between. Majority voting is the quick and easy way of reaching a decision and avoiding impasse, and the method has the advantage of being generally accepted as fair. However, it does little or nothing to satisfy the losers, who may later try to build influence and reverse the decision. A more basic objection is that key decisions, such as how profits from an international joint venture will be distributed among several partners, need to be agreed by all parties. In such cases, the only practical way of reaching an agreement that all the parties will accept may be through consensus.

Consensus

In multiparty business negotiations, the negotiators often decide to make decisions by consensus as a way of avoiding conflict between national subgroups. A frequent result is that facile compromise decisions are made. Options which could trigger conflict are not properly considered. Another disadvantage is that consensus decision-making takes up much time as agreement has to be reached on substantive as well as procedural issues. On the other hand, implementation of consensus decisions is usually swift and decisive. Because they have been closely involved in developing a decision, managers are committed to implementing it smoothly in their own organisations.

Consensus decision-making works well in multilateral business negotiations except when opposing factions have irreconcilable and contradictory interests. Lax & Sebenius (2012) cite Conoco's efforts to build consensus regarding its plans to construct a pipeline in Ecuador's Amazon region. The company had already carried out initial negotiations with a wide range of organisations, including groups opposed to the pipeline project. One such group was composed of Ecuadorean and international advocates for indigenous peoples. Another group comprised environmental nongovernmental organisations (NGOs). Both groups opposed Conoco's plans. Conoco planned to overcome the problem by arranging a consensus-seeking meeting of all stakeholders in a floating hotel on a river in the Amazon region. During this meeting, Conoco executives explained the many benefits of the pipeline to the region. But instead of falling into line, the two opposed combined forces in even more formidable opposition to Conoco, which eventually decided to withdraw from the project.

KEY POINTS

1. The complexity of international multiparty negotiation stems from cultural differences, communication difficulties among multiple negotiators, and legal pluralism. Clashing values and ideologies often make a satisfactory outcome difficult to achieve. Chances of success are improved, however, when the national cultures of the companies involved are close rather than distant, and when the firms have good pre-existing relationships.
2. The parties in multiparty business negotiations can be principals (e.g. companies, governments), representatives, agents, advisers, coalitions of parties, arbitrators and mediators. When principals are unqualified to negotiate on their own behalf – in intellectual property negotiations, say, or international

real estate deals – lawyers, agents or other third parties are sometimes brought in to provide guidance.

3. Blockages in multiparty negotiations stem from cultural differences between negotiators, differences in business norms, and legal and regulatory pluralism. Techniques and approaches used to overcome blockages include tradeoffs, structured information exchanges and clear voting rules. In multiparty business negotiations, voting methods range from top-down decision-making to consensus decision-making methods at the other end of the spectrum. Majority-vote methods fall somewhere in between.

4. Multilateral business negotiations involve negotiation between three or more parties, and are a common feature of international business. The negotiators may be firms, government departments or MNEs which are negotiating with government agencies. Many multilateral business negotiations involve both governments and firms, as in the 2010 and 2011 negotiations for bank and country bailouts in Europe. Multilateral business negotiations are held continuously in the EU, and are central to its functioning.

5. Influential individuals in multilateral negotiations tend to be extroverted personalities, persons who share a common culture and language with many of the other participants, and persons who adopt a collaborative, problem-solving approach to negotiation. These individuals typically manoeuvre themselves into central positions of influence to try to bring about the outcome they think is necessary. They may join a temporary coalition to sway a decision on a particular issue.

6. Reaching an integrative agreement in multilateral negotiations is more difficult than in two-party negotiations, where only two negotiating partners from different countries have to work out the agreement. Where there are, say, five parties, five sets of interests have to be considered simultaneously before a solution can emerge that will work for all. The greater the number of parties involved in a negotiation, the greater the chance that blockages and conflict will retard progress towards agreement.

7. Many conflicting interests and issues have to be addressed in multilateral business negotiations, leading to protracted negotiations. In some cases, to save time, one of the parties will prepare a complete draft contract that resolves all negotiating issues. If this draft contract is accepted by the other parties, it provides a framework for the negotiation and facilitates orderly discussion.

8. Joining a coalition enables negotiators to join forces and negotiate with stronger parties in a collective, organised manner. Weak parties joining a coalition avoid destructive competition with each other, and gain negotiating strength by pooling their resources. An important advantage of coalitions for non-coalition members is that it enables them to negotiate, in effect, with one party rather than many, thus saving time and lowering costs.

9. International agreements and protocols affecting virtually all categories of international business are made by governments and international organisations every year. Companies throughout the world have to conform to the agreed standards. When Airbus, for instance, conducts multilateral or

bilateral negotiations with its many partners, it has to make sure that any agreements reached conform to internationally agreed aviation and safety standards.
10. Companies embarking on multilateral negotiations often underestimate the complexity and difficulty of reaching an agreement. In Northern Ireland, an overall agreement took decades to emerge. Negotiations about climate change among the 192 member states of the UN have tended to fall apart due to a clash between various factions, for example, developed and developing nations, about how to reduce greenhouse gas emissions.

QUESTIONS FOR DISCUSSION AND WRITTEN ASSIGNMENTS

1. Multiparty negotiations are more complex that two-party negotiations and require a different set of skills and procedures. In the context of international business, what are the most important differences between multiparty and two-party negotiations?
2. How are coalitions formed during a multilateral business negotiation?
3. How can coalitions help bring about a negotiated agreement in an international business negotiation where there are multiple participants from diverse cultures with multiple issues to discuss?
4. In a multilateral business negotiation with four parties from different countries participating, what would be the advantages and disadvantages of making decisions by consensus?

BIBLIOGRAPHY

Adair, W. L., Weingart, L. & Brett, J. The negotiation dance: time, culture, and Japanese negotiations. *Journal of Applied Psychology,* 92, 2005, 1056–1068.

Bazerman, M. H. & Neale, M. A. Heuristics in negotiation. In M. H. Bazerman & R. J. Lewicki (eds) *Negotiating in Organisations.* Sage, 1983, 51–67.

Bebchuk, L. & Fried, J. *Pay without Performance.* Harvard University Press, 2004.

Beest, I. V., Van Kleef, G. A. & Van Dijk, E. Get angry, get out: the interpersonal effects of anger communication in multiparty negotiation. *Journal of Experimental Social Psychology,* 44, 2008, 993–1002.

Browning, L. D., Beyer, J. & Shetler, J. C. Building cooperation in a competitive industry: SEMATECH and the semiconductor industry. *Academy of Management Journal,* 38 (1), 1995, 113–151.

Crump, L. Negotiation process and negotiation context. *International Negotiation,* 16, 2011, 197–227.

Crump, L. & Zartman, W. Multilateral negotiation and the management of complexity. *International Negotiation,* 8, 2003, 1–5.

Crump, L. & Glendon, A. Towards a paradigm of multiparty negotiation. *International Negotiation*, 8, 2003, 197–234.

Cullen, J. B. Johnson, J. L. & Sakano, T. Success through commitment and trust: the soft side of strategic alliance management. *Journal of World Business*, 35 (3), 2000, 223–240.

De Dreu, C. K., Weingart, L. R. & Kwon, S. Influence of social motives on integrative negotiations: a meta analytic review and test of two theories. *Journal of Personality and Social Psychology*, 78, 2000, 889–905.

Devine, T. A preemptive approach in multilateral negotiation. *Negotiation Journal*, 6 (4), 1990, 369–381.

Druckman, D. Content analysis. In V. A. Kremenyuk (ed.) *International Negotiation: Analysis, Approaches, Issues*. Jossey-Bass, 1991, 244–263.

Dupont, C. Coalition theory: using power to build cooperation. In I. W. Zartman (ed.) *International Multilateral Negotiation*. Jossey-Bass, 1994, 148–177.

Eisenhardt, K. Agency theory: an assessment and review, *Academy of Management Review*, 14 (1), 1989, 57–74.

Faure, G. O. Negotiations to set up joint ventures in China. *International Negotiation*, 5, 2000, 157–189.

Ghauri, P. The role of atmosphere in negotiations. In P. Ghauri & J-C. Usunier (eds) *International Business Negotiations*. Pergamon, 1996, 173–184.

Graham, J. L., Kim, D. K., Lin, C. Y. & Robinson, M. Buyer-seller negotiations around the Pacific Rim: differences in fundamental exchange processes. *Journal of Consumer Research*, 15, 1988, 48–54.

Gray, N. H. Bahasa, batik, and bargaining: an exploratory study of the negotiation styles and behaviors of Indonesian managers. *Journal of Transnational Management*, 15, 2010, 215–228.

Greenhalgh, L. Relationships in negotiation, *Negotiation Journal*, 3, 1987, 235–243.

Gulliver, P. *Disputes and Negotiations: A Cross-Cultural Perspective*. Academic Press, 1979.

Kern, M. C., Weingart, L. R. & Brett, J. M. Getting the floor: motive-consistent strategy and individual outcomes in multi-party negotiations. *Group Decision and Negotiation*, 14, 2005, 21–41.

Kumar, R. Brahmanical idealism, anarchical individualism, and the dynamics of Indian negotiating behaviour. *International Journal of Cross-cultural Management*, 4 (1), 2004, 39–58.

Kuulaa, M. & Stam, A. A win-win method for multi-party negotiation support. *International Transactions in Operational Research*, 15, 2008, 717–737.

Lax, D. A. & Sebenius, J. K. Deal Making 2.0: a guide to complex negotiations. *HBR*, 90 (11), 2012, 92–100.

Lewicki, R. J., Weiss, S. E. & Llewin, D. Models of conflict, negotiation and third party intervention: a review and synthesis. *Journal of Organizational Behavior*, 13, 1992, 209–252.

Lewicki, R. J., Saunders, D. M. & Minton, J. W. *Negotiation*. Irwin/McGraw-Hill, 3rd ed., 1999.

Meunier, S. What single voice? European institutions and EU-US trade negotiations. *International Organisation*, 54 (1), 2000, 103–135.

Mnookin, R. H. & Susskind, L. *Negotiating on Behalf of Others: Advice to Lawyers, Business Executives, Sports Agents, Diplomats, Politicians, and Everybody Else.* Sage, 1999.

Money, R. B. International multilateral negotiations and social networks. *Journal of International Business Studies*, 29 (4), 1998, 695–710.

O'Connor, K. M. & Adams, A. A. What novices think about negotiation: a content analysis of scripts. *Negotiation Journal*, 15, 1999, 135–147.

Olekalns, M., Brett, J. M. & Weingart, L. R. Phases, transitions and interruptions: modeling processes in multi party negotiations. *International Journal of Conflict Management*, 14 (3/4), 2003, 191–211.

Raiffa, H. *The Art and Science of Negotiation*. Harvard University Press, 1982.

Schuster, C. P. & Copeland, M. J. Global business exchanges: similarities and differences around the world. *Journal of International Marketing*, 7 (2), 1999, 63–80.

Sebenius, J. K. *Negotiating the Law of the Sea*. Harvard University Press, 1984.

Sjostedt, G. (ed.) *International Environmental Negotiations*. Sage, 1993.

Touval, S. Multilateral negotiation: an analytic approach. *Negotiation Journal*, 5 (2), 1989, 159–173.

Weiss, S. E. International business negotiation in a globalizing world: reflections on the contributions and future of a (sub)field. *International Negotiation*, 11, 2006, 287–316.

Winham, G. R. Complexity in international negotiation. In D. Druckman (ed.) *Negotiations: Social Psychological Perspectives*. Sage, 1977.

Wong, T. N. & Fang, F. A multi-agent protocol for multilateral negotiations in supply chain management. *International Journal of Production Research*, 48 (1), 2010, 271–299.

Zartman, I. W. Conclusion: managing complexity. *International Negotiation*, 8, 2003, 179–186.

Zartman, I. W. The structure of negotiation. In V. A. Kremenyuk (ed.) *International Negotiation: Analysis, Approaches, Issues*. Jossey Bass, 2nd ed., 2002.

Part 2
Practice

Negotiator Selection and Training

6

INTRODUCTION

When complex multimillion dollar deals are at stake, an effective negotiating team is a critical factor. Thus a negotiating team chosen to conduct business negotiations abroad should include the best negotiators available, whether male or female. For complex business negotiations, a combination of technical, business and social expertise is usually required, in addition to a competent team leader. A team's wide knowledge and information-gathering resources are needed to enable it to deal with the many commercial, technical and legal issues that are involved in negotiating international business deals. Senior executives who act as team leader when negotiating international business deals achieve a satisfactory final agreement more often than do teams (Weiss, 1993). Potential members of negotiating teams should be assessed for qualities such as flexibility, perspective-taking ability, cultural intelligence and positivity. Negotiators with positive attitudes towards the aim and topic of negotiation are more likely to try to achieve good outcomes. Women should be assessed for emotional resilience if they are being sent to negotiate in a male-dominated country. Women negotiate as effectively as men in international business negotiations and tend to behave more cooperatively than men (Volkema, 2004). The size of a negotiating team often reflects cultural norms. For instance, Chinese negotiating teams are usually twice as large as Western negotiating teams (Stewart & Keown, 1989).

A wide range of training methods is used to develop the skills needed by international business negotiators, including negotiation simulations, behaviour modelling, role plays and case studies. The most effective methods in terms of trainees' subsequent negotiation performance are behaviour modelling and other experiential learning methods (Nadler et al., 2003). Cases are widely used, as they possess sufficient complexity to capture a total negotiating situation. However, individual cases may be recalled by negotiators only in highly similar circumstances, and thus may end up in their store of inert knowledge which is never used. A better approach is to compare *several* brief cases since case comparison leads to greater understanding of negotiation process and strategies.

Simulated negotiations and role plays have become the central focus of negotiation pedagogy (Weiss, 2006). Simulated negotiations involve the trainees emotionally, mentally and physically in a negotiating situation. A weakness of simulated *email-based* negotiations is that participants cannot send and receive nonverbal messages. It is difficult to judge the honesty and reliability of the other party – an aspect that may lead to suspicion and competitive behaviours such as exaggerations and bluffs.

Many negotiator training programmes consist of one- to three-day courses and focus on building practical negotiation skills. Ford, for instance, has run three-day negotiation training programmes for executives who carry out business negotiations in countries worldwide. However, a three-day programme may not be enough to enable a manager to participate effectively in international business negotiations, which, by their nature, are diverse and heterogeneous and often complex. Many negotiator training programmes focus almost exclusively on *bilateral* negotiations – a fact which leaves managers who participate in *multilateral* negotiations with unmet training needs. More specially designed training programmes are required to help managers participate effectively in multilateral business negotiations.

NEGOTIATOR SELECTION

Varying selection criteria

Trompenaars (1993) distinguishes between achievement-oriented or status-oriented cultures. In achievement-oriented cultures, characteristics such as education level, knowledge, skills, experience and so forth are the criteria used for the selection of negotiators. Status-oriented cultures take into consideration such attributes as seniority, age, gender, family background, connections and so on when selecting negotiators. These tendencies are in line with the relationship orientation of high-context cultures, which will typically select their negotiators on the basis of status, whereas the low-context cultures use various abilities and skills as selection criteria.

Selecting negotiating teams

Sometimes a team is sent to negotiate with a foreign company as the result of a very practical decision: "the other company will have a negotiating team and so should we."

At other times a company chooses a team to negotiate when the issues are strategic or complex, and so must have input from a swathe of functional areas. Negotiations to establish a joint venture abroad, for instance, usually need to cover all functional areas of the new company such as production, marketing, financial management and information technology (IT).

In such a case, a negotiating team will have to be selected, with members drawn from corresponding functional areas and departments in the company. Negotiators must truly represent and have the trust of those whom they are representing (Tung & Varma, 2008). If a department or a business unit is left out of the process, its members may become angry and argue that their interests have not been taken into account. Worse still, if constituents do not recognise a negotiating team as their legitimate representative, they may try to block implementation of the negotiated agreement.

Members of multidisciplinary negotiating teams sometimes have inconsistent priorities and goals in an international business negotiation (Brett et al., 2009). Finance, for instance, is preoccupied with costs and margins. Production is worried about the impact on demand of any agreement that is negotiated. The legal department is totally focused on protecting intellectual property rights. Yet negotiated agreements can only be successfully implemented if they reflect the *company's* interests rather than departmental or functional interests. It follows that a way must be found to overcome diversities of approach within the negotiating team.

Inconsistencies of approach in a negotiating team point to the need for company executives to brief the team thoroughly so that members' contributions during negotiating sessions reflect a company approach. Often the mere presence of a senior executive on a negotiating team is all it takes to encourage nonconformists and functional cheerleaders to fall into line. When researchers interviewed negotiating teams from a wide range of sectors, respondents confessed that their team's biggest negotiating challenges came from their own side of the table (Brett et al., 2009). Individuals repeatedly made contributions that were at odds with the company's negotiating position. As the example suggests, the composition of a negotiating team can greatly affect the kind of agreement that emerges from an international business negotiation.

General qualities

As the costs of failure in international business negotiations can be extremely high for the negotiator's employer, whether this is a company, a government or an international agency, selecting the right people in the first place to conduct the negotiation is essential. Studies suggest that a combination of general and specific qualities enables negotiators to be effective in a wide range of international business negotiations. Williams (1971), for instance, found that teams composed of people with neutral attitudes towards the topic of negotiation tend to trade issues as a way of reaching an agreement and so arrive at a compromise solution. The implication is that negotiators with *positive attitudes* towards the topic of negotiation are more likely to try to achieve good outcomes.

Positivity

The importance of the general quality of positivity is reinforced by studies which suggest that the mood of the negotiators at the time negotiations take place affects the outcome of negotiations. Forgas & Vargas (1998), for instance, found that during complex negotiations, people in a positive mood tend to have more ambitious goals, higher expectations and a more cooperative way of negotiating compared to people in a negative mood, and that this positive mood generally leads to a more successful outcome. *Positivity* contributes to a negotiator's performance and can be readily measured and assessed.

Cross-cultural communication ability

Other general qualities which international business negotiators need include cultural sensitivity (Puck et al., 2008) and cross-cultural communication ability (Tung & Varma, 2008). Cui et al. (1998) describe cross-cultural communication ability as a set of abilities and knowledge that enables a person to engage in meaningful communication with business people from other cultures. Such general qualities help individuals make positive responses towards many of the cultural differences encountered when negotiating deals in diverse locations around the world. In Delhi, for instance, positive responses might include liking to eat dal and chapattis for lunch; in Moscow they might include taking a keen interest in the fortunes of the Russian ice hockey team.

Specific qualities

Specific qualities which equip managers to be effective in international business negotiations have been identified by a number of researchers, for example, Liu et al. (2010); Galinsky & Moskowitz (2000); Adair & Brett (2004); and Earley & Ang (2003). According to researchers, specific qualities which contribute to negotiator performance include

- flexibility;
- perspective-taking ability;
- cultural intelligence;
- language skills.

The implication is that potential members of negotiating teams should be assessed for these qualities as they enable negotiators to achieve good negotiating outcomes.

Flexibility

Flexibility helps negotiators cope with the unexpected. In China, different negotiating teams may turn up on different days, for instance. *Inflexibility*, by contrast, can be a fatal flaw. Salacuse (1999) gives the example of an American fast food chain which demonstrated inflexibility during international business negotiations in Australia. The firm steadfastly refused to modify its opening proposal, and this led to the failure of its attempt to negotiate an Australian franchise agreement. Such examples suggest that in international business, simply by being flexible and willing to adjust their negotiating position in response to moves made by the other side, negotiators can gain a negotiating advantage.

International business negotiations are inherently mixed motive and require both competitive behaviour (concern for self) and cooperative behaviour (concern for other) during a single negotiation or set of negotiations (Olekalns et al., 2004).

Indeed, effective negotiators seem to have an inbuilt flexibility that enables them to balance competitive and cooperative behaviours to reach mutually beneficial tradeoffs and secure good negotiation outcomes. When Adler & Graham (1989), for instance, used negotiation simulations with a sample of 462 Japanese, American and Canadian business people, they found that those participating in cross-cultural negotiations were able to adjust their normal intracultural behaviour to match the negotiating behaviour of the other side. Sometimes the matching behaviour extends to body language, with the body movements of a negotiator consistently matching those of the counterpart (Adair & Brett, 2004).

Perspective-taking ability

Perspective-taking ability – the ability to actively consider the other person's viewpoint – is another specific quality possessed by successful negotiators (Galinsky & Moskowitz, 2000). This ability is a strong predictor of effective negotiator behaviour because perspective-taking negotiators are more likely to consider the range of alternative solutions that is open to the other side. Perspective-taking negotiators accurately assess their opponents' bargaining positions, and so tend to achieve better settlements than those without this ability (Liu et al., 2010). Moreover, perspective-taking negotiators are able to avoid stereotyping their negotiating counterparts. Kumar (2004) argues that foreign negotiators who have the capacity to understand the Indian mindset are likely to be successful in negotiations with Indian organisations.

Cultural intelligence

Cultural intelligence is the ability to behave effectively in situations characterised by cultural diversity (Earley & Ang, 2003). This capacity helps a person adapt to communicating with members of other cultures in negotiations and other situations. Culturally intelligent managers are adept at picking up cultural differences during negotiations by listening and observing. Such awareness enables them to adjust their own behaviour and to behave appropriately when conducting negotiations in a foreign country. An example of the use of cultural intelligence is foreign negotiators' careful avoidance of expressions of negative emotions such as anger or irritation when negotiating in China or Japan.

Whereas emotional intelligence and social intelligence are both culture bound, cultural intelligence enables people to bridge cultures by seeking information outside of their own experience to deal with new and confusing social situations, such as the situations often encountered in international business negotiations. There is evidence to suggest that cultural intelligence may increase with practice. Thomas & Inkson (2004), for instance, argue that cultural intelligence is developed incrementally, with each repeat of the cycle building on the previous one.

Language skills

To overcome any language difficulties in an international business negotiation, the negotiating team should ideally include at least one person who speaks the first language of the other negotiating team. This individual may be able to make sense of internal whisperings and discussions of the other team. If this person has previous experience of living and working in the culture of the negotiating opponents, he or she may also be able to correctly interpret the nonverbal signals transmitted by the other team during negotiating sessions.

In other cases, the team may have to rely on interpreters provided by the host organisation – a situation which, in effect, puts them at a considerable disadvantage in negotiating sessions since they can never be completely sure that the interpreter's accounts contain the whole truth.

SELECTION METHODS

Advantages of negotiating teams

When a company decides to send a sole negotiator – it may be a sales manager or a marketing executive – to negotiate a business deal with a foreign company, it is often with the idea of keeping travel and accommodation expenses to the minimum. But sole negotiators seldom have the range of knowledge and experience that will enable them to deal with all the commercial, technical and legal issues that need to be addressed in international business negotiations. That is why negotiating teams often achieve better outcomes than sole negotiators. Teams learn more about the other party's aims and priorities than one person can. They are more likely to prepare adequately for negotiations and to do the necessary research. Moreover, a team's assessment of the other side's priorities and sticking points is usually more accurate than that of a sole negotiator, thus clearing the way to a satisfactory agreement.

International business negotiations deal with complex interrelated issues, and a team's wide knowledge and information-gathering resources are needed so that a thorough understanding of the issues can be gained. Thus when complex multimillion dollar deals are at stake, an effective negotiating team is a critical factor. The costs of failure can be extremely high, so selecting the right people in the first place to be members of the negotiating team is essential. To avoid possible inconsistencies of approach among members of a negotiating team, senior company executives should brief the team with the aim of ensuring that individuals' contributions to the discussion reflect a company approach, not a functional or departmental approach.

Selecting team members

The negotiating team that a company selects to carry out an international business negotiation against strong opposition, needs as a minimum to match the opponent's negotiating team. Team members need to possess the status, skills, and technical and social expertise to match the profile of the other team. This was the case when, in 2003, a European construction company sent a team of experts to negotiate terms for the company's participation in a large construction project in a country in the Middle East.

> The team, drawn from different functional areas of the company, needed a thorough knowledge of all the technical areas that would be covered in the negotiations, that is, procurement, contract negotiation, project management, site management, IT and financial management. The company realised that careful selection of individual members of the team was essential. The company knew that unless the team displayed a thorough knowledge of all the issues to be discussed, it would be eliminated from the project.

The company's human resources (HR) manager subsequently explained to business colleagues how careful selection of individual members of the negotiating team, including technical specialists and the team leader, was an essential first step that led to the team's negotiating very favourable terms for the company's participation in the project.

Technical specialists

In some cases – when companies are setting up an international joint venture, for instance – negotiations may be protracted and last many months. Engineers, manufacturing experts, lawyers, accountants, salespeople and other specialists may have to be involved in such negotiations at different times. In such large and complex negotiations, subgroups of experts are often set up to discuss specialised technical issues, so individual members of the company's team must have the skills and status that will enable them to contribute effectively to technical discussions.

Western companies are likely to emphasise technical know-how, competence and capability when selecting members of negotiating teams. Faure (2000), however, notes that companies in collectivist countries tend to emphasise status and seniority when selecting managers to carry out international business negotiations. Managers from a UK company who were sent to negotiate with a Chinese retailing group told colleagues when they returned that they had been perceived as too young and inexperienced by the Chinese, and that this accounted for their disappointing results. According to Trompenaars (1993), companies in the high-context cultures in Asia and elsewhere select their negotiators mainly on the basis of status as opposed to technical competence.

Team leader

An important responsibility of the team leader is to make sure that team members who are not at the table are kept busy behind the scenes. The legal specialist, for instance, might assess the legal ramifications of any points agreed during the negotiation, reporting these to the team leader, and ensuring that points that are agreed are captured by the language of the contract.

In negotiations that are financially or strategically of high importance, a senior executive often acts as team leader and/or lead negotiator. Weiss (1993) finds that senior executives who adopt this role stress the importance of speed and *limited participation* during the initial negotiations. For instance, they rapidly develop a "heads of agreement" as a prelude to later, more detailed negotiations involving the full team. According to Weiss (1993), such hands-on executives achieve a satisfactory final agreement more often than those who assign complete responsibility, from start to finish of a negotiation, to the negotiating team.

Salacuse's (1998) survey of 12 cultural groups shows that 91 percent of Chinese and Mexicans and 100 percent of Brazilians prefer negotiating teams to have a single clear leader (who is usually the highest-status member of the team). Negotiating teams from the collectivist cultures of Asia, Africa and the Middle East generally leave bargaining and tradeoffs over key issues to this powerful individual (Laroche, 2003). When the leader argues in one direction, that usually ends the discussion as far as the rest of the team is concerned.

Roles played by team members

Robinson & Volkov (1998) argue that a negotiation is executed by managers who act not as autonomous individuals but play different roles. During an international business negotiation, the roles typically include

- *owner* – the main stakeholder of the outcomes of negotiation;
- *negotiator* – conducts the negotiations on behalf of the owner;
- *facilitator* – facilitates the actual negotiation and may also act as mediator;
- *analyst* – formulates goals of the owner and analyses offers and alternatives.

An important responsibility of the team leader is to allocate these or other roles to individual team members. One member of the team may, for instance, be allocated the role of persistently bringing the discussions round to the question of cost control. Another member may be asked to bring up the issue of delivery times and quantities.

Once roles have been allocated, *impromptu role plays* may be held to allow the individuals concerned to practise playing their parts.

Stutman & Newell (1990) argue that this rehearsal of roles to be played by individuals in international business negotiations leads to better control of emotions in the actual negotiation, improved ability to remain rational, more articulated speech and increased overall performance.

Size of team

The size of a negotiating team depends mainly on the subject of negotiation and its complexity and importance. For example, a five-person team was sent by a German engineering firm in 2001 to negotiate the terms of a licensing agreement with an Indian company. The team consisted of a team leader/lead negotiator, supported by technical and engineering specialists. Issues of patent validity and enforceability led the company to add an intellectual property expert to the team. Not all members of the team were present throughout the negotiations.

In international business, the size of a negotiating team may also reflect cultural norms. Stewart & Keown's (1989) survey of Chinese trading companies, for instance, found that Chinese negotiating teams are usually twice as large as the teams sent by Western companies.

Assessment methods

Kelley & Meyers' (1995) Cross-cultural Adaptability Inventory measures flexibility, perceptual acuity and emotional resilience. However, few companies use such instruments when selecting managers to be included in negotiating teams. Some companies use psychological profiling, intelligence and proficiency measures, and standardised tests to identify managers with the required competencies and qualities for conducting international business negotiations. On the other hand, when researchers surveyed chief executive officers (CEOs) of global companies, respondents revealed that they selected managers for key roles based on gut feeling and personal preferences (Fernandez-Araoz et al., 2009). The survey revealed that a "first impression" bias often occurs and distorts selection decisions. Within minutes or even seconds, the interviewer reaches a conclusion about the candidate, pro or con, then spends the rest of the interview seeking confirmatory evidence for the biased judgment.

Intelligence and psychological tests can provide a fair and objective basis for making many selection decisions, but not when they are used without considering their relevance and validity to candidates from diverse cultural backgrounds. Verardi et al. (2010) warn of the dangers of using assessment instruments developed in Western countries with members of other cultures, whose basic assumptions and values are very different from those of the test originators.

When choosing managers to play important roles such as that of lead negotiator, the use of a structured interview format with prepared questions helps reduce interviewer bias. Structured interviews give greater consistency from interview to interview by producing comparable information from candidate to candidate. The risk of biased or freak decisions can also be reduced by diversifying the interview panel.

Female negotiators

When selecting a negotiating team for business negotiations abroad, companies should send the best negotiators available, whether male or female. The low proportion of female managers on international business negotiating teams is mainly due to the reluctance exhibited by many Western organisations to select them (PricewaterhouseCoopers, 2005). Their reluctance often stems from the perceived prejudice against women managers and negotiators in many parts of the world. Most companies, for instance, would not consider sending female managers to negotiate in Saudi Arabia, where women are not involved in business negotiations. Kray et al. (2001) argue that women may do worse in negotiations where stereotypes of women are activated (e.g. agreeable, social, other-focused). To reduce the chances of that happening, women who are sent to negotiate in male-dominated cultures should be assessed for mental toughness at the selection stage. One difficulty of doing so, however, is that "mental toughness" has no universally accepted meaning, and so is difficult to measure with precision.

Stuhlmacher & Walters' (1999) meta-analysis reveals that women negotiators are able to negotiate as well as men and achieve satisfactory settlements in numerous cross-cultural situations. One reason is that women behave more cooperatively than men during business negotiations, leading them to share information and reach agreements amicably and quickly. Volkema (2004), who carried out research in nine countries, concluded that female negotiators are less likely than male negotiators to use competitive and aggressive tactics and questionable negotiating behaviours such as making threats or giving misinformation. Such characteristics help explain why Malaysian business people are more comfortable and exchange information more willingly when negotiating with women rather than men (Ready & Tessema, 2009).

Impact of feminine charm

Effective negotiators combine competitive and cooperative motives and use both competitive and cooperative bargaining approaches at different stages in a negotiation (Olekalns et al., 2004). Kray et al. (2012) argue that effective women negotiators in effect combine competitive and cooperative motives in negotiations by displaying *feminine charm*. Feminine charm combines flirtation (self-oriented, competitive) with friendliness (other-oriented, cooperative). According to the researchers, women negotiators use feminine charm in order to

- mitigate social penalties (e.g. the dislike that competent, assertive women negotiators often incur);
- make male negotiating counterparts feel good;
- flatter and ultimately disarm male negotiating opponents.

Carli et al. (1995) found that women's displays of competence (e.g. behaving assertively, adopting a task-orientation in negotiations) threaten men's higher status and incur social costs such as dislike and resentment. But by combining competence cues with sociability cues (e.g. feminine charm), the social costs are reduced. The effect of using feminine charm is to enable women to become more influential in negotiations. Through a similar mechanism, women who speak tentatively in negotiations and business meetings are more influential than women who speak assertively.

SMALL-GROUP EXERCISE: Discussion questions

Working in small groups, discuss each of the following questions and write down the group's agreed answers. At the end of the exercise, each group presents its answers to the other groups for comment.

1. *What are the advantages and disadvantages of sending a sole negotiator instead of a negotiating team to represent a European company in buying/selling negotiations with companies in Indonesia?*

2. *What qualities do managers need to enable them to be effective team leaders in international business negotiations? How can managers be assessed for possession of these qualities?*

3. *An Australian manufacturer of electronic control equipment is about to enter negotiations with a Korean company to establish a joint venture in Korea. What steps should the Australian company take to ensure that a highly effective negotiating team is selected and sent to Korea? What size of team would be appropriate, and which functional specialists should be included?*

NEGOTIATOR TRAINING

Purpose

An important aim of negotiator training programmes is to equip negotiators with the knowledge and skills that will improve their performance
in negotiations and lead to satisfactory outcomes. International business
negotiators are individuals or negotiating teams who represent companies
or governments, or people who are in business for themselves. They carry
out negotiations in a wide range of cross-border and international business
situations.

Studies show (e.g. Nadler et al., 2003) that the impact made by a particular training programme depends on *training content* combined with *training
method*. The content of many negotiator training programmes is based on
assessment of strategies and tactics used in international business negotiations,
and examination of the psychological, emotional and cultural factors that influence the outcomes (Weiss, 2006). Many negotiator training programmes aim
at developing basic skills, such as gathering and presenting information and
developing a negotiating agenda.

International business negotiations are often emotionally charged, causing
negotiators to take irrational decisions and miss opportunities to maximise their
outcomes. Negotiator training has been found to increase a negotiator's ability
to behave rationally in negotiations and avoid judgmental mistakes (Susskind,
2004). Managers who have attended a negotiation training programme are less
likely to act irrationally and miss opportunities than managers who have not
been trained (Ramarajan et al., 2004). Not all negotiator training delivers effective performance, however. A large US firm spent $350,000 on negotiation
training for senior managers, but the managers subsequently failed to negotiate
a contract renewal with a major client, thus causing high financial losses to the
firm.

Training providers

Many negotiator training programmes are run by universities, companies,
consultants and government agencies. An example of a government-backed
training programme is New Zealand's Exporter Education Programme, which
offers workshops for international business negotiators, international traders and
exporters. The programme includes training in how to develop effective negotiation tactics and strategies, and how to establish and maintain relationships
with foreign business partners. Contract law is covered, together with practical,
country-specific export sales advice. A large portion of the $60 billion annually
that US firms spend on training is invested in designing and running negotiation training courses (Coleman & Lim, 2001). The wide availability of Internet
programmes makes it easy for entrepreneurs and business people worldwide to

participate in online training modules and improve their international business negotiation skills.

Learning approaches

Negotiator training can rapidly develop such practical negotiation skills, and also increase understanding of the psychological, emotional and cultural factors that influence the international business negotiation interaction and outcomes. It does so by using a variety of learning approaches, such as those identified by Rollof et al. (2003):

> *Experiential learning.* Trainees learn through role plays, simulated negotiations and other experiential methods.
>
> *Didactic learning.* Trainees learn negotiation concepts and principles directly through lectures, readings and so forth.
>
> *Reflective.* Trainees learn by analysing and making deductions from the various practical exercises in which they have participated.

Concepts and principles of effective negotiation which are learned in the classroom do not always transfer easily to the world of practice. Successful transfer of negotiation skills from classroom to international business negotiation depends largely on the aims of the training and the training methods used. Lectures, discussions and readings are generally the methods used to give managers knowledge of concepts and principles of negotiation.

The training methods used for building practical negotiation skills sometimes need to be adjusted to fit in with the cultural expectations and preferences of the trainees. In China, for example, both training and feedback sessions have to be group focused.

NEGOTIATOR TRAINING METHODS

Basic skill development

Boyatzis (1982) defines skill competence as the ability to demonstrate a system or sequence of behaviour that is related to achieving a performance goal. Skill competence in the context of international business negotiation can be defined as the effective use of knowledge and skills in developing a sequence of activities to achieve the goals of a particular international business negotiation. Basic skills needed by international business negotiators include active listening skills, cross-cultural communication skills and the ability to respond to the other party in a calm and courteous manner (Thomas & Fitzsimmons, 2008). Ready & Tessema (2009) found that both US and Malaysian subjects needed more training in these basic skills in order to become effective negotiators.

Basic negotiation skills can be acquired through such activities as

- *active listening exercises* – listening to the opponent's arguments, and then restating them; identifying the feelings expressed;
- *responding positively* to offers and proposals;
- *behaving appropriately* – for example, in ways that put other parties at ease, being careful not to threaten or express negative emotions.

Such basic skills are readily acquired in the classroom. The skills can be consolidated and extended through practical experience (e.g. by working as a junior member of a negotiating team).

Advanced skill development

Negotiation training programmes use a wide range of training methods to develop the advanced skills needed for effective performance in international business negotiations. The methods include

- negotiation simulations,
- role plays,
- feedback and debriefings,
- case studies,
- lectures,
- group discussions,
- presentations,
- behaviour modelling.

Nadler et al. (2003), assessing various training approaches used in negotiator training programmes, found that the most effective in terms of the trainee's subsequent negotiation performance was *behaviour modelling*. By watching a "model" negotiator demonstrate behaviours used by competent negotiators, trainees learn how to conduct their own negotiations.

However, trainees themselves often prefer *principle-based learning* (e.g. lectures, case studies, readings). Boyatzis & Mainemelis (2000), for instance, found that 38 percent of MBA students they surveyed had a preference for principle-based learning. Only 32 percent had a preference for learning through experience, by becoming, for instance, temporary members of negotiating teams.

Managers need to see the relevance of a training course to their lives and practical responsibilities (Salacuse, 2010). Thus up to three-quarters of negotiation training programmes designed for inexperienced negotiators who have already acquired basic negotiating skills may need to be devoted to practical interactive exercises, negotiation simulations, role plays, case studies, group discussions, problem-solving activities and other practical skill development exercises.

Lectures

In negotiation training programmes, lectures are a widely used method of presenting information and giving explanations. Lectures are used, for instance, to explain the differences between competitive and cooperative negotiation, or to present models of the negotiation process. International business negotiations are enmeshed in a web of national and transnational laws, so lectures may be used to give details of the laws relating to various international business situations, such as laws governing international buying and selling contracts.

Thus, lectures play an important role. However, when managers and other adult learners listen to lectures their attention span is very brief (Masek, 2000). In many negotiator training situations a 20- to 30-minute lecture followed by practical exercises is generally much more effective than the traditional one-hour lecture in terms of the trainees' being able to recall and use lecture content. Lectures which hammer home two or three key negotiation principles which are easy to apply in an actual international business negotiation are often rated more highly by managers than lectures which describe in detail various negotiation theories, concepts and models.

Experiential learning

The effectiveness of experiential learning – another name for learning by doing – has been demonstrated by many researchers. Brislin et al. (2008), for instance, found that training packages with a core of experiential learning are generally the most effective in achieving training goals. Experiential learning in negotiation training leads to the trainees' engaging with the social, cultural and business aspects of negotiation, and with the dilemmas and problems that occur when, say, a cross-border alliance is being negotiated.

Kolb et al. (2001) stress the importance of learning from others by observation and imitation. Experiential learning theory defines learning as "the process whereby knowledge is created through the transformation of experience" (Kolb, 1984, 41). Although critics of experiential learning claim that it is too lacking in theoretical foundation for it to be established as an accepted methodology, negotiator training providers around the world often design their programmes around a core of experiential learning activities.

Role play

According to Weiss (2006), role plays together with simulated negotiations have become the central focus of negotiation pedagogy because these methods have been found to give trainees a good understanding of the process of international business negotiation. Friedman's (1992) survey found that most negotiation trainers support role plays and negotiation simulations as the most effective methods for developing practical negotiation skills.

Role play is widely used in negotiation training because it improves negotiation outcomes more than most other training methods (Trotman et al., 2005). By stepping into the opponent's shoes for the duration of the role play, the manager gains valuable experience in feeling and arguing the opponent's position. By role playing aspects of a negotiation that are expected to be contentious – a demand for a price reduction, say – a manager can identify arguments which answer these demands, thus reducing the risk of making gaffes during an actual negotiation.

Brett et al. (2009) advocate the use of impromptu role plays shortly before real negotiations begin. Members of the negotiating team are given specific roles, such as confronting the other side about one or more contentious issues (e.g. pricing, delivery dates, installation etc.), and then they practise confronting the other side in role-play simulations. These rehearsals help the role player anticipate the likely emotional responses of the other side and to decide how these responses should be dealt with.

Negotiation simulation

Negotiation simulation is a core component of many negotiation training programmes. The method involves the trainees emotionally, mentally and physically in the simulated negotiating situation. Aspects of international business negotiation that cannot be made meaningful in a lecture become real to trainees in a simulated negotiation, for example, the embarrassment caused by ignorance of a local cultural practice when conducting a negotiation abroad. Simulations give a reference point against which the effectiveness of different negotiation theories and models can be assessed. Students who participate in a simulated negotiation of, say, a contract to set up an international joint venture (IJV) come away with a better understanding of the legal framework of IJVs. Timura (2010), however, argues that the pedagogical power of simulations is limited when they are used without regard for the specific kinds of experiences trainees bring with them to the training.

Salacuse (2010) argues that students participating in simulations should be organised into negotiating teams, since as team members, students derive greater learning from the exercise than students who negotiate individually. Team interaction and the members' diverse backgrounds lead them to think more creatively about the negotiation than they would alone. Groups that spend the initial part of the simulation agreeing on a negotiation process and agenda and discussing basic interests are, according to Salacuse, more successful that those that do not.

Simulated email negotiations

Volkema & Rivers (2008) studied the interactions and outcomes of *simulated email negotiations* that took place between students in two graduate negotiation courses, one in the US and the other in Australia. The study revealed that the main disadvantage of using emails to negotiate international business deals is the inability of the medium to send and receive nonverbal signals. As a result, it is difficult for negotiators to develop personal relationships and trust, and to judge the honesty and reliability of the other party. This characteristic of the medium leads to suspicion and distributive behaviour (e.g. exaggerations, demands and bluffs).

Case studies

The case studies used in negotiation training programmes are often sufficiently complex to capture a total negotiating situation. That is one of the strengths of the method. However, an important weakness is that the negotiator will recall the case and apply the learning only in circumstances highly similar to those presented in the case (Loewenstein et al., 2003). But the circumstances of real-life international business negotiations tend not to be highly similar to the circumstances of a case studied in the classroom. The result is that the manager's learning from the case may become part of the store of inert knowledge that he or she possesses, but never uses.

The danger that case study learning will not transfer to real-life negotiation can be reduced by encouraging trainees to study and compare *several* cases, as opposed to just a single detailed case. Tutors can then lead group discussions about similarities and differences across the cases. Studying several cases, including very short mini-cases, encourages analysis and comparison of cases and the drawing of clear-cut principles and conclusions. Clear guidelines and principles of negotiation are deduced by trainees, and these can be readily applied in "live" negotiations.

Thus, studying several short case studies helps managers to deepen their understanding of the process of international business negotiation. The method helps them to find the right balance between generalisations about international business negotiation and the task-related specificity of actual negotiating situations.

Feedback

The feedback following simulations, role plays and other practical exercises is a key component of negotiation training and contributes to a trainee's superior performance in subsequent real-life negotiations (Thompson & DeHarpport, 1994). Feedback from repeated simulations, for instance, allows trainees to learn how to improve their negotiation strategies and outcomes (Camerer, 1990).

Feedback has long played a central role in theories of learning and performance achievement. Feedback helps the trainees reflect, adapt and self-correct until desired performance standards are achieved. The feedback/debriefing sessions that follow negotiation simulations typically involve tutor-led discussion and feedback about such aspects as whether the teams' negotiation goals were realistic, what the teams' interests and positions were, and whether the participants' behaviour was affected by negative emotion (Van der Vegt et al., 2010).

Feedback and debriefing sessions need to be aligned to the cultural characteristics of the trainees. Hinsz et al. (1997) produce evidence showing that Chinese managers respond better to group- rather than individual-focused training, and to group- rather than individual-focused feedback.

Coaching

One-to-one coaching by an experienced executive or consultant enables a young manager to gain an impartial view of key issues facing the company's negotiating team in an impending negotiation and helps the manager consider how best to resolve those issues. Gosselin et al. (1997) note that coaching practice draws on the conceptual foundations of feedback and behaviour modelling, and that managers generally prefer to receive feedback from their immediate managers rather than from an external coach.

Although one-to-one coaching may be an expensive way of developing negotiating skills, it can be effective. *How* effective depends largely on the quality and experience of the coach.

Length of negotiator training courses

Most negotiator training programmes consist of one- to three-day courses and focus on building practical negotiation skills (Sarkar, 2010). For instance, Ford

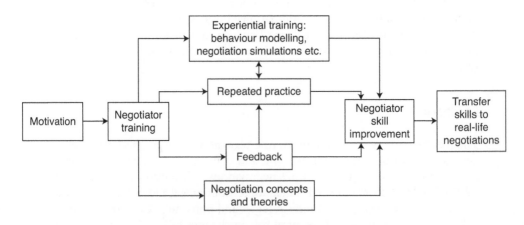

Figure 6.1   Developing negotiation skills

Note: The effectiveness of a particular training programme in building
negotiating skills depends both on training content and the training methods used.

has run three-day negotiation training programmes for executives carrying out international business negotiations in countries around the world. The programme included negotiation simulations, videos and lectures of cultural differences between US and various foreign negotiators, and information about international and contract law. But international business negotiations are, by their nature, diverse and heterogeneous and often complex. That is why three-day programmes may be inadequate for equipping managers with the knowledge and skills needed for effective participation in a range of international business negotiations.

Nevertheless, ElShenawy (2010) finds that even the shortest training programme improves the performance of young or trainee managers who are required to conduct international business negotiations early in their careers. Very short negotiation training courses are used in some professions. A survey of healthcare professionals, for instance, found that a course of one to eight hours provides trainees with the necessary skills to negotiate successfully with behavioural patients (Runkle et al., 2000). Friedman's (1992) survey of negotiation training providers revealed a lack of consensus about the optimum length of negotiation training programmes.

Longer negotiation courses

Relatively long courses are required to equip managers and postgraduate business students with the skills required to conduct international business negotiations. Courses for postgraduate business students, for instance, may need to examine various models of negotiation, such as Pruitt & Kim's (1994) classic "dual concerns" model, and adequate time is required to do so. The extent to which cultural background influences negotiating styles and strategies used in international business negotiations is another important aspect of negotiators' training. Accordingly, the topic is usually included in longer courses, together with the impact made on the interaction and outcomes by the negotiator's personality or disposition.

Raiffa (2003) argues that, as there is no single theory of negotiation, longer courses need to examine various conceptual approaches to negotiation and focus on negotiators' behaviour, the negotiation process, negotiation structure and negotiation strategies. Simulated negotiations are often included in longer courses, allowing students to think about and explain their own negotiating interests and to identify the interests of the other party.

Multilateral negotiations

Trends in global business generate more and more *multilateral* negotiations. Consider, for instance, the multilateral negotiations and linked bilateral negotiations that occur when an MNE negotiates with an overseas government, for instance, to open an assembly plant in the country. In a case such as this, negotiations might be held with national, provincial and municipal governments – sometimes simultaneously – with trade unions, employers' organisations, lobby groups, civil society groups and other interested parties.

Although many multilateral business negotiations take place, very few managers have received training dealing with the problems and processes of international multilateral negotiations (Weiss, 2006). Almost all negotiation training programmes focus on *bilateral* negotiation situations, with the result that the training needs of the many managers who participate in multilateral business negotiations are not catered for.

To make negotiator training more relevant to the needs of companies about to embark on multilateral business negotiations, negotiating teams from the several companies concerned might be *jointly* trained shortly before actual negotiations begin. An appropriate training programme could be designed and run by a university department, consultants, or some other experienced training provider. One result of the training would be to give the various parties a common vocabulary and common concepts on which they could draw once real negotiations begin.

Negotiator bias

The extent to which various kinds of bias occur in negotiations is influenced by cultural factors. Thus Lechuga & Wiebe (2011) found that US subjects displayed less overconfidence bias than Mexicans. Lundeberg et al. (2000) found that negotiators from East Asia, Brazil and Palestine display greater overconfidence than US negotiators. Overconfidence bias involves negotiators' being overconfident that their bargaining position will prevail if they do not "give in" during the negotiations.

Other types of bias that have been identified by various researchers and that lead to negotiators underperforming in negotiations include:

- *Determination-to-win bias.* This leads negotiators to persist in using an initial strategy or course of action in a negotiation even when it is no longer the best choice.
- *Fixed pie bias.* This wrongly assumes that one's own gain can only come at the expense of the other side. As a result, opportunities for tradeoffs are missed that would benefit both sides.
- *Lack-of-perspective bias.* This involves ignoring or being insensitive to the perspective of the other party. For example, a discount deal might be offered to a foreign buyer without sensing that from the perspective of the buyer, an upfront rebate would be much more desirable.

Awareness of the negative effect of bias on negotiation outcomes can be increased by training managers to recognise the cognitive patterns involved in the various types of bias that occur in international business negotiations (Bazerman & Neale, 1992).

Negotiators who are trained to be aware of the causes of overconfidence bias, for instance, are more likely to compromise and reach agreement in an international business negotiation than negotiators who have not received such training.

KEY POINTS

1. Qualities which equip managers to be effective in international business negotiations include flexibility, perspective-taking ability and cultural intelligence. Before a negotiating team is selected to conduct an important negotiation, potential team members should be assessed for these attributes. Women who are sent to negotiate in male-dominated cultures need mental toughness, and women candidates should be assessed for this quality.
2. Effective negotiators combine competitive and cooperative motives and use both competitive and cooperative bargaining approaches at different stages in a negotiation. Effective women negotiators combine competitive and cooperative motives in negotiations by displaying *feminine charm,* which combines flirtation (self-oriented, competitive) with friendliness (other-oriented, cooperative).
3. Team leaders must be carefully selected. Managers in China, Mexico, Brazil and many other collectivist countries prefer negotiating teams to have a single clear leader – usually the highest-status individual in the team. Concessions, trade-offs and other key negotiating tasks are left to this powerful individual. Senior executives who act as lead negotiators tend to achieve a satisfactory agreement more often than those who assign complete responsibility to a team.
4. Training providers disagree about the optimum length of negotiation training programmes. Many practical courses last for one to three days and focus on developing specific negotiation skills, but a three-day programme may not be enough to enable a manager to participate effectively in international business negotiations, which, by their nature, are diverse and heterogeneous and complex.
5. Most negotiator training programmes use several learning methods in combination to develop negotiation skills, for instance, behaviour modelling and negotiation simulations supported by role plays and case studies. Nadler et al. (2003) found that effective learning methods in terms of trainees' subsequent negotiation performance include. Behaviour modelling and other experiential methods are often found to be highly effective. Lectures are used to teach the principles of effective negotiation, but trainees are often unable to transfer the principles learnt to real-life negotiations.
6. Studying single cases only in negotiation courses can be a mistake. Single cases are recalled only in highly similar circumstances. As a result, they become part of the store of inert knowledge that negotiators have but

never use. A better approach is to compare *several* brief cases prior to an actual negotiation. Case comparison promotes learning of the negotiation process and leads to greater understanding and use of effective negotiation strategies.

7. Simulated negotiations and role plays have become the central focus of negotiation pedagogy. Feedback sessions following simulations cover such aspects as whether negotiators' goals were realistic, and negotiators' reasons for making concessions or tradeoffs. Such feedback helps trainees improve their negotiating strategies and outcomes. Managers attending negotiation training courses in collectivist countries such as China generally respond better to group feedback than to individual feedback.

8. Simulated international email-based negotiations between US and Australian MBA students highlighted the inability of the medium to send and receive nonverbal signals. It is difficult to develop personal relationships and trust, and to judge the honesty and reliability of the other party through emails. In real-life negotiations, this characteristic of the medium can lead to suspicion and distributive behaviour (e.g. exaggerations, demands and bluffs).

9. Feedback following training exercises assists skill development. It helps trainees reflect, adapt and self-correct until desired performance standards are achieved. Feedback sessions typically involve tutor-led discussion about such aspects as whether negotiators' goals were realistic, what their negotiating interests and positions were, and whether negotiating behaviour was affected by negative emotion.

10. Global business leads to numerous *multilateral* negotiations being held in numerous locations around the world. But negotiation training programmes focus almost exclusively on *bilateral* negotiations. The result is that the training needs of many managers are not met. More training programmes are needed which will help managers participate effectively in real-world, multilateral business negotiations.

QUESTIONS FOR DISCUSSION AND WRITTEN ASSIGNMENTS

1. "Potential members of negotiating teams should be assessed at the selection stage for flexibility, perspective-taking ability, cultural intelligence, and positivity." Explain why each of these qualities equips managers to negotiate effectively in international business negotiations. What assessment methods might be used to assess whether a manager possesses these qualities?

2. Identify practical negotiating skills required to enable a manager to effectively conduct an international buying/selling negotiation in a culturally distant country. How could the required skills be developed in a training programme?

3. Managers may find it difficult to transfer what they have learned in a negotiator training course to real-life negotiations. Explain why this is the case,
and explain how the transfer rate could be improved.

BIBLIOGRAPHY

Adair, W. L. & Brett, J. M. The negotiation dance: time, culture and behavioral
sequences. *Organization Science,* 16 (1), 2004, 33–51.

Adler, N. J. & Graham, J. L. Cross-cultural interaction: the international
comparison fallacy? *Journal of International Business Studies,* 20 (3), 1989,
515–537.

Bandura, A. *Social Learning Theory.* General Learning Press, 1977.

Bazerman, M. H. & Neale, M. A. *Negotiating Rationally.* Free Press, 1992.

Boyatzis, R. E. *The Competent Manager.* Wiley, 1982.

Boyatzis, R. E. & Mainemelis, C. An empirical study of the pluralism of learning
and adaptive styles in an MBA Program. Paper presented at a meeting of
Academy of Management, Toronto, 2000.

Brett, J. M. et al. How to manage your negotiating team. *HBR,* September
2009, 105–109.

Brislin, R. W. et al. Cross-cultural training: applications and research. In P. B.
Smith et al. (eds) *Handbook of Cross-cultural Management Research.* Sage,
2008, 397–410.

Bülow, A. M. & Kumar, R. Culture and negotiation. *International Negotiation,*
16 (3) 2011, 349–359.

Camerer, C. Behavioral game theory. In R. Hogarth (ed.) *Insights in Decision
Making: A Tribute to Hillel J. Einhorn.* University of Chicago Press, 1990,
311–336.

Carli, L. L., LaFleur, S. C. & Loeber, C. C. Nonverbal behaviour, gender,
and influence. *Journal of Personality and Social Psychology,* 68, 1995,
1030–1041.

Coleman, P. T. & Lim, Y. Y. J. A systematic approach to evaluating the effects
of collaborative negotiation training on individuals and groups. *Negotiation
Journal,* 17, 2001, 363–392.

Cui, G. et al. Cross-cultural adaptation and ethnic communication: two structural
equation models. *The Howard Journal of Communication,* 9 (1), 1998, 69–85.

Earley, C. and Ang, S. *Cultural Intelligence: Individual Interactions across
Cultures.* Stanford University Press, 2003.

Earley, P. C. Redefining interactions across cultures and organizations: moving
forward with cultural intelligence. In B. M. Staw and R. M. Kramer (eds)
Research in Organizational Behaviour, 24, 2002, 271–299.

ElShenawy, E. Does negotiation training improve negotiators' performance?
Journal of European Industrial Training, 34 (3) 2010, 192–210.

Faure, G. O. Negotiations to set up joint ventures in China. *International
Negotiation,* 5, 2000, 157–189.

Fernandez-Araoz, C., Groysberg, B. & Nohria. N. The definitive guide to recruiting in good times and bad. *HBR*, 09 May, 74–84.

Forgas, J. P. & Vargas, P. Affect and behaviour inhibition: the mediating role of cognitive processing strategies. *Psychological Inquiry*, 9 (3), 1998, 205–210.

Friedman, R. (1992) From theory to practice: critical choice for "mutual gains" training. *Negotiation Journal*, 8 (2), 1992, 91–98.

Galinsky, A. D. & Moskowitz, G. B. Perspective-taking: decreasing stereotype expression, stereotype accessibility, and in-group favoritism. *Journal of Personality and Social Psychology*, 78, 2000, 708–724.

Gosselin, A. et al. Ratee preferences regarding performance management and appraisal. *Human Resource Development Quarterly*, 8, 1997, 315–333.

Hinsz, V. B. et al. The emerging conceptualisation of groups as information processors. *Psychological Bulletin*, 121, 1997, 43–64.

Kelley, C. & Meyers, J. The cross-cultural adaptability inventory. In S. M. Fowler & M. G. Mumford (eds) *Intercultural Source Book: Cross-cultural Training Methods*, Vol. 2, Intercultural Press, 1999, 53–60.

Kolb, D. A. *Experiential Learning: Experience as the Source of Learning and Development*. Prentice Hall, 1984.

Kolb, D. A., Boyatzis, R. E. & Mainemelis, C. Experiential learning theory: previous research and new directions. In R. J. Sternberg & L. F. Zhang (eds) *Perspectives on Cognitive. Learning, and Thinking Styles*. Erlbaum, 2001, 227–248.

Kray, L. J., Locke, C. C. & Van Zant, A. B. Feminine charm: an experimental analysis of its costs and benefits in negotiations. *Personality and Social Psychology Bulletin*, 38 (10), 2012, 1343–1357.

Kray, L. J., Thompson, L. & Galinsky, A. Battle of the sexes: gender stereotype confirmation and reactance in negotiation. *Journal of Personality and Social Psychology*, 80, 2001, 942–958.

Kumar, R. Brahmanical idealism, anarchical individualism, and the dynamics of Indian negotiating behavior. *International Journal of Cross Cultural Management*, 4, 2004, 39–58.

Laroche, L. *Managing Cultural Diversity in Technical Professions*. Butterworth-Heinemann, 2003.

Lax, D. A. & Sebenius, J. K. *The Manager as Negotiator*. Free Press, 1986.

Lechuga, J. & Wiebe, J. S. Culture and probability judgment accuracy: the influence of holistic reasoning. *Journal of Cross-cultural Psychology*, 42 (6), 2011, 1054–1065.

Liu, L. A., Chua, C. H. & Stahl, G. K. Quality of communication experience: definition, measurement, and implications for intercultural negotiations. *Journal of Applied Psychology*, 95 (3), 2010, 469–487.

Loewenstein, J., Thompson, L. & Gentner, D. Analogical learning in negotiation teams: comparing cases promotes learning and transfer. *Academy of Management Learning and Education*, 2 (2), 2003, 119–127.

Lundeberg, M. A., Fox, P. W., Brown, A. C. & Elbedour, S. Cultural influences on confidence: country and gender. *Journal of Educational Psychology*, 92, 2000, 152–159.

Masek, L. E. Advice for teaching hands-on computer classes to adult professionals. *Computers in Libraries,* 20 (3), 2000, 32–6.

Nadler, J., Thompson, L. & Van Boven, L. Learning negotiation skills: four models of knowledge creation and transfer. *Management Science,* 49 (4), 2003, 529–540.

Olekalns, M., Anderson, C. & Brett, J. The positive and negative effects of anger on dispute resolution. *Journal of Applied Psychology,* 89 (2), 2004, 369–376.

PricewaterhouseCoopers: *International Assignments: Global Policy and Practice, Key Trends.* PricewaterhouseCoopers, 2005.

Pruitt, D., Kim, S. H. & Rubin, J. *Social Conflict: Escalation, Stalemate and Settlement.* McGraw-Hill, 2nd ed., 1994.

Puck, F. F. et al. Does it really work? Re-assessing the impact of pre-departure cross-cultural training on expatriate adjustment. *International Journal of Human Resource Management,* 19 (12), 2008, 2182–2197.

Raiffa, H. *Negotiation Analysis: The Art and Science of Collaborative Decision Making.* Harvard University Press, 2003.

Ramarajan, L. et al. Relationship between peacekeepers and NGO workers: the role of training and conflict management styles in international peacekeeping. *International Journal of Conflict Management,* 15 (2), 2004, 167–191.

Ready, K. J. & Tessema, M. T. Perceptions and strategies in the negotiation process: a cross cultural examination of U.S. and Malaysia. *International Negotiation,* 14, 2009, 493–517.

Reynolds, M. Wild frontiers – reflections on experiential learning. *Management Learning,* 40 (4), 2009, 387–392.

Robinson, W. N. & Volkov, V. Supporting the negotiation life cycle. *Communications of the ACM,* 41 (5), 1998, 95–102.

Rollof, M., Putnam, L. & Anatasious, L. Negotiation skills. In J. Greene & B. Burleson (eds) *Handbook of Communication and Social Interaction Skills.* Lawrence Erlbaum Associates, 2003, 801–834.

Runkle, C., Osterholm, A., Hoban, R., McAdam, E. & Tull, R. Brief negotiation program for promoting behavior change. *Education for Health,* 13, 2000, 377–386.

Salacuse, J. W. Making deals in strange places: a beginner's guide to international business negotiations. In J. W. Breslin & J. Z. Rubin (eds) *Negotiation Theory and Practice Program on Negotiation,* 1993.

Salacuse, J. W. Teaching international business negotiation: reflections on three decades of experience. *International Negotiation,* 15, 2010, 187–228.

Salacuse, J. W. Ten ways that culture affects negotiating styles: some survey results. *Negotiation Journal,* 14 (3), 1998, 221–240.

Sarkar, A. N. Navigating the rough seas of global business negotiation. *International Journal of Business Insights & Transformation,* 3 (2), 2010, 47–61.

Schuster, C. P. & Copeland. M. J. Global business exchanges: similarities and differences around the world. *Journal of International Marketing,* 7 (2), 1999, 63–80.

Stewart, S. & Keown, C. Talking with the dragon: negotiating in the People's Republic of China. *Columbia Journal of World Business*, 24 (3), 1989, 68–72.

Stuhlmacher, A. F. & Walters, A. E. Gender differences in negotiation outcomes: a meta-analysis. *Personnel Psychology*, 52, 1999, 653–677.

Stutman, R. K. & Newell, S. A. Rehearsing for confrontation. *Argumentation*, 4, 1990, 185–198.

Susskind, L. Negotiation training: are you getting your money's worth? *Negotiation Newsletter*, 7, 2008, 4–6.

Thomas, D. C. & Fitzsimmons, S. R. Cross-cultural skills and abilities. In P. B. Smith, M. F. Peterson & D. C. Thomas (eds) *The Handbook of Cross-cultural Management Research*, Sage, 2008, 201–215.

Thomas, D. C. & Inkson, K. *Cultural Intelligence: People Skills for Global Business*. Berrett-Koehler, 2004.

Thompson, L. & DeHarpport, T. Social judgment, information feed-back, and interpersonal learning in negotiation. *Organisational Behavior Human Decision Processes*, 58 (3), 1994, 327–345.

Timura, C. T. International negotiation pedagogy. *International Negotiation*, 15, 2010, 155–161.

Trompenaars, F. *Riding the Waves of Culture*. Nicholas Beasley, 1993.

Trotman, A., Wright, M. & Wright, S. Auditor negotiations: an examination of the efficacy of intervention methods. *The Accounting Review*, 80 (1), 2005, 349–367.

Tung, R. L. & Varma. A. Expatriate selection and evaluation. In P. B. Smith et al. (eds) *Handbook of Cross-cultural Management Research*. Sage, 2008, 367–378.

Van der Vegt, G. S. et al. Power asymmetry and learning in teams. *Organisation Science*, 21 (2), 2010, 347–361.

Verardi, S. et al. Psychometric properties of the Marlowe-Crowne social desirability scale in eight African countries and Switzerland. *Journal of Cross-cultural Psychology*, 41 (1), 2010, 19–34.

Volkema, R. J. Demographic, cultural, and economic predictors of perceived ethicality of negotiation behavior: a nine-country analysis, *Journal of Business Research*, 57, 2004, 69–78.

Volkema, R. J. & Rivers, C. Negotiating on the Internet: insights from a cross-cultural exercise. *Journal of Education for Business*, 83 (3), 2008, 165–172.

Weiss, S. International business negotiation in a globalizing world: reflections on the contributions and future of a (sub)field. *International Negotiation*, 11, 2006, 287–316.

Weiss, S. E. Analysis of complex negotiations in international business: the RBC Perspective. *Organization Science*, 4 (2), 1993, 269–300.

Williams, J. O. Simulated materials useful in training negotiators. *Improving College and University Teaching*, 19 (3), 1971, 220–222.

Pre-negotiation Activities

7

INTRODUCTION

Managers use the pre-negotiation stage of international business negotiations to increase their understanding of the main negotiation issues and acquire information about the other negotiating team. Setting clear and realistic negotiating goals is another essential pre-negotiation task since clear goals help negotiators decide which concessions they could make, if necessary (Cellich, 1996). A carefully considered small concession can be made in such a way that the other party feels it is achieving a major gain and is motivated to reciprocate by improving its offers. Negotiators need to decide the maximum value of concessions they may be prepared to make. Setting the negotiation agenda is usually done after consulting the other party as well as power centres in the negotiator's own company. An agenda for an international business negotiation might have 10–20 items or more, depending on the number of issues to be addressed. Research should carried out at this stage into any regulatory or policy constraints that could affect the final agreement. By openly referring to these constraints during the negotiations, international business negotiators demonstrate that their offers and proposals are practical and realistic.

Pre-negotiation information gathering can take much time. One reason is that reliable information about companies in some countries is difficult to obtain. In China, for instance, many kinds of information are extremely difficult to extract because they are scattered among various agencies, and often the person responsible for dealing with the information in any one agency is unidentifiable. Professional investigators are sometimes used to obtain information about a negotiating partner in spite of ethical concerns. If there is a danger of ideological conflict disrupting a forthcoming negotiation, the negotiating team should make use of the pre-negotiation stage to decide how they will present their proposals in a way that will be ideologically acceptable to the other side. At the same time they could discuss how the team should handle any issues that may arise concerning nepotism, bribes and other ethical questions.

The team's mandate for a forthcoming negotiation can be established by consulting various power centres in the company such as finance, engineering and marketing. Internal divisions within the negotiating team may also need to be addressed before negotiations begin. Depending on how thoroughly they have been briefed, some members of the team may have priorities and goals that differ from those of the company. Brett et al. (2009) argue that such conflicts of interest should ideally be resolved at the pre-negotiation stage so that during the actual negotiation, all members of the team can be relied on to support *company* goals as opposed to departmental or functional goals. Sometimes there are opportunities for informal communication with the other team prior to negotiations. Informal conversations at pre-negotiation receptions and social events allow individual members of the teams to learn about each other's circumstances, needs, constraints, levels of authority and so on. This kind of information can be helpful when developing arguments and proposals for use in the actual negotiation.

Checks might be made with the host organisation before negotiations start in order to ensure that the negotiating venue is suitable. For example, since sensitive and confidential information is exchanged and discussed in international business negotiations, the room where negotiations are held should be acoustically secure (Oseland et al., 2011).

Will translation, interpreter and catering services be available? Is there adequate air quality and temperature control? For important international business negotiations, a range of information technology (IT) and audiovisual (AV) equipment, including data points for wireless broadband, is increasingly considered to be essential. Geographical location is important because location affects the decision-making. When negotiations are held in a peripheral, not central, location, and when media coverage is limited, negotiators are usually more willing to accept compromise solutions because their decisions are more private, less visible, than in central public locations. In non-central locations, the pressure imposed on negotiators by constituencies – for example, trade unions, national professional bodies, workforces and so forth tends to be limited (Druckman & Druckman, 1996).

PRE-NEGOTIATION PLANNING

Planning tasks

Negotiators who plan better do better. For instance, when Mittal Steel was making plans to acquire Arcelor, Europe's biggest steel company, the negotiations promised to be so complex that they had to be preceded by an entire pre-negotiation campaign of activities. The activities included raising money on the right terms from the right sources, persuading credible figures to join the board, forging agreements with critical employees, and negotiating contracts with various strategic partners (Lax & Sebenius, 2012). Shareholder meetings were planned and held, and multiple financial agreements were made. Regulatory accords in Brussels and Washington, DC, were engineered, allowing Mittal to build sufficient support to overcome blockers of the takeover. The case demonstrates that the more complex the negotiations and the bigger the deal, the greater the amount of pre-negotiation planning required.

Pre-negotiation planning is, from one perspective, the most important stage of an international business negotiation. Lewicki et al. (1999) argue that it lays the very foundation for the process of negotiating. It enables negotiators to acquire information in advance, to define the issues to be debated in the actual negotiation, and to research the interests of the other party. Peterson & Lucas (2001) believe that a fully prepared negotiator should have a reasonable understanding of the other party's needs, interests, resources, negotiating style, and the likely strategy and tactics that the other party may deploy. Acquiring such understanding is an important objective of the pre-negotiation planning stage.

Schuster & Copeland (1999) argue that planning for important international business negotiations must include an analysis of the organisation and of the other side's negotiating team, and information about the company's history, client list and performance statistics. Who will be involved in the forthcoming negotiations, both the total number of those involved throughout and those who will participate in particular phases? Such information will make it easier to structure one's own negotiating team. For high-stake negotiations against formidable opponents, a senior executive may need to be appointed as lead negotiator to improve the chances of a successful outcome.

Role diversity

Deciding the different roles that members of one's own team should play is part of the planning. Role diversity allows the many issues and complexities of international business negotiations to be dealt with in a coordinated way so that a satisfactory agreement can be reached. According to Sjostedt (1993), members of a negotiating team often find themselves playing the role of driver, conductor or defender (among others), as negotiations get underway.

- *Drivers* organise and influence team members to obtain the outcomes they want.
- *Conductors* try to organise team contributions from a neutral position – from the back of the bus.
- *Defenders* are single-issue participants, constantly on the lookout for ways to promote and defend their issue.
- *Cruisers*, by contrast, have no particular axe to grind and are available to be followers.
- *Brakers* block agreement, usually with reference to several issues.

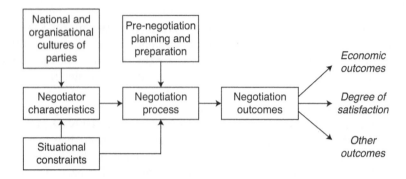

Figure 7.1   International business negotiation model

Note: Pre-negotiation planning is, from one perspective, the most important
stage of an international business negotiation since it affects both the
process and the outcome of negotiation.

A crucial planning task is setting limits – for instance, by determining reservation prices – your minimum price if you are an exporter, your ceiling price if you are an importer, and the maximum value of the concessions you are prepared to make. Cellich (1996) makes the point that international sales negotiators should know the point at which a sale becomes unprofitable, based on a detailed costing of product and associated expenses made before negotiations begin. Inexperienced negotiators often work out one fixed target, and thereby allow themselves little flexibility for making concessions or responding to offers creatively.

Influencing perceptions

In international business negotiations, aspirations are often linked to perceptions. If, for instance, a buyer perceives a foreign property owner as desperate to sell for hard currency, this perception will influence the buyer's aspirations and the price he or she will expect to pay. That helps explain why in international business negotiations, a whole range of behaviours is often displayed at the pre-negotiation stage which are intended to shape the perceptions of the other side regarding the value of the negotiation package to be offered by one's own side.

Consider, for instance, the situation faced by the chief executive officer (CEO) and founder of a small company in Ireland which manufactures veterinary products and which has attracted the interest of a US-based multinational. Persistently poor financial performance by the Irish company has made the CEO desperate to sell his company. However, he feigns indifference and sets about influencing perceptions by nonchalantly deferring for a few weeks a meeting suggested by the Americans to discuss a possible acquisition offer. The effect of this pre-negotiation behaviour is to shape the Americans' expectations of what to anticipate in the initial meeting and, the CEO hopes, to raise their reservation price in the forthcoming negotiation. Other perception-moulding actions which the CEO could take before formal negotiations begin include an opening statement to the press, a memo to shareholders boldly declaring the company's negotiating position, one-sided analyses for the Americans to digest, and other actions deliberately designed to shape the buyers' perceptions and expectations.

As the example suggests, the pre-negotiating stage can be profitably used to develop appropriate negotiating strategies and tactics. Pre-negotiation tactics, initial discussions and opening statements can – in combination – powerfully influence buyers' perceptions of what they are up against, causing them to reduce expectations and raise their reservation price.

Setting limits on prices

Negotiators' aspirations affect their reservation prices, and often both change in the course of negotiations. That is why a crucial part of pre-negotiation planning is to set limits on one's own minimum and maximum prices. It is precisely at the pre-negotiation stage that international business negotiators must decide on the boundaries beyond which there are no longer grounds for negotiation.

Consider, for example, the case of a property company which demands $1 million for the leasehold of an office suite in the city centre. For several weeks after the property goes on the market, the owner of the company argues forcefully in phone calls, emails and letters that the price is fair and reasonable. For weeks he refuses to listen to other offers and just keeps referring to the $1 million price. The aim of this pre-negotiation posturing is to influence the perception of potential buyers about the true value of the building and their expectations of what the property company will accept. Their original aspiration of paying much less may be revised upwards as a result of the pre-negotiation behaviour of the property company.

Lax & Sebenius (1986) point out that once formal negotiations have started, the sequence in which a party makes concessions can also powerfully influence perceptions. For instance, a pattern of concessions that apparently converges to a given point may cause the counterpart to perceive that point as the negotiator's reservation price or limit.

Making useful contacts

Much of the learning about the issues to be negotiated often takes place at the pre-negotiation stage through informal discussions with the other team, enabling the teams to familiarise themselves with each other's negotiating positions on the issues. The pre-negotiation planning period could also be used by managers to make contacts with third parties with expert knowledge of the issues to be negotiated and who might be willing to discuss them with the team. Managers could also use the planning period to obtain and evaluate information about the other party and to learn about their negotiating goals. For Williams (1971), the most effective negotiators are those who

- are thoroughly prepared with relevant information about the topic of negotiation;
- approach the negotiation with a meticulous eye for detail;
- have prepared a range of options for debate;
- are willing to consider options proposed by the other side.

When preparing for multilateral negotiations, the negotiating team might use the pre-negotiation period to hold informal talks with some of the other parties about the possibility of joining forces. By pooling their resources and joining a coalition, parties can increase their bargaining power and avoid destructive competition with each other.

Conditions for successful negotiation

One of the aims of pre-negotiation planning is to create the conditions for successful negotiations, but sometimes the planners' efforts misfire. When senior managers in a US company were given responsibility for planning merger negotiations with a Taiwanese company, the planners were convinced that they had provided the ideal working environment for the negotiations – on board a cruise ship.

> Security was superb and there were absolutely no distractions. The negotiating teams would be able to fully concentrate on the discussions. But after half a day, the negotiations had to be abandoned because most of the participants were seasick.

Planning the agenda

Setting the agenda for an international business negotiation is usually carried out at the pre-negotiation stage as part of the process of getting the negotiators to the table. The agenda is a list of items to be discussed and the order in which they will be discussed. Many sequencing options are possible, from easy to difficult, for instance, or from major issues to minor issues. Part of the agenda-setting task is to consult different departments and power centres in the organisation about issues they would like to see included on the agenda. This should allow a draft agenda to be presented to the other party for comments and approval. Ten to twenty agenda items are typical for international business negotiations (Dupont, 1996). However, complex and protracted negotiations may have more agenda items than this.

Managers authorised by their own organisation and the other party to set the agenda have a powerful means of influencing the structure, interaction and outcomes of a forthcoming negotiation. Keeping to the agenda during the negotiation will force the negotiators to consider matters on an issue-by-issue basis. As Sebenius (2002) points out, keeping strictly to the agenda inhibits the parties from discussing several issues simultaneously, thereby recognising their integrative potential. Sometimes the parties prefer to hold structured negotiations, which keep to the agenda and observe precise time schedules. In other cases the parties prefer negotiations to be more informal, with fewer agenda items and flexible timing.

The extent to which the interaction is controlled by the agenda is strongly influenced by cultural factors. Negotiations held with a Brazilian company, for instance, are likely to meander into other subjects and leave the agenda unfinished (Arruda & Hickson, 1996). Many European negotiators, on the other hand, are used to orderly, agenda-dominated negotiations, and are likely to want to stick to the point and finish on time. Negotiators from some cultures (e.g. Maori culture) may prefer not to use a negotiation agenda. When *virtual negotiations* are being planned, one of the challenges is to involve individuals in different countries in deciding the negotiation agenda. Typically, the manager organising a virtual negotiation invites individuals who will be participating to propose agenda items for each stage of the negotiation.

Goal-setting

Setting clear and realistic negotiation goals in the planning period is an essential first step in developing strategies to achieve the goals. Vague, sweeping goals, such as "to improve business relationships with international business partners," sound good, but are difficult to measure. *Clear, precise goals,* formulated at the planning stage, help negotiators decide, for instance, which concessions and which tradeoffs they could make. A small concession can be made in such a way that the other party feels it is making a major gain, motivating it to reciprocate by improving its offers.

Cellich's (1996) advice to managers formulating their goals for forthcoming business negotiations is the following"

- Know your negotiating position by deciding goals that are clearly defined, prioritised and realistic.
- Find out what the other side's goals and priorities are. This information will help you develop appropriate negotiating strategies, tactics and counter-offers.
- Use a combination of competitive and cooperative strategies to achieve the goals – but with cooperative strategies prevailing towards the end of the negotiation.

Internal consultations

It is at the planning stage that negotiating teams set their negotiating goals and manage their internal negotiations and consultations. Internal consultations are part of the process of persuading various power centres in an organisation to agree on the goals and desired outcomes of forthcoming international business negotiations. Not every company which is involved in business negotiations communicates with a single voice, thus increasing the risk that it will fail to negotiate in a coherent and consistent manner. For instance, a committee – the board of directors or an executive committee – may make important decisions for a company, but may nevertheless lack unity (Crump & Glendon, 2003). As a result, managers throughout the company may be divided on the line that should be taken in a forthcoming international business negotiation where a number of contentious issues will be debated. A way round the problem is for the negotiating team to consult various power centres in the company (e.g. finance, engineering, marketing, senior executives etc.) to clarify management's expectations regarding the forthcoming negotiations. Internal consultations take up valuable planning time, but at least they enable the negotiating team to go into the negotiations with a clear mandate.

Cyert & March's (1963) theory of the firm as a collection of bargaining coalitions highlights the importance of pre-negotiation consultations within the firm. The authors argue that, because of internal divisions and infighting, the official goals of a firm are vague and unhelpful as guides to deciding the strategies needed for an international business negotiation.

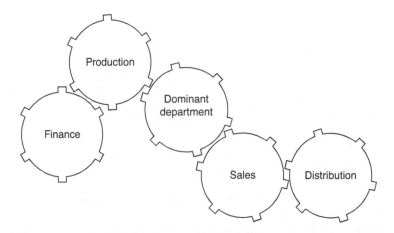

Figure 7.2   Departmental influence on company's negotiating position

Note: Decisions taken in one or two dominant departments may in time affect all the other departments. In international business negotiations, the interests and viewpoints of dominant departments may strongly influence the company's negotiating position.

Divisions within the negotiating team

Internal divisions within the company and within the negotiating team itself need to be addressed at the pre-negotiation stage. Depending on how thoroughly they have been briefed by senior executives, different members of the negotiating team may have diverging priorities and goals. For instance, when negotiations begin, the legal department's representative may focus exclusively throughout the negotiations on protecting intellectual property rights and have no interest in any other issue. The finance department's representative may be preoccupied with costs and margins. Manufacturing may be intent on rejecting any proposals that he or she thinks would disrupt production schedules. If potential conflicts of interest of this kind exist, they need to be resolved before negotiations begin.

When 45 negotiating teams from a wide range of sectors were interviewed, they admitted to researchers that their team's biggest challenges came from their own side of the table when individuals unwittingly started to undermine the team's negotiating strategy (Brett et al., 2009). To reduce the danger that divergent approaches within the negotiating team might create confusion and conflict in an actual negotiation, internal team negotiations may be needed at the pre-negotiation stage with the aim of motivating all team members to unite behind a single set of objectives. Sometimes the mere presence of a top-level manager on the team is all that it takes to persuade functional specialists and departmental champions to fall into line behind company goals.

Case Study

MINI-CASE: Goals and negotiation strategy

International business negotiations are more likely to have a successful outcome if the negotiating parties are flexible and prepared to adjust their negotiating strategies (either in the pre-negotiation stage or later) in line with information acquired about the goals and preferences of the other side. But when an Australian and a Thai team participate in a negotiation simulation aimed at developing their negotiating skills, the teams have a complete lack of information about each other's goals.

As a result, each team misinterprets the other team's negotiating strategy, and the negotiations are getting nowhere – until a short adjournment gives both teams the opportunity to take action to obtain more information. When negotiations resume, the extra information that has been obtained enables each team to make correct deductions about the strategies of the other side, and, as a result, the negotiations make good progress.

Questions:

1. *What methods might each team have used during the short adjournment to obtain information about the negotiating goals of the other side?*
2. *In international business negotiations, what factors besides lack of relevant information typically cause a negotiating team to misunderstand or misinterpret the goals and negotiating positions of the other team?*

PHYSICAL ARRANGEMENTS

Space, layout, equipment, location

Negotiators' level of satisfaction with an international business negotiation is influenced not only by the outcomes but also by physical factors such as a suitable conference room or meeting space, efficient AV equipment and an appropriate setting (Oseland et al., 2011). Ensuring a suitable working environment for a forthcoming business negotiation is an important task that should be carried out by the host organisation at the pre-negotiation stage.

Room size affects the interaction. Anecdotal evidence suggests that the size of room preferred by negotiators from most countries is one that gives the impression of being comfortably full – not crowded – when everyone is present and seated. When negotiations take place in a comfortable, informal setting, cooperative and creative problem-solving is more likely to occur.

Detailed, complex information is often exchanged and discussed in international business negotiations, which suggests the need for an acoustically secure meeting room or space with good projection facilities. According to Oseland et al. (2011), meeting rooms or spaces which lend themselves to successful negotiations have the following features:

- Privacy. Good acoustics to eliminate transmission of sound between rooms or noise from outside.
- Appropriate room size/shape. Appropriate layout and style of furniture that can be arranged to allow different types of activity and interaction.
- Range of IT and AV equipment – for example, data points for wireless broadband. Appropriate AV equipment (with instructions on how to use it, if necessary).
- Adequate daylight (and *control* of daylight, especially when using AV equipment). Air quality and temperature control.
- Efficient interpreter, translation and catering services.

Seating arrangements

Ideally, decisions about seating arrangements should be taken before negotiations begin. Faure (2000) argues that positioning the negotiating teams in two lines facing each other organises the interaction symbolically as conflictual and encourages confrontation. A round-table, or a U-shaped arrangement if many participants are involved, sidesteps this danger and encourages compromise and the abandon-ment of hard-lining. The participants feel psychologically closer to each other than when they take up confrontational positions along opposite sides of a rectangle – an arrangement that risks turning an international business negotiation into a verbal tennis match, with contributions flying to and fro across the table.

An effective seating pattern for multilateral business negotiations is one that encourages maximum interaction by allowing direct eye contact among all participants, as with a circular or U-shaped seating arrangement. Eye contact is important because speakers need to know whether listeners understand what is being said, whether they are pleased or annoyed, agree or disagree. Feedback information is obtained by quickly scanning facial expressions. However, this is impossible if some participants are invisible because of badly thought-out seating arrangements. In such cases, feedback is restricted and interaction inhibited.

Highly competitive negotiating teams usually choose to arrange themselves directly opposite the other team in confrontational positions where direct visual contact represents a challenge to the other, a play at dominance.

Location

Numerous small-scale negotiations are conducted by letter, fax, email or tele-phone, and for the negotiators concerned, location is not an issue since they do not have to travel to participate in a face-to-face meeting. But in other cases, location matters. The location of an international business negotiation and the extent of media coverage, in particular, have strong and consistent effects on the negotiators' decisions (Druckman & Druckman, 1996). When negotiations are held, for instance, in a peripheral – not central – location, and when media coverage is limited, negotiators' decisions tend to be more flexible. A peripheral setting for sensitive negotiations regarding, say, a cross-border merger, encour-ages the negotiators to be flexible and soften their attitudes to compromise solutions. The reason is that the decisions they take are more private, less visible, than when negotiations are held in a central, public location. In peripheral loca-tions, negotiators may be willing to break away from their predetermined scripts because the constraining influence of the media and constituencies (e.g. work forces, trade unions, national professional bodies etc.) is limited.

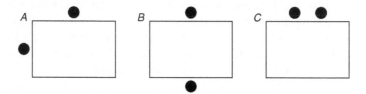

Figure 7.3   Sole negotiators' seating patterns

Note: The most common patterns chosen by sole negotiators for A – conversation;
B – competitive bargaining; C – cooperative tasks, such as
searching for an integrative agreement.

Manrai & Manrai (2010) argue that the location of an international business negotiation can increase the impact made by *time pressure* on negotiation processes and outcomes. In distant locations, for instance, the time sensitivity of American managers is often used against them by foreign negotiating teams.

PRACTICAL EXERCISE: Questions for discussion

Working in small groups, discuss each of the following questions. At the end of the exercise, make a brief presentation of the group's answers to the other groups for comment.

1. *Before an international business negotiation begins, a negotiating team may need to carry out consultations with various power centres in the company. Under what circumstances are such internal consultations required?*
2. *Under what circumstances are internal negotiations or briefings needed within the negotiating team itself?*
3. *A negotiating team representing a US retailer is about to travel to India to conduct buying/selling negotiations with an Indian clothing manufacturer. As part of its pre-negotiation preparations, the US team wishes to develop a draft negotiation agenda to be presented to the Indians before negotiations begin. How should the US team go about this task?*
4. *Explain how negotiators should go about identifying the key issues to be discussed in a forthcoming international business negotiation at the pre-negotiation stage.*
5. *How can understanding of these key issues be increased before negotiations begin?*

ACTIVITIES FOR THE PRE-NEGOTIATION STAGE

Activities checklist

A clear understanding of the activities that need to be carried out at the pre-negotiation stage is essential for managers about to embark on an international business negotiation. Peterson & Shepherd (2010) identify 34 pre-negotiation activities which were used by managers as they prepared for simulated buying/selling negotiations relating to capital equipment for extracting natural gas. The comprehensive list of activities identified by the researchers should help organisations design realistic negotiator training programmes. According to the researchers, it is not known whether negotiators from all cultures carry out all of these pre-negotiation activities.

Peterson & Lucas's (2001) Pre-Negotiation Framework provides a framework for classifying the 34 activities under four headings, as shown in Table 7.1.

Table 7.1   Pre-negotiation planning activities

Information Gathering:
1. Collect primary data (consult with others in your firm, client's firm, third-party firms)
2. Collect secondary data (industry, government, trade publications, Internet, annual reports etc.)
3. Gather data on market conditions, future trends and how they may affect each party
4. Understand other party (general profile, personality profiles and communication patterns of others involved)
5. Knowledge of the competitive alternatives the client may be pursuing
6. Review history of the relationship from internal sources/data
7. Review the previous strategies used by both you and the client
8. Knowledge of client's anticipated preparation
9. Understand the other's decision-making limit (structure and process)

Formulation Activities:
1. Set negotiation objectives
2. Define your interests
3. Define issues to be deliberated
4. Define the bargaining mix (what is on the table and what is not)
5. Set limit levels on issue(s) (optimistic, realistic, pessimistic)
6. Contrive BATNA (Best Alternative to a Negotiated Agreement, point at which you agree not to do business)
7. Create an agenda for negotiation
8. Incorporate potential plans of the other party
9. Create a negotiating team, assign responsibilities, role and deadlines)
10. Outline the role you will assume (if part of a team)
11. Consult with others regarding your plan/strategy

Strategy Development:
1. Develop team strategy (who will speak, who will introduce demands, concessions, solutions)
2. Develop tradeoff strategy on the issues (what you will give for what in return)
3. Devise collaborative strategies (cooperative ideas and options)
4. Devise competitive attacking strategies (options to be highly aggressive)
5. Devise competitive defending strategies (options to defend against attacks)
6. Devise concession strategy (slow, but planned, concessions to appease client)
7. Develop strategies that use a third party to influence client actions (friendly/coercive influence asserted from third party)

Preparation Activities:
1. Role Play
2. Script opening ceremonies (formal opening statement)
3. Prepare questions from client (questions that are in need of answers)
4. Prepare for anticipated questions from client (answers to questions or objections)
5. Prepare a mutual interest business topic (topic both parties find relevant to business concerns)
6. Prepare visual and other aids (charts, graphs, presentation aids)
7. Logistical concerns (seating arrangements, food, drink, room availability)

Source: Adapted from Peterson & Shepherd (2010)

COMMUNICATION AND INFORMATION

Gathering information

> When executives from a US company arrive in Paris to discuss a possible takeover of a French firm, they are invited to join the French board for lunch. But after lunch, the French begin to ask penetrating questions, and it soon becomes obvious that the Americans know next to nothing about the company they wish to acquire apart from its balance sheet. The Americans realise that they have weakened their bargaining position at a stroke by exhibiting inadequate preparation.

As the example suggests, the more significant the negotiation and the more daunting the issues to be resolved, the more important it is to be properly prepared with adequate information. In the context of international business negotiation, adequate information allows options to be weighed and appropriate negotiation strategies to be developed. "Running the numbers and scouting the marketplace are essential before heading to the bargaining table," Leary et al. (2013, 98) insist. So is developing a Plan B in case things do not go as you would like.

The preparatory information-gathering phase is usually longer for international business negotiations than for domestic ones because information in some countries is difficult to obtain. For example, successful outcomes in negotiations with companies in China and former communist countries may depend on finding the answer to such questions as

- what are the company's capabilities?
- who are the company's competitors in regional and international markets?
- will the company be a trustworthy business partner?

In China, such information can be difficult to track down. The information may be scattered among various agencies, and often the person responsible for dealing with the information in any one agency cannot be identified.

Information about the other side

Information about the other party that may need to be obtained at the pre-negotiation stage includes its strong and weak points, its main customers and competitors, and its track record in similar negotiations. Such information will help the team develop negotiating strategies in line with what it has learned about other company. Use the pre-negotiation stage, Wood (2001) advises managers, to find out who will be present from the other team and what their roles are likely to be. The knowledge will help managers anticipate the other team's opening position and prepare an appropriate response. In the absence of information, negotiators have to *infer* the other side's goals indirectly from the pattern of proposals and counterproposals made in the actual negotiation (Adair et al., 2001).

Potential sources of information about a foreign firm include past clients, commercial banks, trade attaches, consultancy, legal firms, chambers of commerce, trade associations and the Internet. Together, these sources of information should provide sufficient information to allow conclusions to be drawn about the other party's strengths and weaknesses and its likely negotiating strategies. Useful information may also be picked up at receptions and other pre-negotiation social events, covering such questions as whether the company is a competitive or cooperative negotiator, whether its negotiators prefer formal or informal negotiations, and so on. Professional investigators are sometimes used to fill in any information gaps that remain, in spite of the ethical questions raised by this type of information gathering.

Information and bargaining power

In international business negotiations, companies with much bargaining power tend to control most of the outcomes (Laubach, 2010). Information is an important source of bargaining power, and companies with greater information are better able to influence the negotiation and the outcomes. Thus managers should use the pre-negotiation stage to

- carry out research to increase knowledge and understanding of the key issues to be negotiated;
- convert the information into quantitative analyses, graphs and charts that negotiators can display to prove their point during the actual negotiation;
- research the legal, regulatory and policy constraints which would affect any decisions taken during the negotiation, and take these constraints into account when developing offers and proposals for discussion at the table so that the team's proposals will be perceived as practical and realistic.

International buying/selling

In carrying out international sales negotiations, a negotiator strengthens his bargaining position if he can show that he thoroughly understands the problems and needs of a foreign buyer, and if he can then show how the products/services offered will help the buyer meet those needs. In most international sales negotiations, an invisible third party – the competition – is also present. Thus, research on the competition should also be carried out at the pre-negotiation stage to identify the strengths and weaknesses of competing firms and so that the sales negotiator knows what he has to beat. Research may reveal, for instance, that a competitor can offer better terms than your own company, but, because of full capacity, may not be in a position to accept further orders, or can only offer

Table 7.2   Preparing information for negotiating team

For top-level negotiations	For lower-level negotiations
1. Investigate the financial aspects. Research the costs, prices, depreciation, credit terms, effects on profit etc.	1. Investigate technical or administrative aspects. Give information relating to specifications, precise changes of procedures needed etc.
2. Make the information general – e.g. the effects of a decision to be made on production over 12-months.	2. Make the information particular. Give concrete details – e.g. a breakdown of maintenanace costs, department by department or month by month. Give many examples.
3. Present the information so that the negotiating team can use it as a decision-making tool in the negotiations – e.g. give several broad alterrnative courses of action, together with the major implications of adopting each one (effects on company turnover, on the business relationship with the other party etc.)	3. Present the information so that its relevance to the company or to a particular department or particular managers is clear – e.g.explain how a decision to be taken in the negotiation will affect the staffing situation in each of these departments.

delayed delivery. Armed with this information, the sales negotiator will be in a good position to resist demands to reduce the price.

According to Lax & Sebenius (2006), building bargaining power is a step-by-step process, with the first step involving the assembly of information about the issues to be negotiated before negotiations begin. The second step is to ensure that the parties have a way of contacting one another in the pre-negotiation period.

Presenting information

The negotiating issues have to be researched and analysed before negotiations begin. Part of the pre-negotiating planning period could be used to decide how the resulting information should be introduced and how it should be presented in the negotiation itself. Charts and graphics might be used, for instance, to communicate information that would be difficult for the other negotiating team to understand if only verbal communication is used. On the other hand, as Schuster & Copeland (1999) point out, charts, graphs, statistics and specific data are not likely to be useful during business negotiations in Latin America, the Middle East or other areas where the negotiating partner is more interested in establishing interpersonal relationships than in understanding the issues.

Presentations made in an international business negotiation must take into account the preferences and expectations of the other side. Kulshreshtha (2009) argues that there is a quasi-academic side to business in some European countries, and that if a presentation is made during a negotiation, it is almost like defending a PhD dissertation. In France, for instance, a presentation made in the middle of a negotiation is expected to be comprehensible, yet to have real depth, and the presenter is expected to answer every question thoroughly.

PRACTICAL EXERCISE: PowerPoint presentation

Working in pairs or small groups, answer the following question. Then prepare a PowerPoint presentation of your answers to be shown to and discussed by other groups.

1. *Identify the pre-negotiation planning activities that will need to be carried out in advance of forthcoming negotiations in Russia between a UK manufacturer of electronic control equipment and a Russian buying team.*
2. *The UK negotiating team intends to make a formal sales presentation early in the negotiation. As the audience will consist of Russian managers from the buying organisation, what kind of presentation will be required, bearing in mind that presenters should familiarise themselves with the characteristics and expectations of their audience?*

Informal communication

It is sometimes necessary for the parties to negotiate about the structure or process of negotiation before live negotiations begin. In informal discussions held before negotiations begin the parties can decide

- the language in which negotiations will be conducted;
- which managers should be at the table;
- what the agenda should be;
- what ground rules and basic procedures are needed;
- what chairing arrangement will be used.

In international business negotiations, there are often contentious and sensitive issues to be negotiated, and such issues are easier to deal with if clear procedures and ground rules have been agreed before negotiations begin.

Informal communication opportunities such as receptions and informal parties before negotiations begin, allow negotiators to learn about each other's needs, goals, constraints, authority, decision-making preferences and so on. This information may give insights into negotiating strategies and tactics that the other side will adopt and the kind of offers that might be the attractive to them – long-term credit, for instance, or early delivery, or an extended warranty period. Moreover, informal communication between the teams at the pre-negotiation stage encourages *relationship building*, which could make the difference between success or failure in some international business negotiations (Chen et al., 2009).

Opportunities for informal communication between members of the negotiating teams are sometimes very limited. In a few high-stake negotiations (e.g. major cross-border acquisitions) in which contacts with other parties are conducted according to protocol, informal contact across ranks may not be acceptable. In other cases, protocol is less important, and informal communication between negotiating teams is encouraged at the pre-negotiation stage.

Al-Khatib et al. (2011, 147) urge negotiators to take advantage of informal communication opportunities to assess the *personality characteristics* of counterparts (e.g. their tendency to exaggerate, be pessimistic, be secretive etc.). Such informal assessments can be a means of predicting the future negotiating behaviour of the other team, and the extent to which it is likely to be influenced by ethical and ideological motivations.

Protocol in negotiations

Negotiators from different countries tend to have different attitudes towards the observation of protocol. Foster (1992) regards American negotiators as notoriously casual about their use of first names, dress, disregard for titles and so on. This casualness goes along with Americans' high risk-taking propensity. In contrast, Hofstede & Usunier (1996) note that risk-averse, high-context cultures prefer highly structured, ritualistic procedures with strict regard to protocol. International business negotiators with a high concern for protocol tend to keep to strict rules regarding dress codes, use of titles, and personal and professional conduct.

ETHICAL AND IDEOLOGICAL QUESTIONS

Managers who frequently travel to foreign countries to participate in international business negotiations sometimes come face-to-face with values and practices that are entirely normal in the country concerned, but which would be unacceptable at home. Examples are child labour in some Asian and African countries, and discrimination against women in some countries in the Middle East. Another example is payments for services rendered that would be seen as bribes in the visitor's own country. In Russia, corruption and bribery in business affairs has been widespread since the collapse of the Soviet Union. Kazakov et al. (1997) argue that commissions and bribes have to be tolerated by foreign business executives in Russia who are anxious to sign a contract or clinch a deal.

Dishonest communication is regarded by some Western sales managers as part of what it takes to do business abroad. For example, a sales manager from a Canadian IT firm participated in sales negotiations with directors of a new publishing company in Eastern Europe.

During the meeting the sales manager tried to convince the directors that the product he was trying to sell them, computer software, would correspond to what the company said it needed. But the sales manager knew that he was being economical with the truth.

To avoid conflict in international business negotiations, managers may have to present their proposals in ways that are ideologically acceptable to the other party. Thus preparations for a negotiation should take into account any known ideological differences between the parties. Schuster & Copeland (1999) advise negotiators to use the pre-negotiation stage to determine how the team will handle any ideological points of conflict that may arise, as well as decide how the team will deal with any issues that may arise concerning nepotism, bribes and other ethical questions.

KEY POINTS

1. Activities carried out at the planning stage aim to create the conditions for successful negotiation. Major negotiating issues can be studied, and information about the other party and the other party's negotiating interests can be obtained and assessed. The pre-negotiation period can also be used to make useful contacts, such as third parties with expert knowledge and experience of the negotiating issues.
2. Negotiators need to know about any regulatory or policy constraints which would affect the decisions taken in a forthcoming negotiation. These constraints should be allowed for when preparing proposals and offers for presentation to the negotiating opponent. Taking these constraints into account will help convince the opposition that the proposals are practical and realistic.
3. Sometimes a negotiating team needs to hold internal consultations with finance, engineering, marketing and other power centres in the company so that their expectations regarding the forthcoming negotiations are clear, and so that the negotiators have a clear mandate. Different members of the negotiating team may have diverging priorities and goals, and such conflicts of interest need to be resolved before negotiations begin so that all team members can be relied on to support *company* goals.
4. The pre-negotiation information-gathering phase usually lasts longer for international business negotiations than for domestic ones since information in some countries is difficult to obtain. In China, many kinds of information are scattered among various agencies, and the person responsible for dealing with the information in a given agency is often unidentifiable. Professional investigators are sometimes used to obtain information about the negotiating partner in spite of ethical questions prompted by this method.

5. Setting the agenda is usually carried out at the pre-negotiation stage. The task may involve consulting the other party as well as different power centres in the company about issues they wish to be included. Ten to twenty items may be on the agenda of a typical international business negotiation, although complex protracted negotiations may have far more agenda items. Managers authorised to set the agenda have a powerful means of influencing the structure, interaction and outcomes of a negotiation.

6. There are often opportunities for informal communication between teams at the pre-negotiation stage, which provides opportunities for negotiators to learn about each other's goals, constraints, levels of authority and negotiating interests. This information can be used to develop persuasive arguments for use in the actual negotiation. Proposals which are known in advance to be attractive to the other side can be developed. The information may give early warning of strategies and tactics likely to be used by the other side.

7. The pre-negotiations stage should be used to decide how to deal with any ideological points of conflict that arise, and how the negotiating team should present its proposals in a way that will be ideologically acceptable to the negotiating partner. Negotiating teams also need to discuss and decide how they will handle any problems that arise due to nepotism, bribes and other ethical questions.

8. Pre-negotiation behaviours intended to shape perceptions include opening statements to the press, memos staking out initial negotiating positions, one-sided analyses and other actions all aimed at shaping counterparts' perceptions and expectations in the desired way. Offensive tactics can influence a negotiator's perception of what he is up against, and cause him to reduce his own expectations and alter his reservation price.

9. Setting clear and realistic negotiating goals at the pre-negotiation stage is an essential pre-requisite for developing negotiating strategies to achieve the goals. Formulating clear goals helps negotiators decide which concessions they could make if necessary. Small concessions can encourage the other party to reciprocate by improving its offers. A useful tactic is to hold a few inexpensive concessions in reserve, in case further concessions are necessary to close the deal.

10. Sensitive and confidential information is often discussed in international business negotiations, so the room where negotiations are held must be acoustically secure. Good acoustics will eliminate transmission of sound between rooms and noise from outside. Other desirable features are a range of IT and AV equipment with data points for wireless broadband, and adequate daylight, air quality and temperature control. Efficient translation, interpreter and catering services should be available.

11. The location of an international business negotiation can affect the decision-making and the outcomes. When negotiations are held in a peripheral, not central, location and when media coverage is limited, negotiators tend

to be flexible and willing to compromise because their decisions are more private, less visible, than in central, public locations. The pressures on negotiators by constituencies – trade unions, professional bodies and so forth – are limited in peripheral locations.

QUESTIONS FOR DISCUSSION AND WRITTEN ASSIGNMENTS

1. "At the pre-negotiation stage of negotiation, behaviours are often displayed which are intended to influence perceptions." Give examples of perception-influencing behaviour before an important international business negotiation, and explain how the behaviours discussed might affect both perceptions and outcomes.
2. What are the advantages of developing clear and realistic goals during the pre-negotiation planning period? How do negotiating goals influence negotiating strategies?
3. Explain how the geographical location of a high-profile international business negotiation can affect the decision-making and the negotiation outcomes.

BIBLIOGRAPHY

Adair, W. L., Okumura, T. & Brett, J. M. Negotiation behaviour when cultures collide: the US and Japan. *Applied Psychology,* 86 (3), 2001, 371–385.

Al-Khatib, J. A. et al. The impact of deceitful tendencies, relativism and opportunism on negotiation tactics: a comparative study of US and Belgian managers. *European Journal of Marketing,* 45 (1/2), 2011, 133–152.

Arruda, C. A. & Hickson, D. J. Sensitivity to societal culture in managerial decision-making: an Anglo-Brazilian comparison. In P. Joynt & M. Warner (eds) *Managing across Cultures: Issues and Perspectives.* International Thomson Business Press, 1996, 179–201.

Brett, J. M. et al. How to manage your negotiating team. *HBR,* September 2009, 105–109.

Cellich, C. Preparing for your business negotiations. *International Trade Forum,* 2, 1996, 20–23.

Chen, Y-R., Leung, K. & Chen, C. C. Bringing national culture to the table: making a difference with cross-cultural differences and perspectives. *The Academy of Management Annals,* 3 (1), 2009, 217–249.

Crump, L. & Glendon, A. Towards a paradigm of multiparty negotiation. *International Negotiation,* 8, 2003, 197–234.

Cyert, R. & March, J. *A Behavioural Theory of the Firm.* Prentice-Hall, 1963.

Druckman, D. & Druckman, J. N. Visibility and negotiating flexibility. *Journal of Social Psychology,* 136 (1), 1996, 117–120.

Dupont, C. A model of the negotiation process with different strategies. In P. Ghauri & J-C. Usunier (eds) *International Business Negotiations*. Pergamon, 1996.

Faure, G. O. Negotiations to set up joint ventures in China. *International Negotiation*, 5, 2000, 157–189.

Foster, D. A. *Bargaining across Borders: How to Negotiate Business Successfully Anywhere in the World*. McGraw-Hill, 1992.

Hofstede, G. & Usunier, J. C. Hofstede's dimensions of culture and their influence on international business negotiations. In P. N. Ghauri & J. C. Usunier (eds) *International Business Negotiations*. Pergamon, 1996, 119–129.

Kazakov, A. Y. et al. Business ethics and civil society in Russia. *International Studies of Management and Organisation*, 27 (1), 1997, 5–18.

Kulshreshtha, A. K. How to carry out international business negotiations for industrial globalization overseas. *Chemical Business*, February 2009, 17–19.

Laubach, C. The executive's guide to successfully negotiating good agreements. *Healthcare Executive*, November/December 2010, 66–71.

Lax, D. & Sebenius, J. *3-D Negotiation: Powerful Tools to Change the Game in Your Most Important Deals*. Harvard Business School Press, 2006.

Lax, D. A. & Sebenius, J. K. Deal Making 2.0: a guide to complex negotiations. *HBR*, 90 (11), 2012, 92–100.

Leary, K., Pillemer, J. & Wheeler. M. Negotiating with emotion. *HBR*, 91 (1/2), 2013, 96–103.

Lewicki, R. J., Saunders, D. M. & Minton, J. W. *Negotiation*. McGraw-Hill, 3rd ed., 1999.

Manrai, L. A. & Manrai, A. K. The influence of culture in international business negotiations: a new conceptual framework and managerial implications. *Journal of Transnational Management*, 15, 2010, 69–100.

Oseland, N. et al. Environments for successful interaction. *Facilities*, 29 (1/2), 2011, 50–62.

Peterson, R. M. & Lucas, G. H. Expanding the antecedent component of the traditional business negotiation model. *Journal of Marketing Theory and Practice*, Fall, 2001, 37–49.

Peterson, R. M. & Shepherd, C. D. Preparing to negotiate: an exploratory analysis of the activities comprising the pre negotiation process in a buyer-seller interaction. *The Marketing Management Journal*, 20 (1), 2010, 66–75.

Salacuse, J. W. Teaching international business negotiation: reflections on three decades of experience. *International Negotiation*, 15, 2010, 187–228.

Schuster, C. P. & Copeland, M. J. Global business exchanges: similarities and differences around the world. *Journal of International Marketing*, 7 (2), 1999, 63–80.

Sebenius, J. K. The hidden challenge of cross-border negotiation. *Harvard Business Review*, 80 (3), 2002, 76–85.

Sjostedt, G. (ed.) *International Environmental Negotiations*. Sage, 1993.

Uher, T. E. & Runeson, G. Pre-tender and post-tender negotiations in Australia. *Construction Management and Economics*, 2, 1984, 185–192.

Williams, J. O. Simulated materials useful in training negotiators. *Improving College and University Teaching*, 19 (3), 1971, 220–222.

Wood, T. Team negotiations require a team approach. *The American Salesman*, November 2001, 22–26.

Negotiation Strategies

8

INTRODUCTION

Strategies are guiding principles for making coherent decisions in complex environments (Kupers et al., 2013). Negotiating strategies guide decision-making in the complex environment of international business negotiations. Only a limited number of strategic orientations are available for international business negotiators, the main choices being between competitive and collaborative orientations (Dupont, 2003). For competitive negotiators, negotiation is about winning or losing – and they try to win. Collaborative negotiators, by contrast, willingly share information, compromise, make reciprocal concessions and try to reach an agreement that benefits both parties. The way in which a negotiating team responds, pro or con, to the other team's opening offers usually reveals whether or not they are collaborative negotiators. A positive response can lay the foundation for the development of trust and cooperation throughout the negotiations. A negative response may be an early warning signal of non-cooperation and conflict between the parties.

Having to answer to shareholders and focus on profitability pushes some international business negotiators to use highly competitive strategies and questionable tactics, such as threats and misinformation. Most negotiators, however, fluctuate between competitive and cooperative approaches in a negotiation (Olekalns et al., 2004). Typically, they begin by making high demands and other competitive moves, but adopt a more cooperative stance at a later stage. Economic models of negotiation – those based on game theory, for instance – have been used to determine negotiation strategies that will lead to maximum gains. But such strategies falsely assume that negotiators make decisions according to principles of economic rationality. In real-life negotiations psychological and situational factors and the impact of culture on negotiator behaviour are always present.

International business negotiations are fundamentally different from domestic negotiations and require a different set of skills and approaches. The appropriateness of a particular negotiation strategy may depend, for instance, on the cultural background of the negotiating partner. *Relationship-oriented strategies* may be appropriate, for instance, when negotiating with the Chinese (Chen, 2008). *Problem-solving strategies* are based on the parties recognising and defining a problem, sharing information and developing options for possible solutions. Typical problem-solving actions in international business negotiations include agreeing to make more resources available, exchanging concessions and creating mutually beneficial options. *Principled negotiation* offers a simple model for maintaining good relations with the other party without necessarily yielding on the issues at stake. Principled negotiation has achieved a high degree of visibility and support from social scientists and business leaders because, in practice, it often leads to integrative agreements.

Strategies used in international business negotiations are, surprisingly often, based on simple rules of thumb. A company may identify one critical process, such as expanding an overseas market, then develop a few guidelines to manage that process. The guidelines are the strategy. Adding more variables might lead the negotiators to give too much weight to peripheral considerations.

Companies need to focus on the organisation's basic interests, not on a swarm of peripheral matters, when developing negotiating strategies. Some companies simplify the strategy selection process by narrowing down the options and considering only strategies that were used successfully in the past. Generic strategies, identified by Porter (1990), which give international companies competitive advantage in overseas markets are cost leadership, niche operations and market differentiation. Often in an international business negotiation the strategy with which a manager begins needs to be changed as the negotiation unfolds. That is why, instead of simply escalating commitment to the original strategy, the manager should use each break as an opportunity to reassess and reformulate the original strategy, perhaps incorporating new information received in the preceding negotiating session. Anything learned in the session about, say, the other party's reservation price or its basic interests could be built into the reformulated strategy.

STRATEGY IN NEGOTIATIONS

Concept and definition

International business negotiators are individual entrepreneurs or teams of managers who represent companies. Effective negotiating strategies enable them to negotiate successfully with managers, suppliers, customers, public officials and other counterparts in a wide range of international and cross-border situations. An effective negotiating strategy is a plan that integrates a negotiator's goals and actions into a cohesive whole (Kupers et al., 2013). Effective strategies contain guiding principles for making coherent decisions in the negotiation. According to Lax & Sebenius (1986, 360), the effectiveness of a specific negotiating strategy depends on the goals and the quality of information that underpins it. The researchers characterise the strategic task as "bringing into being a favourable set of consistent agreements that create value for the parties."

Ghauri & Usunier (1996) see strategies used in international business negotiations as the elaboration of general principles which negotiators intend to keep to during the negotiation in order to achieve their negotiation goals. Viewed from this angle, negotiation strategies can be seen as guidelines prompting appropriate decisions and actions.

Selecting an appropriate strategy for use in a forthcoming international business negotiation is influenced by a negotiator's "frame," which determines whether he sees the negotiation, for instance, as an opportunity for high short-term gains or a means to restrict possible losses. A negotiator's frame can be positive and risk-seeking, or negative and risk-avoiding, and determines whether he sees the possible outcomes in terms of profit or in terms of costs and expenses. Bazerman (1999) advises negotiators to be aware of the part played by their own frame when selecting a strategy. When both parties view a forthcoming negotiation in a positive frame, the prospects for an integrative agreement are greatly increased.

Effective strategies are needed in all aspects of international business, including international sales, international procurement, imports-exports, outsourcing and the formation of strategic business alliances and international joint ventures (IJVs). Ineffective or inappropriate strategies used in any of these areas can lead to poor outcomes, create ill-will and lead to the loss of foreign business. Das & Kumar (2011) make the point that to be successful in these areas, the strategy used must match the specific demands of each negotiation. Just as strategies that work in the software sector would have no hope of working in the far more predictable and stable sector of hosiery manufacture, so strategies needed to successfully negotiate an international alliance are the product of a completely different mindset from those required to negotiate the sale of consulting services to a government in a developing country. Thus managers must negotiate with foreign counterparts using strategies which suit the particular situation.

In international business negotiations, effective strategies are often based on the principles of *simplicity, flexibility* and *measured risk*.

Simplicity principle

Formulating an effective negotiation strategy need not be driven by numbers and extensive analysis, does not have to be an elaborate process. For some companies, the guiding principle seems to be to keep to a few simple rules or guidelines. Companies like Intel and Cisco, for instance, shape their negotiation strategies by relying on simple rules of thumb, not complicated frameworks (Sull & Eisenhardt, 2012). A typical rule-of-thumb might be to identify one critical process (e.g. expanding a particular overseas market), and then develop a few guidelines to manage that process. The rationale underlying such an approach is that adding more variables might lead negotiators to give too much weight to peripheral considerations and prevent them from testing the rule-of-thumb strategy against their own experience and common sense.

German manufacturer Weima Maschinenbau is an example of a company which observes the simplicity principle when formulating negotiating strategies. It created a simple rule to help sales representatives negotiate effectively with international and domestic buyers. The rule was to give an early delivery date for orders for standard products, provided that the customer agreed to pay 70 percent of the price before the product was shipped (Sull & Eisenhardt, 2012). The simplicity principle can be extended to approaches needed to help negotiators to break through deadlocks. For instance, the other negotiating team could simply be asked to explain in greater detail their position on a negotiating issue which is causing conflict or deadlock. In clarifying and elaborating, negotiators often adjust or soften their positions, thus making a breakthrough more likely.

The task of choosing a strategy for a forthcoming negotiation can be simplified by narrowing down the options. Some firms simplify the selection of a suitable strategy by considering only strategies that were used successfully in past negotiations, and that could be used again if adjusted to take account of the new negotiating situation. Spanish retailer Zara's strategic style is related to its flexible supply chain. In both domestic and international negotiations, Zara's strategic vision stays focused on using its flexible supply chain as a principal bargaining counter. Reeves et al. (2012) point out that the company maintains strong ties with 1,400 external suppliers who work closely with the company's designers and marketers. The result is that Zara can design, manufacture and ship a garment in as little as two to three weeks – a huge selling point in cross-border business negotiations.

For some companies, the temptation may be to choose to use strategies that have been used successfully in domestic negotiations. But international business negotiations are fundamentally different from domestic negotiations and require a different set of approaches and skills, for instance, the ability to deal with complexity. Additional complicating factors that have to be addressed in international business negotiations are language and cultural barriers.

Flexibility principle

Managers who participate in international business negotiations must be flexible enough to convert problems into opportunities. For example, when a European

engineering company with limited production capacity entered into sales negotiations with a Chinese firm, it was at a considerable disadvantage vis-à-vis major
competitors. The competitors were international companies with a reputation
for high-quality branded products. But the European company's two-man
negotiating team demonstrated flexibility by adroitly converting an apparent
weakness into a negotiating strength.

> During initial negotiations with top-level managers, the negotiators stressed
> that their firm's small overhead costs allowed it to be extremely price compet-
> itive. They also pointed to the company's small-batch production runs, which
> allowed it to quickly process and despatch even small orders received from
> foreign customers.

In other cases, managers demonstrate their flexibility in the course of a negotiation by being willing to re-evaluate and reformulate strategies which are turning
out to be inappropriate. Early warning signs may come in the shape of new
information received about the other side's goals indicating, for instance, that
the other party is more interested in building a long-term business relationship
than in making short-term gains from the current negotiation. Such information should be carefully assessed, and then incorporated into a revised strategy
which will better meet the demands of the situation.

As the example demonstrates, strategies may have to be modified by negotiators in the course of a single negotiation or set of negotiations. Lewicki et al.
(1999) note that, as negotiations proceed, each side typically proposes changes
to the other party's position and makes changes to its own. This process of give
and take and frequent adjustment of strategic approach is what enables a mutually acceptable agreement to be reached.

When an opening strategy is proving to be ineffective, instead of simply
increasing commitment to the strategy, the team might use each break and
adjournment to reassess and reformulate their original strategy. Did you learn
anything in the last session, Bazerman & Neale (1992) ask, that changed
your assessment of the other party's interests, or the other party's reservation price, or the relative importance of the main negotiating issues to the
other party? In light of what you learned, where should you now be looking
for *tradeoffs*? And what is your present assessment of the Zone of Possible
Agreement (ZOPA)?

No-strategy strategy

Some managers adopt an avoidance strategy by withdrawing from active participation in a particular negotiation. According to Leary et al. (2013, 98), such
managers are practically phobic about going to the negotiating table, and will
sign on the dotted line just to end the stress of dealing with people from different
cultures who have different agendas and styles.

A variation of avoidance strategy is the no-strategy strategy. The no-strategy strategy consists of refusing to make an explicit strategic choice at the start of negotiations and, instead, let things develop before committing oneself. The great advantage of the strategy is that it gives a negotiating team maximum flexibility to adjust their approach based on what the other side does first. Thus the team avoids making a premature commitment to a strategy that may turn out to be ineffective and inappropriate.

According to Janosik (1987), Japanese negotiators avoid early commitment to any particular negotiating strategy, and usually defer making proposals and offers until the other party has revealed its own negotiating position. The underlying rationale seems to be that since the first offer sets the ceiling price, negotiators who are uncertain about the best approach to take should wait for the other party to make the first offer.

Managers also need to demonstrate flexibility regarding negotiating methods. Managers do not have to travel to another country and negotiate face to face with foreign clients in order to clinch a business deal. Instead, they may choose to do the haggling by email or fax or over the phone. However, when negotiators from different countries meet face to face, they gain valuable clues about each other's trustworthiness from nonverbal communication signals, but this information is lacking when negotiations are conducted by phone or email.

Measured risk

Strategies can be high-risk or low-risk. High-risk strategies aim at maximising gains in a negotiation, but can have unintended consequences. In 2007–2008, the credit crisis created an unprecedented demand for affordable mortgages. The high demand prompted American and European banks to make risky lending decisions and equally risky investments. In loan negotiations in several countries, strategies were followed that aimed to maximise short-term returns. Bazerman & Watkins (2008) describe the consequences of these high-risk strategies.

> These strategies blinded mortgage negotiators to disasters waiting to happen. Defaults and foreclosures by overextended homeowners in the US, for instance, led to the fall of Enron and triggered a $700 billion government-funded bank bailout package.

The implication is that before committing themselves to a particular negotiating strategy, managers should first discuss with colleagues how the issues to be negotiated might play out in the long run. What is the company's attitude towards risk and does a proposed strategy reflect this attitude? For instance, is the proposed strategy high risk and aimed at high financial returns? Or is it a low-risk strategy aimed at limiting possible financial losses from participating, say, in an IJV? The risk factors should be assessed before the strategy is used in an actual negotiation.

Relationships

Ghamdi's (2010) survey of British firms which have conducted joint venture and international trade negotiations with Saudi Arabian organisations found that the key factors for successful negotiation with the Saudi firms were not effective negotiating strategies, but rather

- financing arrangements;
- their own firms' good reputation;
- the existence of good interpersonal relationships between the companies concerned.

Relationships in particular, Ghamdi found, contribute more to successful international business negotiations with Saudi firms than do discounts, promises of early delivery or the use of particular negotiating strategies.

It follows that Western negotiators should give time and effort to building good relations with their Saudi counterparts (and perhaps other Arab negotiators) before and during negotiations. In deal-focused cultures such as the countries of North America, relationships grow out of deals. But in relationship-focused cultures, deals arise from already-developed relationships.

A barrier to building relationships before and during negotiations is the strict hierarchy that exists in some negotiating teams. In teams from Asian countries, for instance, hierarchy and protocols usually dictate who speaks to whom, which topics can and cannot be discussed, who speaks first and so on (Chen et al., 2003). Thus, before negotiators can set about building a relationship with the other team, they first need to learn how the hierarchy works and how to penetrate it. Western negotiators are generally less hierarchical, less tradition bound and more direct than their Asian counterparts (Brett & Crotty, 2008). On the other hand, they also tend to be more overtly competitive and self-serving.

Schuster & Copeland (1999) argue that business relationships are not important in many former communist countries because their rapidly changing economies have not enabled lasting business relationships to be established. In these countries, business people tend to focus instead on obtaining the knowledge, expertise, capital and arrangements that lead to business success.

Strategies linked to goals

Effective negotiating strategies help negotiators achieve their negotiating goals. Thus, as Kumar (1999) points out, the ability to develop effective negotiation strategies is improved if a negotiating team already has clear, specific goals – and knows what the goals of the other team are. When information about the negotiating goals of the other party is lacking, negotiators have to infer these indirectly from the pattern of proposals, counterproposals and concessions in the actual negotiation.

Kumar (1999) argues that goals are usually embedded in hierarchies, that is, every goal has different subgoals nested in it. Subgoals increase negotiators' motivation because they appear to be less difficult to achieve. For instance, in an international business negotiation, two negotiating teams may have the same high-level goal –achieving a mutually acceptable agreement – but different subgoals. One team may have a *task-related* subgoal, while the other team may have a *harmony-maintenance* subgoal. For both sides, the subgoal represents an important first step in achieving the final high-level goal of reaching a mutually acceptable agreement. When the subgoals of the parties are incompatible, conflict may erupt and delay the achievement of both parties' main, high-level goal or even lead to impasse.

Tough and soft strategies

Tough, soft and intermediate strategies are used in international business negotiations (Ghauri & Usunier, 1996). Which strategy is used in a particular negotiation depends largely on a party's negotiating goals. If the goals are ambitious, a tough strategy may be used. An example of a *tough strategy* is when a negotiator begins with a very high opening offer, stays firm and expects the other party to make the first concession. A negotiator following a *soft strategy* will make the first concession and expect the other party to reciprocate.

Clear, specific goals allow appropriate negotiating strategies to be developed which, in turn, improve negotiators' performance. Locke & Latham (1990) suggest that *moderately difficult goals* lead to better negotiator performance than either very simple or very difficult goals. Generic strategies which allow multinational enterprises (MNEs) to achieve their goals and gain competitive advantage in international markets are cost leadership, niche operations and market differentiation (Porter, 1990).

Strategies linked to interests

Pruitt (1983) stresses the part played by *basic interests* when managers are selecting a negotiating strategy to be used in a forthcoming negotiation. Basic interests are a set of core outcomes expected by a party as a result of the negotiation process.

If a negotiating team decides to formulate a negotiating strategy which is based on the company's basic interests, it may do so after consulting managers who will be affected by the outcomes of a forthcoming negotiation. This will allow the managers to give their perceptions of the company's basic interests. Examples of the basic interests of companies participating in international business negotiations are

- protection of a trademark or copyright;
- negotiation of a technology transfer package;

- achievement of a certain price range or profit level;
- a supply contract with a potential foreign partner;
- access to a foreign partner's technology.

In international business negotiations a joint problem-solving approach is encouraged by the simple act of the negotiators' focusing on understanding each other's *negotiating interests*, and actively looking for opportunities to create joint gains by tradeoffs among issues that they value differently (Balakrishnan & Patton, 2006).

Focusing on interests affects *outcomes*, which are usually assessed in terms of their effects on the negotiators' interests (Lukes, 2005).

Fast, flexible strategies

Strategies used in international business negotiations may be derived from the company's already formulated corporate strategies. The disadvantage of using negotiating strategies of this kind is that the international business environment is fast moving and unpredictable, and relying on negotiating strategies linked to the company's strategy formulation system can be a mistake. The predictions and assumptions on which top-down negotiating strategies are based may already be out of date by the time they are used in a particular negotiation. That is why a faster and more flexible approach to producing strategies for use in international business negotiations may be needed. Thus people who have to use negotiating strategies – the negotiating team itself – are often the best people to formulate them. The negotiating team has the great advantage of being able to assess the effectiveness of the strategies in real time. On the basis of feedback received in negotiating sessions, it can assess whether the strategy it is using needs to be adjusted or abandoned.

Mantere (2013) argues that, while strategies are written on pieces of paper and in PowerPoint files, corporate strategies are not pieces of paper. The intentions and strategies stated in mission statements and annual reports may turn out to be fantasies – or simply ploys to fool the opposition. Corporate strategies take place in collective actions by members of the organisation. They are conducted by organisational members, in coherence with each other and over time.

Other factors

Other factors that play a part in selecting a negotiating strategy for a particular international business negotiation include

- the importance and urgency of the issues to be negotiated;
- the reputation and power of the negotiating partner;

- the nationality of the negotiation partner;
- the need to build a good business relationship with the other company.

In *multilateral business negotiations*, some parties, faced with the complexities and uncertainties of the multilateral negotiation process, may adopt a pooling-of-resources strategy. Rather than retain expert advisers to advise and in effect to negotiate on their behalf, two or more of the weaker parties who might otherwise be in competition with one another may decide to join forces and pool their resources. The result of adopting this strategy is that it enables them to negotiate in a collective, organised manner.

Case Study

MINI-CASE: Splitting the order

Working in small groups, study the following situation and answer the question that follows. Each group may then make a brief presentation of its answer to the other groups for their comments.

A large multinational company with its global procurement office in Hamburg, Germany, wishes to purchase 10,000 high-specification thermal printers. As a first step, the company's procurement division identifies three prequalified suppliers in Sweden, Germany and Belgium. The next step is for the procurement team to assess the suppliers' capabilities, including quantity capabilities.

Specific issues to be negotiated with the suppliers are

Price: preferred price $1,000 or less.
Delivery: 30–45 days preferred.
After-sales service period: preferred period 3 years.

A batch size of 500 units is considered to be the minimum ordering quantity.

The procurement manager at first considers using an automated procurement system to make the purchase. But most automated systems have to allocate the order to a single supplier even if its price is not competitive or the quantity is inadequate, and they are not able to split orders. Moreover, with most automated systems, the bidding is only based on a single issue – price.

Choice of communication method

Consequently, the manager's negotiating strategy is to negotiate with all three sellers by both email and telephone as this will produce better outcomes for the company. The implication of this approach is that the negotiation will, in effect, be conducted as three bilateral bargaining processes – as opposed to a single multilateral negotiation.

Information exchanged by email and over the phone in initial negotiations eventually leads to the procurement team obtaining the following offers from the sellers:

Swedish supplier:

Price: $1,050
Maximum quantity that could be supplied: 2,000
20 percent discount for orders of 500 and above
30 days delivery
After-sales service: 2 years

German supplier:

Price: $1,100
Maximum quantity that could be supplied: 4,000
10 percent discount for orders of 1,000 and above
60 days delivery
After-sales service: 3 years

Belgian supplier:

Price: $900
Maximum quantity that could be supplied: 5,000
15 percent discount for orders of 2,000 and above
45 days delivery
After-sales service: 3 years

All three suppliers have limited quantity capabilities. After the first round of negotiations, it is clear that none of the suppliers is capable of meeting all of the procurement team's requirements and preferences. However, the buyer's requirement could be satisfied by the three sellers contributing partially to the total order.

After the first round of negotiations, the procurement manager calls a meeting of her team and asks them to decide – based on the information that has been obtained – how many units the company should buy from each of the suppliers.

Question:

1. *How many units should the company buy from each supplier? Explain your reasons.*

STRATEGIC ORIENTATIONS

Competitive strategies

There are only a limited number of strategic orientations in both domestic and international business negotiations. According to Dupont (2003), the main choices are between distributive (competitive) and integrative (cooperative) orientations. A competitive/distributive orientation is characterised by a power-based negotiation style and has clear winners and losers. Competitive negotiations represent zero-sum situations in which the two parties are attempting to secure a larger share of a fixed resource. They are motivated by concern for their own interests, as opposed to joint interests. Lewicki & Robinson (1998) identify typical behaviours used by competitive negotiators. They include

- starting high and conceding slowly;
- exaggerating the value of concessions made by their own side, and minimising the value of concessions made by the opposing side;
- making threats and bluffing;
- misrepresenting information;

Having to answer to shareholders and other stakeholders puts pressure on some negotiators to select and use competitive strategies aimed at maximising financial returns from a negotiation. For many managers in Western countries, international business negotiation is essentially a competitive process of offers and counter-offers (Kumar & Worm, 2004). Highly competitive negotiators may even give up tangible gains and instead concentrate on inflicting losses on the other party (Fisher & Shapiro, 2005).

Highly competitive negotiators

Adopting a highly competitive strategy in international business negotiations can expose a company to greater risks than anticipated. Westbrook & Arendall (2009), for instance, found evidence linking high negotiator competitiveness with unethical or questionable negotiation behaviour such as using threats and providing false information.

Highly competitive negotiators see victory as the goal and often demand one-sided concessions as the price of agreement. Ryckman et al. (1996, 375) conclude that negotiators who are highly competitive are also highly egocentric. They try to win and avoid losing at any cost as a means of maintaining feelings of self-worth. During negotiations they demonstrate an orientation of manipulation, aggressiveness, exploitation and denigration of others. They strongly mistrust their opponent and will take big risks in an attempt to mitigate losses.

Today, negotiations in which the parties focus exclusively on beating the other side are unlikely to be successful. When hard bargainers are confronted by hard bargainers, for instance, the result may be conflict and heavy losses on both sides (Brett et al., 2009). Threats trigger counter-threats and, once started, this pattern of behaviour is difficult to break out of. Thus a decade ago, hard bargaining by both management and unions led to conflict-escalation after Cathay Pacific Airline sacked three employees. The prolonged dispute cost more than $15million, and caused major disruptions of holiday flights during the busiest season of the year.

Cooperative strategies

Cooperative strategies are based on sharing information and being willing to compromise, reciprocate and make concessions and tradeoffs across issues. The process is one of give and take. After making their initial offers, the parties keep modifying them with the aim of coming closer to each other and eventually reaching a mutually satisfactory agreement (Lewicki et al., 1999). Chinese negotiators are highly trained in using cooperative strategies, such as the art of gaining and offering concessions to the other side. Underlying the training is the belief that Chinese negotiators should concede as long as they can reach an agreement that satisfies their basic interests (Chen, 2008). If both sides are willing to concede, an integrative agreement can be reached, and the relationship between the parties is strengthened.

In an international business negotiation, the way in which a negotiating team responds to the other team's opening offers may reveal whether or not they are cooperative negotiators. A positive initial response can lay the foundation for the development of trust and cooperation, whereas a negative response could be an early warning sign of non-cooperation and conflict throughout the negotiation. Negotiators who are conflict-avoiders may be over-cooperative irrespective of the other party's behaviour. An over-cooperative approach may lead to unnecessary concessions being made. Black & Mendenhall (1993) argue that Japanese negotiators tend to be conflict-avoiders because conflict would lead to loss of face for the defeated party and must therefore be avoided.

Walton & McKersie (1965) define cooperative (integrative) negotiation as a process by which parties attempt to explore options to increase the size of the joint gain without respect to the division of payoffs. For managers in many Asian countries, cooperative negotiating strategies are attractive because they facilitate the building of a long-term relationships between the parties, which is seen as an extremely important outcome of negotiations (Chen, 2008).

According to Greenhalgh & Gilkey (1993), female negotiators tend to see the negotiation encounter as just one component of a long-term relationship and thus tend to adopt integrative, cooperative strategies since they desire mutual gain between the parties. Managers who have been dealing with the same overseas customer for several years and who have built up a good business relationship with them are also more likely to adopt a cooperative negotiating strategy.

Cross-cultural aspect

Usunier (2003) argues that it can be difficult to successfully use cooperative, integrative strategies in the cross-cultural setting of an international business negotiation where the nationalistic feelings and resentments of negotiators are easily aroused. In some negotiations – French-Iranian business negotiations, for instance – the two sides may perceive each other as adversaries. In American-Japanese negotiations, the negotiators may be predisposed to regard the other side as unfair trade competitors.

Racial difference is another factor which may frustrate attempts to use cooperative negotiating strategies in an international business negotiation. Rubin & Brown (1975) argue that managers have been found to negotiate more cooperatively with an opponent of the same race than with one of another race, perhaps because similarity induces trust and interpersonal attraction.

Fluctuating strategic stances

Negotiation strategies used in international business negotiations tend to be mixed, as opposed to being exclusively competitive or cooperative. Studies suggest that negotiations can be both competitive and cooperative over time, with phases of resistance, obstruction and abstention (Bruns & Meinzen-Dick 2000). In international business negotiations, cooperative promises and reciprocal concessions may alternate with competitive bluffs and threats of punishment. These fluctuating behaviours may be tactical moves within an overall strategy of either cooperation or conflict.

Olekalns et al. (2004) found that about two-thirds of the way through a negotiation is the tipping point – the point at which negotiators are most likely to change from a competitive to a cooperative stance. They start to focus on resolving important issues and examining options. They make concessions. They begin to seriously consider how the underlying interests of the two sides can be met, and consciously search for agreement. Other studies have identified similarly fluctuating patterns.

- Perdue & Summers (1991) conceptualise problem-solving and aggressive bargaining as two distinct negotiating strategies. They note, however, that both strategies are often used by purchasing managers within a single negotiation.
- Bruns & Meinzen-Dick (2000) note that most negotiations have peaks of conflict but also periods of mutual cooperation. Typically in international business negotiations, there are phases of resistance, abstention, obstruction and compromise.
- Adair & Brett (2005) find that a competitive pattern of spirited posturing and high demands usually marks the first half of a negotiation. The negotiators realise, however, that to continue such competitive behaviour too long might cause the negotiation to break down, and consequently the second half usually becomes more cooperative.

- Daoudy (2009) explains the fluctuating pattern of negotiator behaviour by pointing out that behaviours such as promises or threats of punishment are merely tactical moves within an overall strategy of cooperation or conflict.

Adair et al. (2001) draw attention to the occurrence of *reciprocal sequences* in international business negotiations. These occur, for example, when a negotiator responds to the other side's competitive behaviour with, say, very similar behaviour. When one negotiator makes a very high demand, the other negotiator may respond with an equally high demand. Such reciprocal responses lead to sudden fluctuations in negotiator behaviour which are otherwise difficult to explain.

Other commonly used strategies

Das & Kumar's (2011) framework, which is based on Pruitt's (1983) dual concern model, is founded on four strategies which are widely used in international business negotiations and which are related, to a greater or lesser degree, to the competitive and cooperative strategic orientations described above. The four strategies are

- contending,
- yielding,
- compromising,
- problem-solving.

Contending strategy This strategy is used by negotiators to impose their demands on the other party, through take-or-leave-it proposals, for instance. If the other party reciprocates in kind, the result is conflict. Nonverbal elements associated with contending strategies include aggressive staring, leaning across the table and moving into the other party's territory (Semnani-Azad & Adair, 2011). When contending strategies are used in international business negotiations, conflict may result.

> Conflict was the result when a Malaysian supplier of telecom equipment and a Finnish manufacturer of switching systems opened alliance negotiations. Both companies immediately adopted a contending strategy. The result was that even after five days of negotiation, the atmosphere remained tense and numerous issues remaining unresolved.

As the example suggests, contending is unlikely to be a successful strategy when the opponent also uses a contending strategy. Contending tactics, aimed at improving the negotiator's power position vis-à-vis the opponent, include giving ultimatums, ignoring the opponent's information requests, displaying anger and impatience, and so on.

Yielding strategy In international business negotiation, a yielding strategy usually signals weak bargaining power. In international alliance negotiations, the partner with the lower equity stake sometimes adopts a strategy of yielding to the wishes of its potential partner. Yielding by making unnecessary concessions is a common reaction to unrealistic deadlines being imposed. Neale & Bazerman (1995) make the point that it is harder to yield when concessions imply loss rather than giving up gain. Yielding is an effective way to close negotiations when issues are unimportant and time pressures are high.

Problem-solving strategies These strategies are characterised by each party's sincerely trying to understand the partner's needs, and adjusting its offers to fulfil those needs (Graham, 2002). Problem-solving strategies usually involve carrying out a number of interrelated activities, including

- recognising and defining the problem;
- sharing information;
- jointly developing options for a solution;
- evaluating options and selecting the one that maximises joint gain.

Both parties work together, exchange information about the needs and priorities underlying their negotiating positions, and jointly assess the validity of each proposal that is made on the various issues.

Breaking through deadlocks

A problem-solving approach in international business negotiations can break through deadlocks. If, for instance, the high price proposed for a technology transfer project is causing deadlock, a solution might be to make the price just one item in a package that includes several other components, such as delivery time, warranty and after-sales service, installation and training arrangements. Another move to break the deadlock might be to give the foreign buyer an opportunity to purchase the company's mature technology, developed in the previous generation but still in demand, at a much lower price.

An example of the successful use of a problem-solving approach in an international business context is the alliance between General Electric and Snecma to manufacture jet engines (Das & Kumar, 2011). The new company won no orders for the first eight years, and problem-solving in this context meant modifying expectations, being patient, and working with and not against the partner.

> When the local office manager of an international consulting firm was looking to lease office space in Cape Town, he was offered a ten-year lease on a city centre office. But the manager was unwilling to commit the company to such a long-term deal and turned down the offer. The letting agent countered by offering a shorter lease, but at a much higher annual rent. By consciously adopting a problem-solving approach at this stage and discussing various alternative arrangements, the manager was able to negotiate a win-win solution. This consisted of signing a three-year lease at a somewhat higher rent than the ten-year lease offered, but which could be renegotiated at any time before the lease expired.

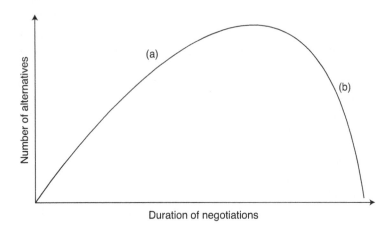

Figure 8.1   Typical problem-solving approach used by negotiators

Note: A problem-solving approach used in international business negotiations involves
(a) generating alternative possible solutions to major problems and
(b) filtering out the less attractive alternatives.

Principled negotiation

The aim of principled negotiation, a variant of problem-solving strategy is, according to Fisher & Ury (1991), to find a mutually beneficial outcome from negotiation by keeping to several principles:

- Be hard on the issues but soft on the people.
- Focus on interests, not positions.
- Invent options for mutual gain.
- Agree on objective criteria to judge solutions.

A disadvantage of principled negotiation is its lack of proven validity. Fisher & Ury (1991) do not cite research on which the model is based. Nevertheless, principled negotiation serves as a simple, practical model for maintaining good relations with the other party without necessarily yielding on the issues at stake. It can be an effective strategy to use in international business negotiations when there is scope for a negotiated agreement that benefits the different parties. For example, negotiations to decide the terms of participation in an international consultancy project might be based on the principle that consulting firms should be allowed to recover the costs of doing the work, plus a reasonable fee for time and effort.

Trotman et al. (2005) argue that principled negotiation involves

- thinking of the other as a problem-solving partner in negotiations rather than an adversary;
- understanding the other negotiator's negotiating position;

- creating efficient two-way communications;
- defining each negotiating issue in terms of the interests of the different parties;
- seeking creative options so as to maximise the joint gain.

Compromise strategy. Compromise strategies are often used when the negotiator's main aim is to build or maintain a friendly relationship with the negotiation partner. The strategy usually involves seeking agreement and offering concessions easily. Such an approach reduces the risk of conflict but also increases the possibility of one party exploiting the other. In most international business negotiations, there are issues on which the negotiators are flexible, or willing to consider trading for gains elsewhere. Flexibility is revealed by negotiators' posturing on issues which are important to both parties. Agreement is usually reached on such issues by the parties compromising (Druckman, 1991).

Different types of conflict are associated with different types of negotiation strategies (Harinck et al. 2000). For instance, conflict generated by a proposal to repatriate a proportion of an IJV's net profits may spur the negotiators to formulate new and more creative strategies aimed at reconciling the interests of the parties over the long term. Compromise strategies in international business negotiations involve mutual give and take in which each party gives a little in order to achieve an agreement. Such strategies have the effect of reducing tension and conflict, thus increasing the chances of reaching a satisfactory negotiated outcome (Lee et al., 2006).

Case Study

MINI-CASE: Compromise strategy in Poland

A Swedish manufacturer of bedroom furniture is holding negotiations with a long-time business associate, a major retailer in Poland. At stake is a $2 million export shipment of bedroom furniture manufactured by the Swedish company. Early in the negotiation, the parties clash on price.

The Swedish firm insists that it cannot reduce the price without taking a loss, but the retailer counters by disclosing that it has been offered a better price for similar-quality furniture by a well-known German manufacturer. The Swedish firm's furniture always sells well in Poland, but on this occasion it is not price competitive.

Slipping into problem-solving gear, the Swedish export sales manager proposes a compromise. He points out that, although three months ago the German competitor offered a better price than the Swedish company, that was three months ago. Since then the situation has changed. At the present time, because of full capacity, the Germans would definitely not be able to guarantee early delivery and might even be unable to accept any order for a large shipment.

The best way round the problem, the export manager suggests, would be a compromise. If the retailer will agree to go ahead with the purchase at the stated price, the Swedish firm will guarantee early delivery. It will also agree to share the retailer's expenses, on a 50/50 basis, for advertising and promoting the Swedish furniture.

This compromise solution, which creates value to both sides, turns out to be acceptable to the Polish team, and the negotiation quickly proceeds to the contract stage.

Questions:

1. *What are the advantages and disadvantages of using a compromise strategy in an international business negotiation?*
2. *Which alternative strategy or strategies could the Swedish negotiator have used in the negotiation which might have led to favourable outcomes for the Swedish company?*

MAXIMUM GAIN STRATEGIES

Approaches based on economic models of negotiation are widely used in simulated negotiations to determine strategies that will lead to maximum gains for the negotiator. But game theory and other economic models of negotiation falsely assume the rationality of negotiators. Such assumptions ignore the psychological and dispositional factors and the impact of culture on international business negotiations.

Minimax strategies. When minimax strategies are used in international business negotiations, the aim is usually to minimise financial risk as opposed to maximising financial gain. Minimax is a decision rule used in decision theory for minimising possible loss in a worst-case negotiating scenario. Minimax strategies involve refusing options presented by the other party that appear too risky, such as an offer to accept payment for an export shipment in a foreign currency which is known to be subject to sudden exchange-rate fluctuations.

Sufficing strategies. Like minimax strategies, sufficing strategies have the effect in negotiations of reducing risk by leading negotiators to accept what seems to them to be sufficient, even if more might have been obtained. In international business negotiations, ideas of what is sufficient are linked to the national cultural standards of the parties (Brett, 2001). Studies suggest that negotiators from certain cultural groups are predisposed to adopt strategies that reduce risk. Ready & Tessema's (2009) study, for instance, refers to the risk-averse negotiating strategies used by Malaysian negotiators.

Strategies used in aid negotiations

International aid negotiations usually involve negotiations about financial, technical and physical support to be provided by developed countries to less developed countries. A major challenge facing the negotiating teams, which represent donors and recipients respectively, is to find strategies which deal with the complex issues involved in these negotiations, including issues of governance and corruption.

In the negotiations, power differences between the parties can create formidable problems (Spector & Wagner, 2010). For example, since donor countries maintain the ultimate power of being able to provide or withhold funds, they can safely use hard-bargaining strategies to protect their interests. They often do so by imposing tough conditions on loan or grant agreements. These "conditionalities" force the recipient country to take actions to improve governance, gender equality, human rights and so on. But sometimes recipient countries adopt counter-strategies in an effort to equalise the power balance. According to Zartman & Rubin (2000), such counter-strategies include the following:

- *Compliance strategy.* A recipient country accepts what it regards as unfair conditions imposed by the donor, but immediately starts to make plans for changes to be negotiated in the post-agreement period.
- *Protest strategy.* The recipient forcefully complains during negotiations about the unfair conditions on the grounds that they impinge on the recipient country's sovereignty.

In some cases the protests spread to the streets. For example, in 2009, street demonstrations occurred in Pakistan against conditions placed on a US$7.5 billion development assistance package from the United States. The conditions required Pakistan to report back on its use of the funds and to strengthen its anti-corruption programme. Spector & Wagner (2010) found that the protesters saw these conditions as humiliating and believed that they undermined Pakistani sovereignty.

PRACTICAL EXERCISE: Questions for discussion

Working in small groups, discuss each of the following questions. At the end of the exercise, make a brief presentation of the group's answers to the other groups for discussion and comment.

1. *"Effective strategies are needed in all types of international business negotiation."* In the context of international business negotiations, what is an effective strategy?
2. Give examples of two effective strategies that are commonly used in international business negotiations. Describe their impact on the interaction and outcomes of negotiation.

---

3. *Why do negotiating strategies used in international business negotiations often change and fluctuate during a negotiation? Explain the causes and effects.*
4. *What are the advantages of knowing the negotiating interests of the other side in an international business negotiation? How can knowledge of the other side's interests be acquired?*

NEGOTIATING TACTICS

Purposes

Negotiating strategies are developed and used in order to achieve negotiators' goals regarding profitability, business relationships and other outcomes (Das & Kumar, 2011). *Negotiating tactics*, used in support of negotiating strategies, tend to be offensive or defensive and involve calculated responses to the opponent's proposals and intentions. Sebenius (2002) urges negotiators to map the different roles played by members of the opponent's team as a way of anticipating the offensive or defensive tactics they are likely to use.

Offensive tactics may be used to support highly competitive strategies, and include the use of threats and ultimatums and time pressures of various kinds designed to put pressure on the opposing party (Peterson & Lucas, 2001). *Defensive tactics* are used to deflect attacks of this kind, and include using the "higher authority" ploy.

Examples

Researchers have identified various tactics, offensive and defensive, that are used in international business negotiations. They include the following:

Bidding. Several parties who want the same thing – it might be a foreign distributorship – are pitted against one another by means of a formal or informal bidding process designed to drive up the price (Gates, 2011).

Brinksmanship. One party convinces the other party that they have no choice but to accept the offer and the proposed agreement – or to walk away (Goldman, 1991).

Good Guy/Bad Guy. This is a widely used tactic to encourage cooperation. One member of a negotiating team makes unreasonable demands, and another offers a more rational approach (Gates, 2011). The good guy appears more reasonable.

First concession tactic. The tactic of making the first concession signals willingness to enter into a long-term, cooperative relationship with the opposing party (Zhao, 2000).

Information overload. The opponent is deliberately overloaded with information so that they have difficulty separating important from unimportant facts. The idea is to confuse the opposing team.

Deadlines. Force the other party to make a decision by giving them a deadline.

Questionable tactics

Lewicki & Robinson (1998) raise questions about the acceptability of some of the negotiating tactics used by international business negotiators. These tactics include exaggerations – exaggerating the value of concessions, for instance – pretending not to be in a hurry, hiding one's bottom line, and more questionable tactics such as misrepresenting information and bluffing.

Volkema & Fleury (2002) found that situational factors can have a dramatic effect on a negotiator's willingness to use questionable tactics. If, for instance, the *issues* and the *outcomes* of an international business negotiation are very important to a negotiator, the individual will be more inclined to protect his or her self-interest by using hard-bargaining tactics or by engaging in unacceptable behaviours such as bribery or paying someone for restricted information. Yukl et al. (1976) found that negotiators under high *time pressure* engage in less truthful communication in negotiations.

Carson (1993) argues that a negotiator has a moral right to protect him- or herself by using questionable tactics when faced with an unethical opponent. Some countries, for instance, are known to have tough negotiators who make exaggerated first offers and few concessions, and who try to intimidate opponents with emotional or combative arguments (Acuff, 1997). If a manager anticipates having to negotiate with such an opponent, the manager is, according to Carson (1993), justified in taking pre-emptive actions (e.g. bluffing or providing false information) in order to protect him- or herself against potential loss.

Volkema & Fleury (2002) studied negotiating tactics used by business people from Brazil and the US and concluded that the use of either offensive or defensive negotiating tactics is influenced by

- the importance of the negotiating issue being debated;
- the reputation of the opposing party;
- the negotiating context (location, urgency, etc.).

KEY POINTS

1. A strategy contains guiding principles for making coherent decisions in negotiations. It is a plan that integrates a negotiator's goals and actions into a cohesive whole. Economic models of negotiation such as game theory have been widely used to determine negotiation strategies that lead to maximum gains, but such strategies falsely assume that business negotiators make deci-

sions according to principles of economic rationality. In international business negotiations, psychological and situational factors, and the impact made by culture on negotiations, are always present.

2. The main choices for negotiators are between competitive and cooperative strategies and tactics. For Western managers, negotiation is a competitive process of offers and counter-offers, whereas many Asian managers use cooperative strategies based on information sharing, reciprocal concessions and compromises. Examples of competitive tactics are starting high and conceding slowly, exaggerating the value of concessions made by one's own side, and minimising the value of concessions made by the opposing side.

3. Highly competitive negotiators may use threats, misinformation and other kinds of questionable behaviour (Westbrook & Arendall, 2009). Having to answer to shareholders and strive for profits may motivate a negotiator to use highly competitive strategies. The way in which a negotiating team responds to the other team's opening offers often reveals whether they are highly competitive. A negative, dismissive response can be an early warning sign of non-cooperation and conflict between the parties throughout negotiations.

4. Stances adopted by international business negotiators often fluctuate. About two-thirds of the way through a negotiation the negotiators change from being competitive to being more cooperative (Olekalns et al., 2004). They start to focus on resolving important issues and begin to seriously examine options. They make concessions, start to consider how the underlying interests of the two sides can be met, and search for an agreement that will be acceptable to both sides.

5. A strategy may have to be adjusted in response to new information received about the other party's goals and intentions. The new information should be assessed and incorporated into a reformulation of the original strategy. Some managers refuse to make an explicit strategic choice at first, preferring to let things develop before committing themselves. This gives them maximum flexibility to adjust their approach based on what the opponent does first. Each break and adjournment might be used to reassess and reformulate the original strategy. Anything learned, say, about the other party's reservation price should be built into the reformulated strategy.

6. Some collectivist negotiators – notably Japanese and Chinese negotiators – tend to avoid early commitment to any particular negotiating strategy. They are more likely to defer making proposals and offers until the other party has committed and revealed its own strategic stance. The underlying rationale seems to be that the first offer sets the ceiling price; therefore, negotiators who are uncertain about the best approach to take should wait for the other party to make the first offer.

7. The process of strategy selection can be simplified by narrowing down the options – by considering only strategies that were successful in the past, for instance. Effective negotiating strategies are often based on a few clear guidelines. Shaping a strategy need not be driven by numbers and extensive analysis. In creating a negotiating strategy, companies should focus on their

basic interests, not a swarm of peripheral matters. High-risk strategies aim at maximising gains, but may have unintended consequences.

8. Problem-solving strategies in international business negotiations involve recognising and defining a problem, sharing information and developing options for possible solutions. *Principled negotiation* provides a simple model for maintaining good relations with the other party without yielding on the issues at stake. It can be an effective strategy when there is scope for an agreement that benefits the different parties.

QUESTIONS FOR DISCUSSION AND WRITTEN ASSIGNMENTS

1. What are the main features of *principled negotiation*? In the context of international business negotiation, what are the strengths and weaknesses of this approach to negotiation, and how can the weaknesses be overcome?
2. What considerations might influence a manager's choice of a negotiation strategy to be used in buying/selling negotiations with a state-owned company in a former communist country? Identify three strategies which might be considered and list the main pros and cons of adopting each of these strategies.
3. What are the dangers of using economic models of negotiation (e.g. game theory) to develop strategies for use in an international business negotiation?
4. Explain the difference between negotiating strategies and negotiating tactics, as used in international business negotiations.

BIBLIOGRAPHY

Acuff, F. L. *How to Negotiate Anything with Anyone Anywhere around the World.* AMACOM, 1997.

Adair, W. L. & Brett, J. M. The negotiation dance: time, culture, and behavioural sequences in negotiation. *Organization Science*, 16 (1), 2005, 33–51.

Adair, W. L., Okumura, T. & Brett, J. M. Negotiation behavior when cultures collide: the U.S. and Japan. *Applied Psychology*, 86 (3), 2001, 371–385.

Balakrishnan, P. V. & Patton, C. *Negotiation Agenda Strategies for Bargaining with Buying Teams.* Pennsylvania State University Press, 2006.

Bazerman, M. H. & Watkins, M. D. *Predictable Surprises: The Disasters You Should Have Seen Coming.* Harvard Business School Books, 2008.

Bazerman, M. H. Negotiator judgment: a critical look at the rationality assumption. In J. W. Breslin & J. X. Z. Rubin (eds) *Negotiation Theory and Practice. Programme on Negotiation*, Harvard Law School, 1999, 197–209.

Bazerman, M. H. & Neale, M. A. *Negotiating Rationally.* Free Press, 1992.

Black, J. S. & Mendenhall, M. Cross-cultural training effectiveness: a review and theoretical framework for further research. *Academy of Management Review*, 15, 1990, 113–136.

Brett, J. M. *Negotiating Globally*. Jossey-Bass, 2001.

Brett, J. M. & Crotty, S. Culture and negotiation. In P. B. Smith, M. F. Peterson & D. C. Thomas (eds) *The Handbook of Cross-cultural Management Research*. Sage, 2008, 269–283.

Brett, J. M. et al. How to manage your negotiating team. *HBR*, September 2009, 105–109.

Bruns, B. R. & Meinzen-Dick, R. (eds) *Negotiating Water Rights*. International Food Policy Research Institute, 2000.

Carson, T. Second thoughts about bluffing. *Business Ethics Quarterly*, 3, 1993, 317–341.

Chen, M. Negotiating a supply contract in China. *Thunderbird International Business Review*, 50 (4), 2008, 271–281.

Chen, Y-R., Mannix, E. A. & Okumura, T. The importance of who you meet: effects of self – versus other – concerns among negotiators in the United States, the People's Republic of China, and Japan. *Journal of Experimental Social Psychology*, 39 (1), 2003, 1–15.

Daoudy, M. Asymmetric power: negotiating water in the Euphrates and Tigris. *International Negotiation*, 14, 2009, 361–391.

Das, T. K. & Kumar, R. Interpartner negotiations in alliances: a strategic framework. *Management Decisio,n* 49 (8), 2011, 1235–1256.

Druckman, D. Content analysis. In V. A. Kremenyuk (ed.) *International Negotiation: Analysis, Approaches, Issues*. Jossey-Bass, 1991, 244–263.

Dupont, C. A model of the negotiation process with different strategies. In P. Ghauri & J-C. Usunier (eds) *International Business Negotiations*. Pergamon, 2nd ed., 2003.

Fisher, R. & Shapiro, D. *Beyond Reason: Using Emotions as You Negotiate*. Viking Penguin, 2005.

Fisher, R., Ury, W. & Patton, B. *Getting to Yes: Negotiating Agreement without Giving In*. Penguin Books, 1991.

Gates, S. *The Negotiation Book*. Wiley, 2011.

Ghamdi, S. M. Al. The attitude of British firms towards Saudi-British business negotiations: an empirical examination. *International Journal of Management*, 27 (2), 2010, 226–234.

Ghauri, P. & Usunier, J-C. (eds) *International Business Negotiations*. Pergamon, 1996.

Goldman, A. *Settling for More: Mastering Negotiating Strategies and Techniques*. The Bureau of National Affairs, 1991.

Graham, J. L. Culture's influence on business negotiations: an application of Hofstede's and Rokeach's ideas. In F. J. Contractor & P. Lorange, P. (eds) *Cooperative Strategies and Alliances*. Pergamon, 2002, 461–492.

Greenhalgh, L. & Gilkey, R.W. Our game, your rules: developing effective negotiating approaches. In R. Lewicki, J. A. Litterer, D. M. Saunders & J. W. Minton (eds) *Negotiation: Readings, Exercises, and Cases*. Irwin Professional, 1993, 414–423.

Gulliver, P. *Disputes and Negotiations: A Cross-Cultural Perspective*. Academic Press, 1979.

Harinck, F., De Dreu, C. K. W. & Van Vianen, A. E. M. The impact of conflict issues on fixed-pie perceptions, problem solving, and integrative outcomes in negotiation. *Organizational Behavior and Human Decision Processes*, 81 (2), 2000, 329–358.

Janosik, R. J. Rethinking the culture-negotiation link. *Negotiation Journal*, 3, 1987, 385–396.

Kumar, R. Communicative conflict in intercultural negotiations: the case of American and Japanese business negotiations. *International Negotiation*, 4, 1999, 63–78.

Kumar, R. & Worm, V. Institutional dynamics and the negotiation process: comparing India and China. *International Journal of Conflict Management*, 15 (3), 2004, 304–334.

Kupers, W., Mantere, S. & Statler, M. Strategy as storytelling: a phenomenological collaboration. *Journal of Management Inquiry*, 22 (1), 2013, 83–100.

Lax, D. A. & Sebenius, J. K. *The Manager as Negotiator: Bargaining for Cooperation and Competitive Gain*. Free Press, 1986.

Leary, K., Pillemer, J. & Wheeler, M. Negotiating with emotion. *HBR*, 91 (1/2), 2013, 96–103.

Lee, K., Yang, G. & Graham, J. L. Tension and trust in international business negotiations: American executives negotiating with Chinese executives. *Journal of International Business Studies*, 37 (5), 2006, 623–641.

Lewicki, R. & Robinson, R. Ethical and unethical bargaining tactics: an empirical study, *Journal of Business Ethics*, 17, 1988, 665–682.

Lewicki, R. J., Saunders, D. M. & Minton, J. W. *Negotiation*. Irwin/McGraw-Hill, 3rd ed., 1999.

Liu, L. A., Chua, C. H. & Stahl, G. K. Quality of communication experience: definition, measurement, and implications for intercultural negotiations. *Journal of Applied Psychology*, 95 (3), 2010, 469–487.

Locke, E. A. & Latham, G. P. *A Theory of Goal Setting and Task Performance*. Prentice Hall, 1990.

Lukes, S. Power and the battle for hearts and minds. *Millenium*, 33 (3), 2005, 477–494.

Mantere, S. What is organisational strategy? A language-based view. *Journal of Management Studies*, 50 (8), 2013, 1408–1426.

Neale, M. A. & Bazerman, M. H. The effect of framing on confidence and negotiator overconfidence. *Academy of Management Journal*, 28, 1995, 34–49.

Olekalns, M., Brett, J. M. & Weingart, L. R. Phases, transitions and interruptions: modeling processes in multi party negotiations. *International Journal of Conflict Management*, 14 (3/4), 2003,191–211.

Perdue, B. C. & Summers, J. O. Purchasing agents' use of negotiation strategies. *Journal of Marketing Research*, 28 (2), 1991,175–189.

Peterson, R. M. & Lucas, G. H. Expanding the antecedent component of the traditional business negotiation model: pre-negotiation literature review and planning-preparation propositions. *Journal of Marketing Theory and Practice*, 9, 2001, 37–49.

Pruitt, D. G. Strategic choice in negotiation. *American Behavioural Scientist*, 27 (2), 1983, 167–194.

Pruitt, D. G. Strategy and negotiation. In V. A. Kremenyuk (ed.) *International Negotiation: Analysis, Approaches, Issues.* Jossey-Bass, 1991, 78–89.

Ready, K. J. & Tessema, M. T. Perceptions and strategies in the negotiation process: a cross-cultural examination of U.S. and Malaysia. *International Negotiation*, 14, 2009, 493–517.

Reeves, M., Love, C. & Tillmanns, P. Your strategy needs a strategy. *HBR*, 90 (9), 2012, 76–83.

Ryckman, R., Hammer, M., Kaczor, L. & Gold, J. Construction of a personal development competitive attitude scale. *Journal of Personality Assessment*, 66, 1996, 374–385.

Schuster, C. & Copeland, M. Global business exchanges: similarities and differences around the world. *Journal of International Marketing*, 7 (2), 1999, 63–80.

Sebenius, J. K. The hidden challenge of cross-border negotiations. *Harvard Business Review*, 80 (3), 2002, 76–85.

Semnani-Azad, Z. & Adair, W. L. The display of "dominant" nonverbal cues in negotiation: the role of culture and gender. *International Negotiation*, 16 (3), 2011, 451–479.

Spector, B. I. & Wagner, L. M. Negotiating international development. *International Negotiation* 15, 2010, 327–340.

Sull, D. & Eisenhardt, K. M. Simple rules for a complex world. *HBR*, 90 (9), 2012, 69–74.

Tinsley, C. How negotiators get to yes...constellation of strategies used across cultures. *Journal of Applied Psychology*, 86 (4), 2001, 583–593.

Volkema, R. J. & Fleury, M. T. L. Alternative negotiating conditions and the choice of negotiation tactics: a cross-cultural comparison. *Journal of Business Ethics*, 36 (4), 2002, 381–398.

Walton, R. & McKersie, R. *A Behavioural Theory of Labour Negotiations*, Sage, 1965.

Westbrook, K. W. and Arendall, C. S. Negotiator hypercompetitiveness and unethical negotiation strategies: examining the effects of performance goals. *Ethics and Critical Thinking*, 3, 2009, 117–150.

Yukl, G. A., Malone, M. P., Hayslip, B. & Pamin, T. A. The effects of time pressure and issue settlement order on integrative bargaining. *Sociometr,y* 39 (3), 1976, 277–281.

Zartman, I. W. & Rubin, J. Z. Symmetry and asymmetry in negotiation. In I. W. Zartman & J. Z. Rubin (eds) *Power and Negotiation.* University of Michigan Press, 2000.

Zhao, J. J. The Chinese approach to international business negotiation. *The Journal of Business Communication,* 37 (3), 2000, 209–237.

International
Buying/Selling
Negotiations

9

INTRODUCTION

Globalisation is transforming industries and markets around the world and providing new international business opportunities for companies. Companies wishing to expand their international activities can reduce the risks by selling into foreign markets indirectly, through distributors and agents. Many companies succeed in international business by emphasising decentralised and autonomous operations by subsidiaries in one or more foreign countries (Briscoe et al., 2009).Systematic planning is essential for international sales success: the bigger and more complex the transaction, the longer the planning period required (Cellich, 1996). Major international sales deals are usually built on a series of smaller ones. The big final deal is usually a culmination of smaller, earlier negotiations among various interested parties.

International buying and selling is made easier when automated information systems are available. Motorola's automated system allows the company to negotiate over 50 percent of its annual spending online. Negotiating by Internet facilitates the international buying/selling process, allowing it to be completed quickly and without travel. Emails are widely used for negotiating international business deals because of email's response flexibility and the ease of communicating with multiple parties. But email's inability to send and receive nonverbal messages makes it difficult for negotiators to assess the honesty and intentions of the other party – an essential step in building trust between buyer and seller. In many poor countries, there is distrust of foreign business people. Fukuyama (1995) argues that trust of others is linked to economic prosperity. In rich countries, there is trust because deterrents to fraud and malpractice exist in the form of financial services authorities, compliance officers and contract enforcement mechanisms. The importance of trust in international business helps explain why no universal sales appeals are effective at all times in all countries.

Buying and selling *teams* are now commonplace in a wide range of business settings, including advertising, aircraft manufacturing, materials handling, packaging, retailing, steel making and telecoms (Morgan, 2001). In international buying/selling negotiations, teams with their wider knowledge and information-gathering resources have a deeper understanding of the issues to be negotiated than a sole negotiator. A negotiating team has a pool of competencies from which to draw. Moreover, teams take pains to do the necessary research and to adequately prepare for important sales negotiations. International sales teams find it easy to develop options. They can, for instance, produce a range of payment and delivery options to accommodate all possible contracts. A package containing various prices, alternative terms of payment, free servicing, free training, early delivery and so forth could be used to justify a higher price than that offered by competitors. Some negotiating teams, however, fall into the over-optimistic trap and reject offers that are well above the company's best alternative to a negotiated agreement (BATNA). In international sales negotiations, over-optimistic sellers typically value their own possessions more highly than those of others and consequently ask too much for their products or services. As a result they may fail to make a sale.

When many issues have to be negotiated in an international buying/selling negotiation, the negotiators must decide whether to deal with the issues *simultaneously* or *sequentially*. Sequential negotiation restricts the ability of the negotiators to make tradeoffs and may lead to competitive bargaining and a distributive agreement. Simultaneous bargaining, in which all issues are discussed together, is more likely to result in an integrative agreement and higher joint gains.

EFFECTS OF GLOBALISATION

Growth of international sales

Globalisation is the absence of borders and barriers to trade, the ever-increasing interaction, interconnectedness, and integration of people, companies and countries (Briscoe et al., 2009). An important effect of globalisation is the rapid growth of markets worldwide. In Asia, for instance, Singapore, Hong Kong, South Korea and Taiwan have all emerged as important economic powers in recent decades. Goldman Sachs predicted in 2003 that the BRIC countries of Brazil, Russia, India and China would be among the world's dominant economies by 2050. By 2013, China and India were already well on track to overtake the US as the world's biggest car markets. The process of globalisation seems certain to accelerate due to continuing advances in communications technology and growing economic and financial interdependence among countries and regions worldwide.

Driven by globalisation, *international trade* has grown nearly twice as fast as world gross domestic product (GDP) since 1970, and hundreds of thousands of firms have started selling to international markets (Hill, 2002). Markets around the world are being radically transformed and providing new business opportunities for companies. For instance, the World Investment Report ranks Saudi Arabia twelfth in the top 20 host economies for foreign direct investment (FDI) inflows (UNCTAD, 2011). As the volume of international trade increases, so too does the frequency of buying and selling negotiations between people from different countries, so that today nearly all business has an international dimension.

Vietnam is an example of a developing country which has been transformed by globalisation. With 80 million inhabitants, high population growth and rapidly rising per capita incomes, Vietnam offers a large potential market for consumer goods. As Meyer et al. (2006) point out, many Vietnamese consumers associate quality of life with consumption of branded products – and they are willing to pay a premium to acquire them. For foreign companies wishing to expand their international selling efforts, the opportunity is immense. A major problem facing foreign sales negotiators is that accessing the Vietnamese market is difficult and expensive. The marketing and distribution infrastructure is not well established. However, the example of Vietnam illustrates that selling to international markets is potentially more profitable but also more difficult than selling to domestic markets.

International marketing effort

IKEA is the largest global furniture retail firm with some 250 stores in 35 countries. According to Jonsson (2008), IKEA's international growth strategy is to use *replication* as the means to achieve international expansion. In spite of the varied economic and political environments in which the company operates and in spite of all the cultural differences, IKEA implements a *standardised concept and range* in all markets. In the Chinese market, the company is able to offer low-price products in huge volumes by producing locally. The challenges facing companies like IKEA become more complex as the level and scale of its overseas sales activities increases.

International marketing focuses on marketing goods and services across national borders and coordinating marketing activities in multiple countries and regions. Typical goals of international marketing activities are to achieve local, regional and global balance, together with economies of scale and brand (Doyle, 2011). After a certain level of expansion has been reached, effective international marketing may depend on a network of distributors, agents, foreign business partners and suppliers – and overseas subsidiaries. Many Western-based multinational enterprises (MNEs) obtain their results through a network of overseas subsidiaries, strategic alliances and joint venture partners.

On the other hand, many firms which are very successful domestically over-estimate their chances of becoming equally successful in international markets. Hubbard et al. (2007) point to the many Australian companies, for instance, which are successful in domestic markets, but which have overestimated their ability to succeed internationally.

MNEs and international selling

An MNE is a firm with operations in more than one country, with interna-tional sales, and with managers and employees of various national backgrounds (Doh & Teegen, 2003). Most of the revenues of MNEs come from overseas subsidiaries and foreign sales. Large, technologically sophisticated markets are the most likely to have high strategic importance to an MNE, even though markets in some developing countries are easier to penetrate. Generic strategies which may give an MNE competitive advantage both in developing and devel-oped markets are cost leadership, niche operations, and market differentiation (Porter, 1990).

Briscoe et al. (2009) distinguish between multinational MNEs and global MNEs. In *multinational* MNEs, each overseas subsidiary is usually decentralised and becomes nationally self-sufficient. Overseas subsidiaries play a key role in their international marketing plans because of the subsidiaries' superior understanding of local and regional markets. Philips' many self-sufficient national organisations carry out everything from design and production to marketing and sales– a typi-cally multinational strategy which gives Philips competitive advantage in sectors where local responsiveness is essential for international sales success.

In *global* MNEs, little account is taken of national differences. Products for global markets are often standardised, and economies of scale are impor-tant. Global MNEs typically integrate local activities into worldwide opera-tions through communication linkages and interdependencies (Jackson, 2002). Within a global MNE, knowledge and innovations originating from subsidiaries are transferred to other subsidiaries worldwide.

Risk factors

International selling activities entail risk. Accordingly, the *degree of risk* must be carefully assessed before a company launches its products into a new overseas market. Most companies operating abroad, for instance, are exposed to legal risk. In some countries, national laws require foreign companies in the country to take on local partners or to employ a high proportion of local workers. Some countries have "buy local" and other regulations to protect local industry. Such laws and regulations increase the risks and make it difficult for a foreign company to succeed financially. In such countries, a less risky way of selling its products may be through a *local distributor*.

Foreign distributorship agreements

Negotiations with foreign distributors typically involve discussing market conditions, whether import quotas will apply, the distributor's plans for advertising and promotions, and possible political or legal changes which may affect implementation of the agreement. Details of prices, discounts, commissions and exclusivity are normally covered in the agreement, as are the duration of the agreement, the disputes procedure in case of future disputes between the parties, and the national law under which the agreement will be interpreted (McCall, 1996).

When negotiating with a local distributor, a foreign firm has more bargaining power if its products are covered by patent, trademark or copyright. Where this is the case, a company can try to use its bargaining power to attempt to establish a lasting relationship with the distributor since it depends on the distributor for implementing its international marketing plans.

Licensing agreements

Licensing is another low-risk way for a firm to generate income from abroad. For a fee, the licensee gains access to some of the company's patents, trademarks and technology. A licensing agreement may be a simple patent licence or a production or process technology licence. The main advantage of the licensing agreement to the licensor is the income produced by the licence fee. The main advantage to the licensee is that the company gains an immediate position in the market without having to develop its own technology.

The licensing agreement specifies how costs, expenses and licence fees are calculated.

Complicated issues of patent validity and enforceability in foreign markets sometimes require expert advisers to be available during the negotiations. According to Parker (1996), the negotiating team sent out to negotiate a high-value licensing agreement with a foreign company typically comprises a project manager supported by technical, engineering, legal and Internet Protocol (IP) specialists.

INTERNATIONAL SALES NEGOTIATIONS

Cultural influences

Barry et al. (2004) note that buying/selling negotiations between parties from very different cultures often exhibit sources of stress and tension over and above those inherent in the bargaining situation. Additional pressures are caused by differences in nationality, language, nonverbal behaviours, values and patterns of thought. Anecdotal evidence suggests that in international business negotiations, cultural differences between buying and selling teams are usually much less than cultural differences between the teams' countries. A possible reason is that both buying and selling teams tend to share a common international business culture.

Hofstede's (1980) four dimensions have implications for the way in which managers from different countries approach international buying/selling negotiations. Negotiators from *collectivist* countries, for instance, tend to prefer verbal to detailed written agreements, and they are often more concerned with relationship building than with making a quick profit (Schuster & Copeland, 1996). Bagozzi et al. (2003) point out that collectivist negotiators make concessions and unattractive compromises in order to maintain good interpersonal relationships with the opposing team.

Buyers from countries high in *uncertainty-avoidance* may feel overwhelmed if presented with too many options and may postpone making a buying decision (Medvec & Galinsky, 2005). International sales negotiators should perhaps consider limiting the number of options offered to such buyers to no more than two or three. When a two-person sales team representing a Dutch software company conducted buying/selling negotiations with a Greek retailer, the Dutch team presented just two equivalent software packages to the retailer simultaneously:

- a $700,000 package with payment in 30 days;
- the same software for $900,000 with payment in 120 days.

The Greek team responded well to the super-simple approach. After carefully weighing the pros and cons of each option, they committed themselves to purchasing the 30-days package.

Indonesian negotiators

Strong *collectivist* and *power-distance* orientations in Indonesia were revealed by the Hofstede (1980) and GLOBE studies (House, 2004). Gray (2010) describes how these orientations typically play out in international buying/selling negotiations. Indonesian negotiators, for instance, assume that the senior manager on each negotiating team will make all major decisions during the negotiation since Indonesian negotiators have a high degree of respect for specific roles within each negotiating team, such as buyer and seller roles and the role of team leader.

At the table, Indonesian managers can be expected to value and encourage cooperative approaches and, in accordance with Indonesian communicative norms, to use *indirect* communication. Accordingly, Western sales negotiators, with their direct and explicit communication styles, need to use cultural intelligence and read between the lines when bargaining with Indonesian buyers.

Cultural intelligence

Adler & Graham (1989) found that managers involved in international business negotiations effortlessly adapted their "normal" behaviour to match the expectations of the other side, thereby demonstrating cultural intelligence. Cultural intelligence is the ability to adjust one's behaviour and interact effectively with people from diverse cultures (Thomas, 2006). Johnson et al. (2006) argue that people with cultural intelligence are flexible and have

- cognitive skills that allow them to function effectively in various cultural contexts;
- motivational impetus to adapt to a different cultural environment;
- the ability to engage in adaptive behaviours in international business negotiations and other social contexts.

A Canadian executive demonstrated cultural intelligence by adapting to the expectations of his Brazilian counterparts during a business trip to Brazil. Colleagues in Canada told him that Brazilians prefer to do business with people they like and trust, and who are outgoing and easy to get on with. The Canadian, normally an unassuming, unassertive person, realised that during the trip he would need to adjust his normal communication style.

> Subsequently, in Brazil he made a real effort to be outgoing and friendly with the people he met while negotiating various business deals. His willingness to adjust his "normal" style laid the foundation for what turned out to be a commercially successful business trip.

Business practices

Negotiators from different countries have different business practices, and the differences impinge on international selling efforts. Cold-call selling, for instance, is an accepted practice in North America, but not in cultures that emphasise relationships, such as those of Latin America, Asia and the Middle East. Being aware of practices that are expected– and others that are not acceptable–can mean the difference between success and failure for foreign sales negotiators in China (Chen, 2008). For companies about to enter sales negotiations in a foreign country, a way of reducing the risks is to make arrangements with a local consultant to give advice on such matters as

- business practices which are required – and those which are unacceptable – in the country;
- degree of formality required in negotiating sessions;
- methods of decision-making likely to be used in negotiations;
- important points of etiquette that need to be observed in negotiating sessions;

- whether government officials will need to approve any agreement that is made and, if so, the length of time this will take.

PERSONALITY FACTORS

Personality factors affect the interaction and outcomes of international sales negotiations (Kale, 1996). Latin American or Arab buyers, for instance, may base a buying decision more on the personality of the sales negotiator than on the quality of the product (Muna, 1980). Graham (1985) points out that when a foreign seller and a local buyer first meet and attempt to establish rapport in advance of formal negotiations, *interpersonal attractiveness* can make a lasting positive impact and lead to cooperative behaviour in the actual negotiation.

The relationship between extroversion and sales performance has been noted by many researchers. However, extroverted sales negotiators may not be adept at eliciting information from members of a foreign buying team about their needs and preferences. In pre-negotiation social events, for instance, extroverted managers may not be good at sizing up or deducing strategies likely to be used by the buying team because the managers may be too busy performing an active, self-conscious social role.

Low-risk and high-risk negotiators

In international buying/selling negotiations, both positive, risk-seeking behaviour and negative, risk-averse behaviour can be predicted (Kahneman & Tversky, 1979). Positive, risk-seeking behaviour is likely when individuals are keenly aware of large potential gains. Negative, risk-avoiding behaviour can be predicted when individuals are aware of and are evaluating possible losses.

Managers conducting buying/selling negotiations in a foreign country can reduce the risks of failing to achieve negotiating goals by remembering that there are many possible ways – in addition to face-to-face negotiations with prospective buyers – to secure an international sales deal. An export sales manager could, for instance, search for alternative buyers or better prices on the Internet while continuing to negotiate face-to-face with the current foreign sales prospect.

Winning trust

A challenge that confronts any international buying/selling team is winning the trust of foreign clients. In international business negotiations, trust is the extent to which the negotiators believe in the good intentions of the negotiating partner (Rao & Schmidt, 1998). Trust influences the negotiation process by encouraging buyers and sellers to share information and to reach agreement. But in poor countries there is often *distrust* of foreigners, and winning the trust of prospective customers is more difficult for foreign sales negotiators than it is in the developed world. Fukuyama (1995) points out that trust of others is linked to economic prosperity. In rich countries, there is trust because deterrents to fraud and malpractice exist in the form of financial services authorities, compliance officers and contract enforcement mechanisms.

The importance of trust in international business helps explain why no universal sales appeals are effective at all times in all countries. For instance, the most trusted brands and the most frequently purchased in countries worldwide are local brands. Thus the most trusted and popular car in France is Renault, for instance. In Germany and Austria, it is Volkswagen; in the Czech Republic, Skoda; in India, Maruti and so on.

A further complication for companies wishing to sell more of their products in foreign markets is that consumer attitudes towards foreign products are often influenced by ethnocentrism. Highly ethnocentric consumers are usually older people who believe that buying imported products damages their domestic economy and causes unemployment (Usunier & Lee, 2005).

Case Study

MINI-CASE: Arab-style negotiation

Working in small groups, study the following situation and answer the question that follows. Each group may then make a brief presentation of its answer to the other groups for their comments.

The focus of much research has been on examining the negotiating behaviour of a few countries, notably the US, China and Japan. Only limited research has been done on how buying/selling negotiations are conducted in the Arab world (Weir, 2000). This is in spite of the fact that the Middle East is an important economic region due to its natural resources and its strategic importance. The World Investment Report (UNCTAD, 2011) ranks one country in the region, Saudi Arabia, twelfth in the top 20 host economies for FDI inflows.

International business people need to have a good understanding of how culture affects the way in which negotiations are conducted and business decisions taken in such an important economic region. Khakhar & Rammal (2013) address this need by exploring key cultural and socioeconomic factors that influence the negotiation process between Arab negotiators and foreign counterparts. The researchers interviewed 30 Arab managers in Lebanon with experience in conducting international business negotiations. As English is widely spoken in the Lebanese business community, there was no need to conduct the interviews in Arabic.

At the time of the interviews, political conflict and uncertainty was influencing business activities in Lebanon, and the managers said that sometimes they had to hold important commercial negotiations with foreign firms in another country in the Arab world, such as the United Arab Emirates, where there were no signs of political instability, and where there was a more favourable climate for deal making and relationship building.

Wasta at work

In the Middle East, wasta (networks and connections) is similar to guanxi in Chinese business culture (Hutchings & Weir, 2006). The researchers found that using wasta is an accepted business practice in the Arab world, and that business relationships are strengthened by its use. In the Arab world, negotiations are conducted with several businesses simultaneously, and usually the organisation with the strongest wasta connections is the one that secures the deal. One manager explained that the connections he had in the Ministry of Economy and Trade helped him speed up registration procedures for a foreign business partner that would normally take several weeks.

Role of trust

The interview data suggests that in the Arab world the concept of trust is linked to the size of company with which negotiations are being held. Many managers said they would trust a large foreign MNE more than they would a smaller company looking to enter the Arab region. The managers thought that trust precedes business in most countries in the Middle East, and the managers themselves tended to spend much time and effort at the pre-negotiation stage building a personal relationship with foreign negotiators, and considered this investment in relationship building as a vital part of the negotiation process.

Several respondents made the point that they found it difficult create a trusting personal relationship with negotiators from the US and UK because of their business-like, time-conscious attitudes. This business-like approach allowed formal negotiations to begin quickly, but because of the lack of a personal relationship and trust, the Arab negotiating team normally required much more detailed information about the options that were on the table before an agreement could be reached. As a result, more time was required to complete the negotiations than would have been the case had some time initially been spent on building a personal relationship between the negotiators.

Decision-making

The Arab negotiators interviewed by Khakhar & Rammal (2013) deviated sharply from the emotional pattern of decision-making and persuasion often ascribed to negotiators in the Middle East. Glenn et al. (1977), for instance, contrast the emotional persuasion styles used by negotiators in the Middle East with the rational styles used in the US. The Arab managers interviewed by Khakhar & Rammal (2013), however, made their decisions rationally rather than emotionally, and took into consideration the various contextual factors of negotiations. They carefully assessed business opportunities and potential financial outcomes.

Direct communication

The Arab negotiators also deviated from stereotype by using direct rather than indirect communication. In negotiations with a foreign negotiating team, they would, for instance, openly state the importance of their business networks and how their opponents could benefit from these networks. Information provided by the managers revealed that the concessions they made in international business negotiations were carefully planned. The managers made sure that they did not deviate too much from their desired outcomes and goals.

Monochromic approach

Unlike Hall's (1966) classification of Arab countries as polychronic societies in which deadlines are not adhered to, the Arab managers – in another deviation from stereotype – tended to display monochronic attitudes about meeting negotiating deadlines. According to Hall, negotiators in polychronic societies engage in multiple activities simultaneously and view time schedules as flexible. For instance, they will permit a negotiating session to continue until everything has been covered.

Source: Khakhar & Rammal (2013)

Questions:

1. *Arab managers conduct buying/selling negotiations with several companies simultaneously. What are the advantages of conducting simultaneous negotiations? What steps could a foreign sales team take to improve its chances of securing the deal?*
2. *When conducting buying/selling negotiations with Arab negotiators, the business-like approach adopted by many Western negotiators can be counterproductive. Explain why.*
3. *"Using wasta is an accepted business practice in the Arab world." What is wasta? What are the advantages of using it, as seen through the eyes of Arab managers?*

NEGOTIATING TEAMS

Pool of competencies

Both in domestic and international buying/selling negotiations, multifunctional *teams* of negotiators are becoming increasingly common (Balakrishnan & Patton, 2006). A survey of 192 organisations in North America, for instance, found that buying teams were used in domestic and international business negotiations by three out of four firms (Pelletier, 2004). Individual members of the teams were highly specialised and played specific roles in a negotiation (e.g. devil's advocate, lead negotiator).Team size varies according to contextual factors. Stewart & Keown's (1989) survey of Chinese trading companies found that Chinese firms send large negotiating teams consisting of highly trained individuals to conduct buying/selling negotiations with Western companies.

The use of buying and selling teams by companies is now commonplace in a wide range of international business settings, including advertising, aircraft manufacturing, materials handling, packaging, retailing, steel making and telecoms (Morgan, 2001). A key advantage of a negotiating team is that it has a pool of competencies from which to draw, whereas a sole negotiator has only his or her own resources to rely on. Negotiating teams can effectively collaborate to break down a complex international business negotiation, and the wide capacity base of the team reduces the amount of blunder in negotiations. A team's wider knowledge and information-gathering resources give it a deeper understanding of the issues to be negotiated. Moreover, because of peer pressure, teams take pains to prepare adequately for negotiations and do the necessary research.

Sole negotiators versus teams

A sole international sales negotiator is at a considerable disadvantage when bargaining against a team of foreign buyers due to the inherent imbalance of bargaining power and resources. For example, when facing a three-member buying team, each of them responsible for dealing with a particular negotiating issue, a sole negotiator must decide whether to hold a separate negotiation with each team member or to negotiate with all three members at the same time. If the seller opts for three separate negotiations, he or she has an additional decision to make – the order in which the separate meetings should be held. If, on the other hand, the seller opts for a single negotiation, he or she may be forced to wait in an expensive foreign hotel while a meeting can be arranged at which all three members of the buying team can be present.

Balakrishnan & Patton (2006) point out that such decisions taken by a sole negotiator affect both the process and the outcomes of an international buying/selling negotiation. If the seller takes on the whole buying team in a single negotiation, he or she has a further decision to make, that is, whether the negotiating issues should be negotiated *simultaneously* or *sequentially. Sequential bargaining* restricts the ability of the two sides to make tradeoffs and is likely to lead to competitive interaction and a distributive agreement (Mannix et al., 1989). *Simultaneous bargaining*, in which all of the issues are discussed together, is more likely to result in an integrative agreement and higher joint profits for the parties.

Case Study

MINI-CASE: Sole negotiators

Two sales negotiators from a Western country are about to enter into negotiations with the same large state-owned organisation in the Middle East. They have identical proposals and packages to offer, and their warranty arrangements are very similar. However, the ways in which they approach the task of securing the deal are very different.

The first negotiator knows very little about the culture or the organisation, but he is an experienced presenter and puts a lot of effort into developing a slick PowerPoint presentation which puts across the key features of the package he is offering. He is quietly confident that his proposal will speak for itself.

The second negotiator's approach is different. He makes a great effort to learn about the culture and the organisation, including the organisation's style of negotiation. During the meeting, the information he has acquired enables him to take a customer-focused approach and show that he understands the organisation's needs.

Subsequently, the second negotiator is awarded the contract.

Questions:

1. *Where did the first negotiator go wrong?*
2. *Why did the second negotiator win the contract?*
3. *In an international sales negotiation, what are the different components of a "customer-centred" approach?*

EFFICIENCY FACTORS

Automated systems

Robins et al. (2002) point to Walmart's world-class capabilities in managing mass retailing operations worldwide, including supply chain management, logistics, inventory management and automated information systems. An important function of the company's automated systems is to facilitate numerous large-scale buying negotiations by obtaining accurate and timely information about quantities, prices, delivery times and other details.

Automated systems improve the speed and efficiency of carrying out multiple negotiations with buyers or sellers worldwide. An example of an automated system is ECN Pro, which handles interactions in which a buyer has to negotiate with numerous suppliers. The system is able to split an order to more than one supplier, thereby achieving a better negotiation payoff for the buyer (Wong &

Fang, 2010). An offer is negotiated using a few simple criteria such as product, quantity, price, sales tax and so forth. An order is then produced, and payment made.

Motorola's experience

In the past, teams of Motorola commodity managers met with teams from all the potential suppliers for a particular commodity group, often over several weeks (Metty et al., 2005). Negotiations frequently entailed international travel and its costs for both the firm and its suppliers. Once back in the office, the commodity manager would create elaborate spreadsheets to model different award scenarios. But that was before Motorola transformed its supplier negotiation processes.

Transformation was achieved by implementing a complete supplier negotiation software platform (MINT), which changed the way in which the firm conducts negotiations with its suppliers. The effect was to move Motorola away from loosely coordinated efforts by individual sectors towards conducting global negotiations with suppliers jointly across business units. The company has been able to cut the cost of negotiating purchases worldwide, while maintaining relationships with more than 1,000 suppliers. The negotiation software allows Motorola to negotiate over 50 percent of its annual spending online. Online requests for quotations lead to suppliers' bidding against one another, usually on the Internet. Internet negotiation speeds up the buying/selling process, and allows it to be completed quickly and without travel.

The case demonstrates that managers do not necessarily have to travel to another country and carry out major international business negotiations face-to-face. International buying/selling negotiations can be conducted efficiently by using automated systems, supported, where necessary, by fax, letter, phone, videoconference, telex and email.

Careful planning

The planning phase is usually much longer for international than for domestic buying/selling negotiations because assembling the preliminary information takes so much longer. Thus the bigger the transaction, the longer the planning period required (Cellich,1996). Large international sales deals are usually built on a series of smaller ones, with the big final deal being a culmination of smaller, earlier negotiations among various interested parties. Lax & Sebenius (2012) describe how, when Boeing set out to sell $11billion worth of aircraft to Air India in 2005, the company's planning effort incorporated initial negotiations to build support with Boeing's internal departments, banks, export agencies, aircraft leasing companies and the Indian government.

Appropriate communication method

A wide range of communication technologies, including automated systems, is increasingly used to support international buying/selling activities. In an international management workshop organised by a university, an Australian sales manager explained to participants how he successfully negotiated a major contract with a Taiwanese company using computer-based document sharing to support the bargaining.

In international buying/selling negotiations which are conducted entirely by phone or email, personal relationship may need to be boosted by friendly introductory chitchat, which helps a human connection to be made even in the absence of any face-to-face presence. As Blume (2010) points out, when two negotiators are in different countries, what each of them most needs is to establish a comfort level with the other person before serious negotiations begin. A major disadvantage of using email to negotiate a sales deal is the medium's inability to send and receive nonverbal messages, which makes it difficult to develop trust and a personal relationship with the other party.

Case Study

MINI-CASE: "Cloud" support for negotiators

Managers and design and construction professionals employed by a global contractor based in the UK spend much of their time negotiating deals with potential partners and clients overseas. Experience has shown them that, when conducting negotiations in a foreign country, they often need to have instant access to schedules and other large files, cost estimates, photos, drawings and other kinds of information in order to participate effectively in the negotiations.

For years, the company relied on an internal server to upload and download all these documents. But the system was slow and difficult to use, and – worse still – was rapidly running out of capacity. That prompted the company to make an arrangement with a provider of cloud-based file sharing. The company's negotiators immediately benefited from the change.Resources stored by the provider are easily and instantly accessed via a web browser or applications developed for computers, tablets and smart phones. Now, when the company's negotiators travel abroad and try to sell the company's services to foreign clients, as long as they have an Internet-connected device, they can immediately access all their files when required for use in the negotiations.

Source: McAfee (2011)

Questions:

1. *"In international sales negotiations, it is more important to provide accurate information than to produce unchecked information instantly on demand."Under what circumstances should this rule be ignored?*
2. *"Much of the information needed in international buying/selling negotiations can be anticipated before negotiations begin." To what extent is this a true statement?*

CLIENT-CENTRED OPTIONS

Options, designed to meet buyers' needs, help sales negotiators sell their products. In the context of business negotiations with overseas clients, customer-centred options might be

- various payment plan options;
- an extended warranty option;
- packaging options;
- packages with and without free installation;
- delivery options.

Delivery options, for instance, might be based on free on board (FOB) or cost, insurance and freight (CIF) alternatives. An FOB price is much lower than the CIF price. Packaging options might be for bulk packaging and unit packaging. Bulk packaging is much less expensive than unit packaging. The price quoted for the outright purchase of an expensive piece of machinery might at first be rejected by a buyer in a developing country – but not when free initial training is added to the package.

Alternatively, the sales negotiator might table a "total package" containing alternative prices, various terms of payment, servicing and training options, packaging options, delivery options and so on. If the buyer is interested in the package in principle, each component of the total package can then be negotiated so that the final negotiated agreement is the product of the agreements made on the separate components.

Influence of the first offer

In international business negotiations, first offers – irrespective of which side makes them – act as anchors. According to Mussweiler et al. (2000), anchors in the shape of initial numerical values sway the judgment of both novice and experienced negotiators. First offers anchor negotiation counterparts around a *starting value* which influences both the counteroffer and the final settlement price (Galinsky et al., 2005). Attention to an anchor, such as the opening offer price, is precisely what underlies the influence of the opening offer. Mussweiler & Strack (1999) identify the mechanism involved. A high opening offer (for a car, say) focuses the buyer's attention on attractive features of the car such as prestige or high resale value. A low opening offer, on the other hand, focuses attention on negative features of the car such as manual locks, lack of power steering and so forth.

Studies conducted by Gunia et al. (2013) demonstrated that negotiators achieve better outcomes when making the first offer than when receiving it. From this it can be inferred that many international business negotiations agreements favour the first mover – which helps explain why final prices are typically higher when sellers make the first offer than when buyers do. Thus Gunia et al.'s (2013) studies challenge Dell & Boswell's (2009) claim that going second is the wiser move for negotiators. It is not known, however, whether or not the first-offer effect extends across cultures.

Ceiling and floor prices

Know your negotiating limits, Cellich (1996) advises buying/selling negotiators, that is, your ceiling price if you are a buyer, and your floor price if you are a seller. An international sales negotiator's first offer sets the ceiling of the price range, and negotiators who are uncertain about the state of the market often wait for the opposition to make the first offer.

Negotiators' responses to offers vary, however. American and Japanese negotiators, for instance, respond to an opponent's opening offer in different ways (Janosik, 1987). Americans respond very quickly, but Japanese negotiators wait for additional information before committing themselves. They defer committing to a particular approach or making major concessions until the opponent has compromised. Kazuo (1979, 541) compared Japanese and Chinese negotiating tactics and found that Japanese managers were unable to maintain a wait-and-see attitude when faced with Chinese insistence that the Japanese present their own proposal first.

Avoid over-optimism

An important factor in international buyer/seller negotiations is the parties' perception of the price established through bargaining. If the price is perceived as fair and equitable by both parties, the effect is to increase buyer satisfaction but without incurring a negative effect on the seller's profit (Maxwell et al., 1999).

Some international sales negotiators, however, fall into the over-optimistic trap. This leads them to set too high a price on their products or services and to reject offers that it are not in their company's best interests to reject, offers, for instance, that are well above the company's BATNA best alternative to a negotiated agreement. Lax & Sebenius (1986) argue that a price that is better than both companies' BATNAs can be considered to be a mutually satisfactory agreement.

Medvec & Galinsky (2005) explain seller over-optimism by pointing out that sellers, being human, typically value their own possessions more highly than the possessions of others. In international sales negotiations, a sales negotiator may demonstrates this tendency by asking too much for the products or services offered. The result is that, even after making concessions, the negotiator fails to make a sale.

Case Study

MINI-CASE: French-Brazilian bargaining

A Brazilian food processing firm embarks on negotiations with a French engineering company regarding a technology package consisting of machinery and equipment to be supplied by the French company. Partly because the Brazilian firm is experiencing cash flow problems, the Brazilian negotiating team insists that the price proposed by the French company is far too high. The French team dismisses the Brazilians' argument, and simply reiterates that in terms of value for money, the French equipment is highly competitive.

It is only when the Brazilians threaten to break off negotiations that the French team is startled into formulating and tabling a win-win proposal that the French believe will create value for both sides. The price will remain unchanged, as specified in the draft contract. But in exchange, the Brazilians will be required to make a down payment of only 5 percent as opposed to the 20 percent specified in the draft contract.

The lead negotiator on the French team argues that by demonstrating flexibility in the terms of payment, they have, in effect, eased the Brazilians' cash flow problems, and on this basis the Brazilian company is strongly urged to go ahead with the deal. The Brazilians, however, are not sure what to do and reserve a decision until the following day.

Questions:

1. Should the Brazilians accept the French offer? If not, why not?
2. What additional information should the Brazilians demand from the French which would help them to reach a firm decision?
3. What additional concessions might the French team make to convince the Brazilians to sign an agreement?
4. If the deal goes ahead, how should the French company prepare technical personnel for the assignment? What would be the role in Brazil of French technical staff?

SALES NEGOTIATIONS IN CHINA

Chinese negotiators

Chinese firms often send large negotiating teams to conduct negotiations with Western companies (Stewart & Keown, 1989). A third of their time in negotiations might be spent discussing technical specifications and another third discussing price. Zhao (2000) investigated what Chinese negotiators are trained to do by examining China's international business negotiation textbooks and interviewing Chinese negotiators. Virtually all textbooks describe and recommend *cooperative win-win negotiating strategies*. Such strategies are based on traditional Chinese values such as nurturing mutual trust and long-term relationships, and working cooperatively. These cultural dimensions have repeatedly been shown to be important to successful negotiations with Chinese managers (Ralston et al., 1992).

Negotiations between parties from very different cultures – between Western and Chinese negotiators, for instance –often generate tension and anxiety caused by differences in language, nonverbal behaviours, values and patterns of thought (Barry et al., 2004). Yet according to Kumar (2004), Chinese negotiators may consider the expression of emotions by their Western counterparts as dangerous, irrelevant or juvenile. Such reactions may create additional tension, which can affect the outcomes of a negotiation.

Tough bargaining

Chinese negotiating behaviour usually entails slow decision-making and tough bargaining, with price reductions of as much as 50 percent being demanded as the price of signing an agreement (Hout & Ghemawat, 2010). Moreover, long delays in reaching agreement are common because of bureaucratic procedures and the need to get approval from top-level officials or managers. In the early stages of a negotiation, the Chinese stress personal interaction and friendship, but when serious negotiation begins, the Chinese become highly bureaucratised and require coordination with layers of hierarchical committees and senior officials (Pye, 1986).

At the end of buying/selling negotiations in China, a draft agreement may have to be revised so that it reflects the needs and interests of the Chinese government. It may need, for instance, to include plans to provide free training for the Chinese company's workforce. Western managers in China to carry out long-term negotiations with the Chinese invariably find that they need to establish *guanxi* (connection) with provincial branches of the Communist Party in order to achieve results. Faure (2000) points out that local, provincial and even central government authorities can strongly influence negotiations between Chinese firms and foreign sellers.

The right products

Understanding the Chinese mindset and possessing a knowledge of Chinese culture no doubt contribute to sales success in China, but today a foreign company's ability to offer technologically advanced products is more important. As Stalk & Michael (2011) point out, Chinese companies have already displaced global names and become market leaders in some high-growth markets in China. Examples are Midea in consumer appliances and Xizi in elevators. The rise of China's own markets makes the country less dependent on Western companies than in the past, and successful selling to the Chinese depends on offering the right products and services to the right customers at the right price.

Concessions

Foreign sales negotiators in China should plan in advance the concessions they might make in a negotiation, calculate their cost, and decide how and when to make them. Making concessions is interpreted by Chinese and other Asian companies as a sign of cooperation and willingness to find a mutually agreeable outcome (Chen, 2008).A few inexpensive concessions made in the final stages of negotiations with the Chinese can help to close the deal.

The agreement

In shaping a sales agreement, many Western negotiators first try to win agreement on just a few proposals and work to build up to a wider, more comprehensive agreement, but Chinese negotiators do it the other way round (Sebenius, 2002). Chinese negotiators generally prefer to first seek agreement on general principles and afterwards work through the details.

KEY POINTS

1. National laws may require a foreign company to take on local partners or employ a high proportion of local workers. Some countries have "buy local" and other regulations to protect local industry. Such laws increase the risk of operating in the country and make it more difficult for a foreign company to be financially successful. The risks of selling into foreign markets can be reduced by selling through local distributors and agents.
2. Buying and selling teams are commonplace in a wide range of international business settings, including advertising, aircraft manufacturing, materials handling, packaging, retailing, steel making and telecoms (Morgan, 2001). A negotiating team has a pool of competencies from which to draw, whereas a sole negotiator has only him- or herself to rely on. Teams, with their wider

knowledge and information-gathering resources, are likely to have a more thorough understanding of the issues to be negotiated.

3. Automated systems improve the speed and efficiency of carrying out multiple negotiations worldwide. Motorola's system allows the company to negotiate over 50 percent of its annual spending online. Online requests for quotations lead to suppliers' bidding against one another, usually on the Internet. Internet negotiation accelerates the buying/selling process, allowing it to be completed quickly and without travel.

4. Emails are widely used for negotiating international business deals because of email's response flexibility and ease of communicating with multiple parties. Email also offers easy storage and retrieval of messages. But email's inability to send and receive nonverbal messages makes it difficult to assess the honesty of the other party – a characteristic that can contribute to questionable bargaining behaviour such as bluffs, threats and exaggerations.

5. Managers from collectivist countries are often concerned with relationship building. They make concessions and unattractive compromises to maintain good interpersonal relationships, and often they prefer verbal to detailed written agreements. The example shows how the cultural characteristics of buyers and sellers influence international buying/selling negotiations. Buyers from high uncertainty-avoidance countries may feel overwhelmed if presented with too many options and should be offered no more than two or three.

6. Satisfaction of the parties with an international sales negotiation depends largely on whether the *price* established by bargaining is seen as fair. If it is perceived by both parties as fair and equitable, buyer satisfaction is increased, but without incurring a negative effect on the seller's profit. Some international sales negotiators fall into the over-optimistic trap and set too high a price on their products. They reject offers that it is not in their company's best interests to reject, for example, offers that are well above the company's BATNA.

7. Generating options contribute to successful international sales negotiations. Price is only one of the issues to be negotiated. Options designed to meet buyers' needs typically include alternative payment plan options, extended warranty options, delivery options, packaging options and so forth. Packaging options, for instance, might be based on bulk packaging and unit packaging. Bulk packaging is much less expensive than unit packaging.

8. Sales teams must try to win the trust of their foreign customers. But *distrust* of foreigners is a characteristic of many poor countries. Fukuyama (1995) shows that trust of others is linked to economic prosperity. In rich countries, there is trust because deterrents to fraud and malpractice exist in the form of financial services authorities, compliance officers and contract enforcement mechanisms. The importance of trust in international business helps explain why no universal sales appeals are effective at all times and in all countries.

9. As a result of globalisation, industries and markets around the world are being radically transformed and providing new international business opportunities for companies. Many MNEs succeed in international markets by emphasising decentralised and autonomous operations within wholly owned subsidiaries. Other MNEs integrate local activities of overseas subsidiaries into worldwide operations through communication linkages and interdependencies.

10. IKEA's international expansion strategy is based on the replication principle. In spite of the many different economic and political environments in which the company operates, and in spite of all the cultural differences, IKEA implements a standardised concept and range in all markets. In the Chinese market, the company is able to offer low-price products in huge volumes by producing locally.

QUESTIONS FOR DISCUSSION AND WRITTEN ASSIGNMENTS

1. "The most trusted brands and the most frequently purchased in countries worldwide are local brands."When negotiating with foreign buyers, what can a company's sales negotiators do to overcome this buy-local tendency?
2. What are the advantages and disadvantages of using only email to conduct buying/selling negotiations between managers or entrepreneurs in different countries?
3. When participating in international buying/selling negotiations a sole sales negotiator is at a disadvantage when faced with a small team of buyers. Explain why.
4. Describe the risks and opportunities of selling to international markets. Identify several ways in which the risks can be reduced.

BIBLIOGRAPHY

Adler, N. J.&Graham, J. L. Cross-cultural interactions: the international comparison fallacy. *Journal of International Business Studies*, 20 (3), 1989, 515–538.

Bagozzi, R. B., Verbeke, W. &Gavino Jr., J. C. Culture moderates the self-regulation of shame and its effects on performance: the case of salespersons in the Netherlands and the Philippines. *Journal of Applied Psychology*, 88 (2), 2003, 219–233.

Balakrishnan, P. V. & Patton, C. *Negotiation Agenda Strategies for Bargaining with Buying Teams*. Pennsylvania State University Press, 2006.

Barry, B., Fulmer, I. S. & Van Kleef, G. A. I laughed, I cried, I settled: the role of emotion in negotiation. In M. J. Geldand & J. M. Brett (eds) *The Handbook of Negotiation and Culture*. Stanford Business Books, 2004, 71–91.

Blume, A. *Your Virtual Success*. Career Press, 2010.

Briscoe, D. R., Schuler, R. S. & Claus, L. *International Human Resource Management*. Routledge, 3rd ed., 2009.

Cellich, C. Preparing for your business negotiations. *International Trade Forum*, (2), 1996, 20–25.

Charles, M. Language matters in global communication. *Journal of Business Communication*, 44, 2007, 260–283.

Chen, M. Negotiating a supply contract in China. *Thunderbird International Business Review*, 50 (4), 2008, 271–281.

Dell, D. & Boswell, J. *Never Make the First Offer (Except When You Should)*. Portfolio/Penguin, 2009.

Doh, J. P. & Teegen, H. *Globalisation and NGOs*. Praeger, 2003.

Doyle, C. *A Dictionary of Marketing*. Oxford University Press, 2011.

Faure, G. O. Negotiations to set up joint ventures in China. *International Negotiation*, 5, 2000, 157–189.

Firth, A. The discursive accomplishment of normality. On "lingua franca" English and conversation analysis. *Journal of Pragmatics*, 26(3), 1996, 237–259.

Fukuyama, F. *Trust: The Social Virtues and the Creation of Prosperity*. Hamish Hamilton, 1995.

Galinsky, A. D. et al. Regulatory focus at the bargaining table: promoting distributive and integrative success. *Personality and Social Psychology Bulletin*, 31, 2005, 1087–1098.

Graham, J. L. Cross-cultural marketing negotiations: a laboratory experiment. *Marketing Science*, 4 (2),1985, 130–146.

Gray, N. H. Bahasa, batik, and bargaining: an exploratory study of the negotiation styles and behaviors of Indonesian manager. *Journal of Transnational Management*, 15, 2010, 215–228.

Gunia, B. C. et al. The remarkable robustness of the first-offer effect: across culture, power, and issues. *Personality and Social Psychology Bulletin*, 39 (12), 2013, 1547–1558.

Hall, E. T. *The Hidden Dimension*. Doubleday, 1966.

Hill, C. W. L. *International Business: Competing in the Global Marketplace-Postscript 2002*. Irwin/McGraw-Hill, 3rd ed., 2002.

Hofstede, G. *Culture's Consequences: International Differences in Work-related Values*. Sage, 1980.

House, R. J. et al. (eds) *Culture, Leadership and Organisations: The GLOBE study of 62 Societies*. Sage, 2004.

Hout, T. M. & Ghemawat, P. China vs. the world: whose technology is it? *HBR*, 2010, 95–103.

Hubbard, G. et al. *The First XI: Winning Organisations in Australia*. Wiley, 2007.

Janosik, R. J. Rethinking the culture-negotiation link. *Negotiation Journal*, 3, 1987, 385–396.

Johnson, J. P., Lenartowicz, T. & Apud, S. Cross-cultural competence in international business: toward a definition and a model. *Journal of International Business Studies*, 37 (4), 2006, 525–543.

Jonsson, A. A transnational perspective on knowledge sharing: lessons learned from IKEA's entry into Russia, China and Japan. *The International Review of Retail, Distribution and Consumer Research,*18 (1), 2008, 17–44.

Kahneman, D. & Tversky, A. Prospect theory: an analysis of decision under risk. *Econometrica*, 47, 1979, 263–291.

Kale, S. How national culture, organizational culture and personality impact buyer-seller interactions. In P. N. Ghauri & J. C. Usunier (eds) *International Business Negotiations*. Pergamon, 1996.

Kazuo, O. How the "in scrutables" negotiate with the "in scrutables."*China Quarterly*, 79, 1979, 529–552.

Khakhar, P. & Rammal, H. G. Culture and business networks: International business negotiations with Arab managers. *International Business Review*, 22, 2013, 578–590.

Kumar, R. Brahmanical idealism, anarchical individualism, and the dynamics of Indian negotiating behaviour. *International Journal of Cross-cultural Management*, 4 (1), 2004, 39–58.

Lax, D. A. & Sebenius, J. K. Deal Making 2.0. A guide to complex negotiations. *HBR*, 90 (11), 2012, 92–100.

Lax, D. A. & Sebenius, J. K. *The Manager as Negotiator*. Free Press, 1986.

Mannix, E. A., Thompson, L. L. & Bazerman, M. H. Negotiation in small groups, *Journal of Applied Psychology*, 74, 1989, 508–517.

Maxwell, S., Nye, P. & Maxwell, N. Less pain, some gain: the effects of priming fairness in price negotiations. *Psychology & Marketing*, 16 (7), 1999, 545–563.

McAfee, A. What every CEO needs to know about the cloud. *HBR*, 89 (11), 2011, 124–132.

McCall, J. B. Negotiating sales export transactions and agency agreements. In P. Ghauri & J- C. Usunier (eds) *International Business Negotiations*. Pergamon, 1996, 187–202.

Medvec, V. H. & Galinsky, A. D. Putting more on the table: how making multiple offers can increase the final value of the deal. *Negotiation*, April 2005, 3–5.

Metty, T. et al. Reinventing the supplier negotiation process at Motorola. *Interfaces*, 35 (1), 2005, 7–23.

Meyer, K. E. et al. Doing business in Vietnam. *Thunderbird International Business Review*, 48 (2), 2006, 263–290.

Morgan, J. P. Cross-functional buying: why teams are hot. *Purchasing*, 130 (7), 2001, 27–32.

Muna, F. A. *The Arab Executive*. Macmillan, 1980.

Mussweiler, T. & Strack, F. Hypothesis-consistent testing and semantic priming in the anchoring paradigm. *Journal of Experimental Social Psychology*, 35, 1999, 136–164.

Mussweiler, T., Strack, F. & Pfeiffer, T. Overcoming the inevitable anchoring effect: considering the opposite compensates for selective accessibility. *Personality and Social Psychology Bulletin*, 26, 2000, 1142–1150.

Ohmae, K. Managing in a borderless world. *HBR*, May-June 1989, 152–161.

Parker, V. Negotiating licensing agreements. In P. Ghauri & J-C. Usunier (eds) *International Business Negotiations*. Pergamon, 1996, 203–229.

Pelletier, B. Process makes perfect. *Packaging Machinery Technology*, 1, 2004, 68–73.

Porter, M. E. *The Competitive Advantage of Nations*. Free Press, 1990.

Pye, L. W. (1986). *Chinese Commercial Negotiating Style*. Cambridge, MA: Rand Corporation

Ralston, D. A., Gustafson, D. J., Elsass, P., Cheung, M. & Terpstra, R. H. Eastern values: A comparison of managers in the United States, Hong Kong, and the People's Republic of China. *Journal of Applied Psychology*, 77 (5), 1992, 664–671.

Rao, A. & Schmidt, S. M. A behavioural perspective on negotiating international alliances. *Journal of International Business Studies*, 29 (4), 1998, 665–694.

Robins, J. A., Tallman, S. & Fladmoe-Lindquist, F. Autonomy and dependence of international cooperative ventures: an exploration of the strategic performance of US ventures in Mexico. *Strategic Management Journal*, 23 (10), 2002, 881–901.

Schuster, C. & M. Copeland: *Global Business: Planning for Sales and Negotiations*. Dryden, 1996.

Sebenius, J. K. The hidden challenge of cross-border negotiation. *Harvard Business Review*, (March), 80 (3), 2002, 76–85.

Stalk, G. & Michael, D. What the West doesn't get about China. *HBR*, 89 (6), June 2011.

Stewart, S. & Keown, C. Talking with the dragon: negotiating in the People's Republic of China. *Columbia Journal of World Business*, 1989, 68–72.

Thomas, D. C. Domain and development of cultural intelligence: the importance of mindfulness. *Group Organization Management*, 37, 2006, 78–99.

Usunier, J-C. & Lee, J. A. *Marketing across Cultures*. Pearson Education, 4th ed., 2005.

Volkema, R. & Rivers, C. Negotiating on the Internet. *Journal of Education for Business*, 83 (3), 2008, 165–172.

Wong, T. N. & Fang, F. A multi-agent protocol for multilateral negotiations in supply chain management. *International Journal of Production Research*, 48 (1), 2010, 271–299.

Zhao, J. J. The Chinese approach to international business negotiation. *The Journal of Business Communication*, 37 (3), 2000, 209–237

Alliance, IJV and International M&A Negotiations

10

INTRODUCTION

International business alliances are partnerships between firms based in different countries that may result in joint ventures, joint research and development (R&D) programmes, co-production agreements, licensing arrangements, multinational franchising deals and other agreements. Partner selection criteria include superior technology, managerial capability and international experience. The network position of potential partners is increasingly important in partner selection (Shi et al., 2012). In the global liner shipping industry, for instance, forming an alliance boosts a company's position in interorganisational networks and leads to higher innovation rates and lower financing costs. Forming an alliance with a suitable partner often involves lengthy and difficult negotiations, especially if the potential partner is an actual or potential competitor. The fear of opportunism may make the partners wary of sharing information that could potentially be detrimental to their interests – a tendency which may be enhanced if the partners have not cooperated with each other before.

This leads to inhibited information sharing in the negotiation since each partner worries that the other partner will use the information obtained to gain competitive advantage.

Managers enter alliance negotiations in either a competitive or a cooperative spirit (Rao et al., 1999). Cooperative negotiators try to reach integrative agreements that benefit the different parties. Competitive negotiators try to maximise outcomes for their own side regardless of the impact on the prospective partner. Negotiators may struggle in evaluating the optimal scope and the nature of an alliance. The partners may have congruent goals, yet fail to arrive at an agreement because of the noise and uncertainty that intrudes in negotiating sessions (Kumar & Patriotta, 2011). Das & Kumar (2011) point out that few studies have investigated such key aspects of the negotiation process as the impact made by national cultural differences on international alliance negotiations.

Different kinds of alliances have different emphases. A *strategic alliance* is a long-term relationship aimed at increasing the strategic operating capability of two or more firms (Vanpouckeab & Vereecke, 2010). Strategic alliances help companies gain competitive advantage in international business by enabling production and marketing to be optimised between the partners, business and technological knowledge to be exchanged, or joint R&D programmes to be carried out. Thus, when Microsoft and Sony teamed up, it was with the aim of moving closer together on technology standards for digital television and other electronic products. An *exploitation alliance* enables the partners to share their complementary assets to maximise joint profits. An *exploration* alliance focuses on developing new technologies. With anticipated outcomes and paybacks distant in time, an exploration alliance needs to be long lasting. There is a dearth of reliable guidelines for effectively conducting *multiparty* alliance negotiations.

In international joint venture (IJV) negotiations, a number of basic policy issues have to be addressed. These may include equity split, guidelines for reporting to the parent companies, transfer of financial and technological assets to the IJV, and protection of intellectual property rights. Other issues that have to be addressed are management structure of the new company, staffing and operating methods that will enable the venture to function efficiently. When international companies negotiate joint ventures with companies in the developing world, the international firm usually contributes equity capital and technology, while the local company provides human resources and specialised market knowledge (Liu, 2008).

In some IJVs, local managers may have no experience of efficient decision-making processes or of sophisticated governance structures. Marketing incompetence by local managers may lead to poor pricing and purchasing decisions, inadequate product-line selection, and poor distribution and promotion arrangements. Thus, the responsibilities of the parent companies for ensuring that local staff are adequately trained need to be discussed and specified in the agreement. Negotiators need to be realistic about the possibility of future disputes occurring between the partners, and should ensure that the national law that will be used in the case of future litigation is stated in the contract.

During international merger and acquisition (M&A) negotiations, the cultures of acquirer and acquired frequently clash. Many cross-border M&As eventually fail because of incompatible national and organisational cultures. Another reason for eventual failure is lack of caution at the negotiation stage. In acquisition battles, a determination to win at any cost may lead to irrational decision-making – and may involve losing a lot of money in the process.

ALLIANCE NEGOTIATION

Purpose

Resource dependency theory (Pfeffer, 1988) gives insights into the motivations of firms seeking to form alliances. The theory is based on the assumption that firms are interdependent entities seeking to manage and reduce the uncertainty in the surrounding environment. Firms lacking control over scarce resources, for example, cutting-edge technology or international marketing reach, may try to manage the resulting uncertainty by forming international alliances. It is for such reasons, as Dyer et al. (2001) point out, that negotiating alliances with innovative companies worldwide is an important component of many firms' global strategy. The innovativeness of companies in emerging markets is exemplified by Tata's $2,500 car in India, Embraer's advances in jet design in Brazil, and BYD's battery technology in China. By negotiating alliances with such companies, a firm can reach new markets and tap the potential for innovation in products and services that exists worldwide.

Alliance activities

International business alliances are partnerships between firms based in different countries that may result in multinational R&D activities, international joint ventures, licensing arrangements, co-production agreements, multinational franchising deals and so forth (Vanpouckeab & Vereecke, 2010). The wide-ranging issues have to be addressed in alliance negotiations, leading to protracted negotiations. International alliances evolve through the stages of formation, operation and outcome (Das & Teng, 1999).

Negotiations are held not only in the initial formation stage but also throughout the later stages when the alliance becomes operational and management control issues have to be negotiated.

Negotiations at the formation stage give alliance negotiators the opportunity to test the suitability of their potential partners and to assess whether there is a good strategic, organisational and cultural fit among the alliancing firms (Lasserre, 2007).

Making the assessment can be a lengthy process if the potential partner is a competitor or a potential competitor. Information sharing during initial negotiations is often inhibited because of the risk of an actual or a potential rival's using the information gained for competitive advantage. When Renault and Nissan formed an alliance, because of the cultural distance between the companies, the negotiators had to grapple with both *task* and *relational* issues (Das & Kumar, 2011). The dual interests of the partners had to be reconciled and integrated throughout the lengthy negotiations and also over the life cycle of the alliance.

Alliance negotiations have to be studied without the support of an integrated theoretical framework. Existing research throws little light, in particular, on the dynamics of *multiparty* alliance negotiations and on the risks involved in providing business information to multiple potential partners who are also potential competitors and who may use the information against you. In such cases, each negotiating team knows that it can influence the other teams' outcomes – and that its own outcomes can be influenced by the other teams. This knowledge prompts negotiators to keep modifying their negotiating positions from time to time to avoid conflict and keep the talks alive (Lewicki et al., 1999).

Seeking alliance partners

Firms embark on alliance negotiations after seeking information about potential partners' capabilities and motivations. Companies generally base partner selection on a company's financial viability, technological capability, quality of products and services, and market reach (Shi et al., 2012). Specific partner selection criteria include

- superior technology,
- proven managerial capability,
- international experience,
- network position of potential partners.

Nearly three-quarters of firms in developing countries seek alliances with international companies which possess *superior technology* (Miller et al., 1997).

However, the network position of a company is increasingly important in selecting an alliance partner. In the global liner shipping industry, for instance, a company's position in interorganisational networks is boosted through alliances, leading to higher innovation rates and lower financing costs (Greve et al., 2010).

Relationship fit

Many alliances fail outright or achieve only a few of their initial goals (Segil, 2004). Inkpen & Ross (2001) calculate the outright failure rate to be around 50 percent. The inference is that in international alliance negotiations, the relationship fit of the potential partners should be carefully assessed. Relationship fit is the ability of potential partners to maintain a strong relationship throughout the life cycle of the alliance. A good fit implies a good strategic and organisational compatibility among the alliancing firms. Segil (2004) produces evidence to show that companies that evaluate relationship fit at the outset tend to be more successful at building strong and lasting alliances than firms that neglect to do so.

Hewlett-Packard's self-help manual for executives involved in alliance negotiations included a candidate-evaluation form to help this kind of assessment to be made. It also included a template for making the business case for an alliance (Dyer et al., 2001).

Trust between alliance partners

Trust is the extent to which the negotiators believe in the good intentions of the negotiating partner (Rao & Schmidt, 1998). Trust allows negotiators to talk frankly about their interests and their constituents, and to float tentative proposals without fear the other will construe them as concessions.

Whereas trust enables effective negotiation, *distrust* between the parties leads to contentious behaviour and makes a satisfactory agreement harder to achieve. An example of contentious behaviour occurring long after the original agreement was signed relates to the alliance between Meiji Milk and Borden Products. The alliance had been in existence for 20 years when sales of Borden's products in Japan began to slow down. Borden responded in a combative way by accusing Meiji of seeking to develop its own products and causing the slowdown (Das & Kumar, 2011). Shortly thereafter, Borden exited from the alliance.

Consider the contrasting case of Air France and KLM which, in 2001, entered into informal discussions about a possible strategic alliance. Lander & Kooning (2013) explain how these informal talks gave an opportunity for mutual trust to develop so that in time the talks became a platform for discussing the timing and conditions of an outright merger. Both companies realised that for the merger to be successful, managers and employees from the two organisations would have to go through a similar process of trust development during the *integration phase* of the merger.

In both alliance and IJV negotiations, trust is vital because it helps mitigate opportunistic behaviour (Faems et al., 2008). Trust in negotiations encourages the parties to candidly share information and views. Information exchange is often seen as a key component of the negotiation process, but in alliance negotiations may be highly problematical if levels of uncertainty and suspicion are high (Kumar & Patriotta, 2011). Researchers have noted what happens when task-oriented Americans negotiate with relationship-oriented Japanese. While the Americans exchange information directly, the Japanese do it only indirectly. This makes it difficult for the Americans to understand or fully appreciate their counterpart's perspective and leads to difficulty in creating joint gains (Brett & Okumura, 1998).

Problem-solving approach to negotiations

When Fiat negotiated with Tata to establish a joint venture, both companies adopted a problem-solving approach to the negotiations (Mitchell & Hohl, 2008). The two sides met once every month over a 12-month period to exchange information and discuss various options for managing the venture. These initial negotiations were marked by a high degree of trust and cooperation – and by the absence of legal advisers. The negotiators realised that dealing with the other side's concerns in a constructive, problem-solving manner would be difficult if company lawyers, worried about liability, were present. Both companies' commitment to avoiding legalistic complexities enabled them to freely share information, build trust and achieve good results in terms of the eventual outcomes of negotiation.

Mistrust emerged as an issue following Disney's successful negotiations to open Euro Disney outside Paris. Disney's American management rashly assumed that French employees would conform to American work codes. But by assuming that French employees would conform to American expectations in their work practices, they made little effort to build up trust (Kulshreshtha, 2009). Lengthy conflict with French trade unions was the main result of this miscalculation. Finally, Disney gave up and appointed French managers to top-level positions. Labour difficulties gradually subsided when managers and workers started to trust each other. As the example suggests, irrespective of whether negotiators represent an international company or a government, they need to be sure that the person on the other side of the table is reliable and trustworthy.

Clashing corporate cultures

The corporate culture of a company usually reflects the national business environment. Hofstede (1980), for instance, found that within a single multinational company, IBM, there were wide variations of corporate culture depending on the national location. IBM's organisational culture had, in effect, adjusted to the national culture in each country.

Negotiations to form international alliances or international M&As of companies based in different countries bring both national and corporate cultures into play. The chances of a successful negotiation are reduced when the national and corporate cultures of the companies involved are distant from each other. Research shows that negotiations tend to be more successful in terms of interaction and outcomes when the negotiators are culturally close (very similar), and less successful when they are culturally distant (totally foreign) from each other (Fehr, 1996).

Cultural distance

The complexity and ambiguity of alliance negotiations is greater when there is great cultural distance between the partners. Cultural distance implies that the partners may find it difficult to understand each other's intentions, and equally difficult to accurately communicate their own (Kumar & Nti, 2004). The most obvious effect of cultural distance between the negotiating partners is that they may miscommunicate and misunderstand each other's intentions.

When cultural distance between alliancing firms is high, it may be difficult for them to agree on the nature of the problems which must be solved to allow the alliance to operate effectively (Kumar & Patriotta, 2011). The negotiators may be unsure about each other. Does the partner trust them? Can they trust the partner? In the event of future disagreements, will it be possible to resolve the conflict quickly without rancour? There may be worries about possible opportunistic behaviour by the partner, and about whether the partner will be fully committed to the alliance if the deal goes through. Cultural distance between the negotiators may increase their willingness to use hard bargaining and other questionable tactics (Rao & Schmidt, 1998).

Other cultural factors

Alliance negotiation is a more complex undertaking than negotiating a foreign distribution agreement or signing an agreement with a foreign supplier. Complexity is further increased when cultural barriers between the parties emerge. Negotiators' *nonverbal behaviours*, for instance, are cultural products, and in an alliance negotiation, the differing nonverbal communication behaviours of negotiators may create mutual misunderstanding. Typical nonverbal behaviour by Japanese negotiators, for instance, includes apologising by bowing and smiling. European negotiators, in accordance with their cultural norms, are likely to interpret this behaviour as a sign of insincerity and untrustworthiness. To overcome such misunderstandings, negotiators must try to adopt the perspective of the other negotiator This ability, deriving from cultural empathy, may give a negotiator insight into the counterpart's mindset and therefore into their possible negotiating strategies.

Negotiating teams from different countries have different ideas about how alliance negotiations should be conducted. Asian teams, for instance, may prefer negotiations to start with a broad agreement on general principles. Western negotiators, on the other hand, generally prefer to address one issue at a time in detail. Negotiators who are flexible are able to adjust to either approach. In large power-distance countries such as India, France and Indonesia, negotiations usually have to be conducted with high-level decision-makers. Usually, terms of address must be carefully assessed and protocol observed at all times.

TYPES OF ALLIANCE

Strategic alliances

A strategic alliance is a long-term cooperative business relationship designed to increase the strategic operating capability of two or more individual firms

(Vanpouckeab & Vereecke, 2010). Strategic alliances are motivated mainly by the desire to gain competitive advantage in the international marketplace, as demonstrated by Shanghai Auto's alliance with General Motors to serve India's car market. By pooling resources, the partners aimed to gain competitive advantage over global business rivals.

Other reasons which motivate companies to form alliances are to enable the companies to carry out joint R&D programmes, to optimise production, to improve quality standards or to increase international marketing effectiveness. Das & Kumar (2011) point to the alliance negotiated between General Electric and Snecma to manufacture jet engines as an example of the successful application of a problem-solving approach to alliance formation. Problem-solving involved constantly looking for creative ways to resolve disagreements that arose between the partners while waiting for the first orders to arrive.

Chrysler-Fiat negotiations

In 2009, following six months of negotiation, Chrysler Group and Fiat finalised an alliance agreement, and the new Chrysler became operational. Fiat's technology in fuel efficiency and its distribution network in Europe and South America have since enabled the new Chrysler to become efficient and profitable. An excerpt from the draft agreement illustrates the partners' success in converting numerous complex and difficult issues into a workable plan:

> The agreement grants the US automaker access to Fiat technology, platforms and powertrains for small and medium-sized cars, which are amongst the most innovative and advanced in the world. This will enable Chrysler to expand its product offering with the addition of low environmental impact models. Chrysler will also have access to Fiat's international distribution network. The alliance represents an important step toward positioning both Fiat and Chrysler among the next generation of leaders of the auto industry globally.
>
> As consideration, Fiat received an initial equity interest of 20 percent in the newly formed Chrysler Group LLC, which could increase up to a total of 35 percent upon achievement of specific pre-established targets. The agreement does not contemplate any cash investment in Chrysler by Fiat or commitment to fund Chrysler in the future. Fiat will also have the right to acquire a majority interest in Chrysler once all government loans have been fully repaid. The alliance is expected to bring enormous benefits to both companies by giving them the critical mass necessary to compete at a global level.

Technology alliances

Technology alliances are voluntary arrangements between firms to exchange and share knowledge as well as resources with the aim of developing their processes, products or services (Gulati, 1998). An example of a successful technology alliance is that formed by Microsoft and Sony, who teamed up to link personal computers and consumer electronics devices. The alliance enabled the companies to move closer together on technology standards for digital television and other products. Technology alliances are an important strategic tool for technology-based firms even though, according to Wittmann et al. (2009), 70 percent of technology alliances are not successful. An important reason for eventual failure is that technology alliances require excessive resources and capabilities to create and maintain relationships between partners. They also divert attention from internal R&D in the partner firms (Park & Kang, 2013).

Western companies which form alliances with Chinese enterprises often share their technologies with their Chinese partners as a condition of operating in China. In return, the Western companies gain marketing knowledge and access to the huge Chinese market.

Exploitation and exploration alliances

At a given stage of its development, a firm can either exploit its existing routines and systems or explore new possibilities. Rothaermel & Deeds (2004) extend the concept to international business alliances:

- Firms can exploit the technology and know-how gained from alliance partners, for instance, by minimising production costs and expanding sales.

or

- They can work with their partners to explore and create new technology that did not previously exist in the firms.

Exploitation and exploration alliances are fundamentally distinct types of alliance because they deal with different types of alliancing problems. In exploitation alliances, the partners share their complementary assets to maximise joint value creation. In exploration alliances, on the other hand, the partners are searching for something novel, such as a breakthrough technology. Consequently, in exploration alliances, long-term commitment by the partners to the alliance is needed since the hoped-for paybacks are distant in time (Koza & Lewin, 1998). The distinction between the two types derives from March's (1991) dichotomy.

The level of task ambiguity is higher in exploration alliances since alliances of this kind are associated with the development of new technologies – an uncertain process. What is the "right" way to discover or develop a new technology?

SMALL-GROUP EXERCISE: Discussion questions

Working in small groups, discuss and write down the group's answers to each of the following questions. At the end of the exercise, the group presents its answers to the other groups for comment.

1. *What motivates firms to negotiate strategic alliances with partners in other parts of the world? In seeking an alliance partner, what selection criteria is a manufacturing country likely to use?*
2. *Explain the difference between exploitation and exploration alliances and give examples of each type. How is the success of each type of alliance assessed?*
3. *An Irish manufacturer of electronic control equipment is about to enter into negotiations with a Canadian company to establish an alliance to share business and technological knowledge and to carry out joint R&D programmes. What are the most important negotiating issues that will have to be addressed in the negotiations?*

IJV NEGOTIATIONS

Purpose

IJVs are basic building blocks for companies trying to establish a global network. Bosch, for instance, has negotiated several ventures with Japanese companies. Japanese employees are trained in production processes at Bosch factories in Germany, and Bosch managers are sent to Japan to ensure that quality control standards are being achieved. A large organisation such as Bosch may have numerous IJVs which must be managed without the company having full ownership and control of the human, financial and physical resources involved.

The immediate purpose of IJV negotiations is to set up a new firm with its own legal identity to carry out a joint activity as specified in the agreement for a stated length of time. An underlying, longer-term purpose may be to extend and strengthen an already-established business relationship. This was the case when DreamWorks Animation negotiated an IJV in 2012 with Shanghai Media Group and China Media Capital, two state-owned Chinese media groups. The agreement covered the building of a studio in Shanghai to develop film and television productions for the fast-growing Chinese market. An important effect of the negotiation has been to strengthen the rapidly evolving relationship between the partners in China and the US.

There are many cases of IJVs being formed between firms with complementary assets. A firm that has developed a valuable new technology, for instance, may set up a joint venture with a firm in another country that holds a dominant position in local and regional markets. A typical result of forming an IJV is that new products are developed and many new customers are acquired. Parent firms from highly developed economies often rely on the parent of the local partner to take a major role in activities such as marketing or labour management (Robins et al., 2002).

Limited research

Only a limited amount of research-based information exists about the way in which IJV negotiations are actually carried out. When Reus & Ritchie (2004) analysed three internationally renowned journals, they found that over a 15-year period, only six articles appeared that were devoted to joint venture negotiation. However, frameworks designed to assist research into international business negotiations, including IJV negotiations, have been developed by several authors.

Faure (2000) points to four distinct phases of IJV negotiation:

- preliminary investigation;
- business proposal;
- contract negotiation;
- implementation of the agreement.

Since all aspects of the alliance – financial, legal, production, marketing, management control and so forth – have to be covered in the agreement, it may take the negotiators many months to pass through all these phases. For managers wishing to negotiate a successful alliance, there are no easy textbook answers, no off-the-shelf approaches – apart from the need to identify appropriate partners.

Resources

In IJV negotiations, practical details that must be settled at an early stage include

- the IJV's purpose;
- the level and type of equity and other resources to be committed by each partner;
- when the joint venture will begin to function;
- each partner's responsibility for appointing key managers in the new company.

The amount of equity to be committed by partners is a key negotiating issue. When the parties are an international company and a local partner, it is usually the international company which contributes equity capital and technology (Liu, 2008). The local partner, on the other hand, often provides human resources and specialised market knowledge. Both parties usually benefit from this arrangement.

Multinational firms bring to an IJV resources that cannot be readily obtained through the market, that is, resources that are scarce, valuable and difficult to imitate or substitute, such as patents, licenses, and brand names, or less tangible resources, such as management skills and experience. Beamish et al. (2000) make the point that Starbucks's ventures with Jardine in Asia have brought competitive advantage over rivals who do not have access to comparable management skills.

Large international companies form ventures with smaller firms in developing countries because often the local firms have important resources to offer. Resources such as land-use rights, distribution networks, links with government departments and low labour costs. If the local firm is a state-owned enterprise (SOE), however, problems can follow. For instance, in many developing countries, SOEs are subject to interference from their controlling ministry or provincial government (Meyer et al., 2006).

Negotiating issues

Major issues that have to be addressed in IJV negotiations include the following:

- *Basic policy issues.* Distribution of positions on the board. Number of managers and employees to be taken from each/all of the parent companies. Protection of intellectual property.
- *Financial aspects.* Transfer of financial and technological capital and expertise to the new company. Level and type of resources to be contributed by each partner. Royalties to be paid for use of brand names. Licensing fees. Targeted return on investment (ROI) of the IJV.
- *Legal issues.* The joint venture company is necessarily created under the national law of the country in which it operates (giving a great advantage to the partner from that country). Negotiators should be realistic about the possibility of future disputes occurring between the partners and should specify in the contract the national law to be used in case future litigation is necessary.
- *Integration issues.* In IJVs, the faster the different partners can knit the venture together, the sooner they can reap the benefits. Joint task forces might, for instance, be formed and tasked with identifying operational areas – purchasing, manufacturing, logistics, financial reporting and so forth. – where synergies could be achieved.
- *Issues of trust.* Trust in IJV negotiations is more likely to exist if there are prior ties among the potential partners A previous business relationship gives each party knowledge of how the other party reacts to problems and conflict. Once an IJV has been set up, trustworthy behaviour among IJV managers

is influenced by the quality of governance in the country where the venture is located. Partners may stray from ethical behaviour in countries where laws and regulations are seen as unenforceable.

Negotiations need to cover the management structure of the IJV and the operating principles that will enable it to function efficiently and profitably. Robins et al. (2002) studied a sample of established US-Mexican ventures and found that more than half were shared-equity IJVs. In these, the Mexican parent was majority owner in 57 percent of cases. In 90 percent of the IJVs, major decisions were taken without direct governance by the parent companies. The IJVs were relatively long lived, with an average age of 12 years.

IJVs do not necessarily involve equity participation. There are many forms of international ventures, such as licensing agreements, technology transfer deals, arrangements for sharing R&D expenditure, joint promotion or joint product design etc. Dupont (1991) draws attention to the long time span that generally separates preliminary contacts from final agreement. When cultural differences are severe, governments or consultants may be called on to provide answers to governance questions and provide guidelines for resolving future disputes between the partners.

The channel tunnel project, with an Anglo-French IJV company in charge of the construction, took several years from official start-up in 1984 to pre-negotiations and operative agreements. As in many IJV companies, cultural factors became crucial, especially dissimilarities in economic and management systems as well as different priorities and expectations.

Issue linkage

In IJV negotiations, differences in the technological, financial, engineering and marketing capabilities of the partners can form the basis for a mutually beneficial linkage of negotiating issues. The issue of equity contributions, for instance, might be linked to the issue of royalty payments, licensing fees or the number of managers appointed to senior positions. Under the IJV agreement negotiated between Cambridge Biostability (UK) and Panacea Biotec (India), Panacea purchased £1.935 million of Cambridge's equity upfront, and at the same time signed a long-term licensing agreement that provides gross royalty income to Cambridge over the agreement period (Dai & Lahiri, 2011).

IJV PERFORMANCE ISSUES

Management performance

IJV performance criteria include growth, sales or profitability, and typically these are linked to performance in specific areas such as human resource management or quality control (Robins et al., 2002). Human resources (HR) development and quality control are among the best-researched areas of IJV operations, and the concerns most widely cited by managers of emerging economy ventures.

Key functional areas in which poor decision-making can cause an international venture to be unsuccessful are production, marketing and finance (Ricks, 1999). For example, technical incompetence in the IJV's marketing department can lead to wrong pricing, inadequate product-line selection, and poor distribution and promotion arrangements. Poor procurement decisions may reduce profitability. A decision taken at the negotiation stage to set up a production plant in an unsuitable location can lead to the new company's incurring heavy initial losses.

Björkman et al. (2007) examine how cultural differences and poor management in IJVs affect the organisation's performance. Other performance problems, identified by Urban (1996), stem from

- incompatible corporate cultures;
- divergence of strategic interests of the partners;
- mistrust among the partners;
- achievement of only superficial integration;
- over-complicated or inappropriate decision-making processes.

Management control

Joint ownership of an IJV leads to questions of who controls what, and how control will be exercised. Yan & Gray's (1994) analysis of four Chinese-US joint ventures shows that the question of management control is a key issue that needs to be addressed by the partners at the negotiation stage.

Child & Yan (1999) note that during negotiations to set up an IJV in China, managers of a US and a Chinese pharmaceutical company quickly agreed that equity holdings would be 50/50. But the remaining negotiations lasted three years because of the numerous issues the negotiating teams had to address, such as plant location, staffing levels, and Chinese access to the US company's technology. Negotiations about managerial staffing and composition of the board of directors of the new company were particularly contentious and took up a lot of time.

Control function of IJV boards

IJV boards usually consist of representatives of the partners in proportion to their equity and non-equity contributions to the venture. In practice, this may lead to large international companies appointing most of the board members and so controlling the strategic direction of the company (Li et al., 2009). Higher equity investment gives a company greater bargaining power in IJV negotiations, which it can use to negotiate for the right to appoint most of the board members and senior managers. The advantage of a dominant foreign ownership structure is that, according to Ding (1996), it minimises opportunistic behaviours of local partners and reduces potential partner conflict.

Klijn et al. (2013) studied how IJV governance structures, particularly the board of directors, influence performance outcomes of an IJV. The board is an important instrument of IJV control. An IJV's directors engage in *control* of the IJV on behalf of the partners' parent companies. The directors also carry out an important *coordination* function. For instance, they coordinate the activities of the IJV and the parent companies, they participate in drawing up strategic plans, and so on.

Klijn et al. (2013) found that the level of *control* and *coordination* functions of boards affect the performance of IJVs positively. This positive effect is magnified in IJVs that are broader in functional scope. The researchers' results therefore support Boone et al.'s (2007) finding that the value of board involvement grows as firms become more complex in response to the increasing benefits of control and specialisation of board members when firms become more complex.

Underinvestment

IJVs have a high potential for gain but also a high potential for loss. That helps explain why many negotiated IJV agreements are never implemented – more than half in China, according to Demirbaga & Mirzab (2000). IJVs that are implemented may underperform because of underinvestment by one or more partners who delay full investment until they are sure that market conditions are favourable (Carter et al., 2011). Such behaviour creates frictions that may eventually lead to one or more partners withdrawing from the venture altogether.

For companies that wish to enter an IJV but that are worried about investment failure, *real options* provide an attractive psychological hedge. A real option is a right to invest resources at a future point in time. In IJV negotiations, "real option" thinking is at work when one of the partners agrees to make a small initial investment of resources while information about the likely success of the venture is accumulating. Later, the option to make a larger investment can be exercised by the partner.

Case Study

MINI-CASE: Japanese-Pakistani venture

Working in small groups, study the following description and answer the questions that follow. Each group may then make a brief presentation of its answers to the other groups for their comments.

When negotiations were held between Mitsubishi and the Pakistani firm Packages to establish a joint venture to produce Biaxially Oriented Polypropylene (BOPP) film in Pakistan, the equity contributions of the partners were quickly agreed. Mitsubishi would contribute 30 percent of the equity fund and Packages 40 percent. The remaining 30 percent would be financed through a public offering. According to the business plan, the new company would gain 30–35 percent market share in the first year, gradually increasing to 60 percent in the fourth year. The Pakistani government offered a five-year sales tax exemption and an eight-year income tax holiday if the new plant was established in Hattar in Pakistan.

Once these details had been settled, the partners agreed that Mitsubishi would appoint two directors, and Packages three directors to the board of the new company. Public shareholders would select two directors. Packages would nominate the Chairman and the Managing Director of the company. At this stage in the negotiations, Mitsubishi wanted a clause to be inserted in the agreement saying that Packages would reimburse Mitsubishi's investment if there were repeated losses in operations, but the proposal was dropped after the Packages team rejected it as unfair.

Mitsubishi agreed to transfer technology to Packages by training plant operators. Then the price of equipment to be installed in the new company became an issue. Much equipment was to be purchased from Mitsubishi Corporation. But later it became clear that some items – boilers, for instance – could be obtained elsewhere at a much lower price. Negotiations were suspended while a Packages procurement team visited equipment manufacturers in Europe. When talks resumed, Mitsubishi agreed to revise the price down to allow for some items of equipment to be supplied by other manufacturers.

The Packages-Mitsubishi case shows how implementation challenges can affect the realisation of the partners' joint venture objectives, and brings out the specific challenges which may arise in a technology-intensive international joint venture operation. The negotiations suggest that in setting up an IJV, some non-problematical issues can be agreed at a very early stage of negotiations. Details regarding more complicated issues, such as organisation structure, management positions, dispute resolution procedures and so forth – can be negotiated at a later stage in the negotiations.

Source: Arif & Butt (2006)

Questions:

1. *Identify 3 major negotiating issues regarding the IJV which were addressed and settled at an early stage of the negotiations. Which other issues would it have been helpful to discuss and settle early in the negotiations?*
2. *Based on the information given, identify possible performance problems that the IJV could eventually experience as a result of cultural and other differences. What specific actions by management could help to reduce these problems?*
3. *How could Mitsubishi have structured its joint venture with Packages to improve the probability of achieving its goals?*

Training issues

Many failures in IJVs can be traced back to inadequate selection and training of local employees (Vaara et al., 2012). Managers in local firms may not be familiar with the governance structures, management techniques and decision-making processes used in mature market economies. In some IJVs, the management knowledge and management techniques used by local management are inadequate compared to international standards, and lead to poor bottom-line results. To guard against such risks, the negotiating parties should make sure that responsibilities for training local managers are discussed, agreed and specified in the contract. Expatriate managers are often made responsible for carrying out or arranging the training required.

Performance measurement

Profitability and *satisfaction* are criteria which are widely used to measure IJV performance. It is in the partners' interests not only to achieve profits but also to keep each other satisfied and committed to the venture. Moreover, satisfaction reduces the likelihood of future disputes between the partners occurring. Studies have found that negotiators often experience satisfaction with regard to the amount of trust generated between partners at the negotiation stage and throughout the life cycle of the partnership (Shankarmahesh et al., 2004).

CROSS-BORDER M&A NEGOTIATIONS

High risk

Cross-border M&As are the dominant form of FDI and one of the most widely used strategies to achieve international diversification.

In the 1990s, GE capital integrated more than 100 mergers, increasing its workforce by 30 percent, globalising its business and doubling its net income. The example shows that cross-border mergers can be highly successful and have profitable outcomes. On the other hand, merging or making an outright acquisition of a company in a culturally distant country can be a risky undertaking. Even though negotiating a cross-border merger takes two to three times longer than does a domestic merger, more than half of attempted mergers fail (Zweifel, 2003).

An example of a cross-border merger that failed spectacularly was BMW's merger with Rover. The merger failed when BMW was forced to sell the Rover group after posting losses of billions of dollars. BMW attributed the failure to the culture gap between the two companies and their incompatible management styles. Marks & Spencer found that its famed distribution systems could not cope with Canadian geography when it acquired Peoples Department Stores.

Cultural differences and differences in management approach make integration in merged companies difficult. When Daimler merged with Chrysler, German management board members had executive assistants who prepared detailed position papers on numerous issues (Bower, 2001). The Americans however did not have assigned aides. They formulated their decisions by talking directly to engineers or technical specialists. German decisions worked their way through the bureaucracy for final approval at the top. The Americans' style of decision-making involved middle managers' proceeding on their own initiative without waiting for top-level approval.

Bringing two companies together requires disconnecting and reconnecting hundreds of processes and procedures as quickly as possible, and usually the people involved in cross-border mergers are strangers thrown together against their will. Employees of both companies need to keep day-to-day business going, but they also need to build relationships, which involves bridging formidable language and culture gaps. That is why *integration planning* is needed in order to find ways to clear paths between two distinct cultures.

Bankers Trust-Deutsche Bank merger

When New York-based Bankers Trust merged with Frankfurt-based Deutsche Bank in 2007, the Americans soon discovered that the pace of business is slower in Europe than in the US. Kulshreshtha (2009) notes that the American executives found that they could not fathom their German partners. Accustomed to making split-second decisions and used to working in an environment in which planning rarely extended beyond a given deal, the New York executives found themselves working with German bankers who planned systematically – often several years at a time.

Integration activities were needed, and these included management seminars in which the Americans were taught to slow down and think in different terms, in accord with European banking culture. The Germans, for their part, needed a crash course in merchant banking and a whole new vocabulary rooted in international business deals.

Essential stages of M&A negotiations

Due diligence

Carrying out due diligence is an essential stage of international M&A negotiations. Due diligence is a term used for an investigation of a business prior to signing a contract. It can be a legal obligation, but the term usually applies to voluntary investigations. An example of due diligence is the process through which a potential acquirer evaluates a target company or its assets for an acquisition (Hoskisson et al., 2004). In this case, the due diligence consists mainly of fact checking. Is the foreign company, for instance, everything it says it is? Is it as financially sound as its annual report suggests? Not surprisingly, many potential international M&A deals collapse at the due diligence stage.

The due diligence process varies for different types of companies. In the case of a foreign manufacturing company, the areas investigated might include the financial, legal, labour, information technology (IT), intellectual property and market situation of the company Together, these various audits should enable the potential acquirer to value the company (Gillman, 2002).

Negotiating price, workforce reductions

Negotiating price, management structure and workforce reductions is a highly sensitive stage in M&A negotiations. Aiello & Watkins (2000) found that successful acquirers usually divide their team into two or three separate negotiating groups to deal with these sensitive aspects of the negotiations, especially if the negotiations are held in a foreign country. The groups consist of

- *managers* (who negotiate personnel and strategic issues including workforce reductions);
- *lawyers* and/or investment bankers (who negotiate terms and structure of the financing);
- *top executives*, who can use the bankers and lawyers to deliver hard messages without poisoning relationships with the other company.

Incompatible cultures

Shortly before China joined the WTO in 2000, the Chinese government permitted Chinese companies to acquire overseas enterprises. Williamson & Raman (2011) note that the first wave of M&As consisted mostly of failures. They included Ping An's investment in the European financial services group Fortis. Another merger that failed was when TCL, China's largest colour television manufacturer, acquired a 67 percent stake in France's Thomson. The new company was dysfunctional partly because of cultural differences. For instance, when Chinese executives tried to hold meetings on weekends – a regular occurrence in China – their French counterparts would turn off their phones and be unavailable. Such frictions contributed to TCL's closing five of its seven European centres in 2007.

Kanter (2009) looks at successful international acquisitions ranging from global deals such as Proctor & Gamble's purchase of Gillette, to regional acquisitions such a Shinhan Bank's acquisition of Chohung Bank in South Korea, and notes that the organisational cultures of acquirer and acquired frequently clash.

Shinhan Bank's strong corporate culture was very different from Chohung Bank's culture, and triggered resistance from Chohung staff. About 3,500 Chohung employees and managers shaved their heads and piled their hair in front of Shinhan offices. To quieten the labour union, Shinhan agreed to delay formal integration for three years. However, de facto integration was achieved before then through joint task forces and various integration events including sing-alongs and mountain climbing.

Three-quarters of companies in one survey believed that M&A failures are caused by incompatible national and corporate cultures (Global Workforce, 11, 1998). That helps explain why the probability of a company choosing an IJV in preference to a merger or outright acquisition increases with cultural distance (Kogut & Singh, 1988). International mergers are risky. In acquisition battles, the desire to win at any cost can lead to irrational decision-making and may involve losing a lot of money in the process. During cross-border acquisition battles, negotiators may become obsessed by the belief that escalating their commitment one stage further will lead to victory. Bazerman & Neale (1992, 13) believe that the best way to eliminate irrational escalation in acquisition battles is to try to understand the psychological factors that feed it:

> When you commit yourself to a course of action, this commitment biases your perception and judgment, causes you to make irrational decisions to manage the impression of others.

Schweiger (2002) argues that an *integration programme* designed to minimise cultural frictions and capture anticipated synergies greatly increases the chances of an international merger's being successful. Such an approach worked well at the time of Hewlett Packard-Compaq merger negotiations in 2001–2002. Both sides considered a smooth integration so important that initial plans for an integration programme were mapped out at an early stage in the merger negotiations.

Case Study

CASE STUDY: The HP-Compaq merger

Working in small groups, study the following description and answer the questions that follow. Each group may then make a brief presentation of its answers to the other groups for their comments.

Potential competitive advantages

When Hewlett-Packard and Compaq announced their intent to merge in 2001, the worldwide response was mostly negative. International media high-lighted the difficult challenge of operationally and strategically integrating two very large and successful multinational companies in the context of a highly dynamic competitive environment. Nevertheless, the HP-Compaq merger has turned out to be highly successful, whether measured by increased shareholder value, market leadership or market share.

Pre-merger talks and formal negotiations focussed on the potential competitive advantages that a merger would bring. These included

- a much stronger product-market position across the computing businesses. HP was strong in mid-range and high-end UNIX servers, which was a weakness for Compaq. Compaq, on the other hand, was strong in low-end industry standard (Intel) servers, which was a weakness for HP.
- Compaq was a clear second in the personal computer (PC) business and stronger on the commercial side than HP, while HP was stronger on the consumer side. Together, they would have the capacity to offer the industry's most complete set of IT products and services for businesses and consumers worldwide, including
  - storage and management software,
  - servers,
  - access devices (PCs and hand-helds),
  - imaging and printing.

Merger of equals?

Companies typically pursue mergers and acquisitions to create value by acquiring technologies and products, by accessing valuable overseas markets, or by establishing global brand presence. Results vary depending on whether the integration is a merger of equals or the absorption of one company by another. In a merger of equals, a new company with a new and vibrant corporate culture often emerges, whereas in an unequal situation, the acquirer's culture and systems usually dominate. HP's merger with Packard was not quite a merger of equals, as the new company would be 64 percent owned by HP, 36 percent by Compaq.

The combined company would have 145,000 multicultural employees in more than 160 countries. Thus, an important focus in the merger negotiations was agreeing upon an outline plan for *country-level integration*. In the post-merger period, top management took six months to develop detailed country-level integration plans. These included identifying and appointing country managers.

During the negotiations, the companies calculated that the merger could generate cost synergies of around $2.5 billion annually. On the other hand, both sides recognised that *cultural differences* between HP and Compaq could act as a barrier to effective integration. Pre-merger due diligence checked financial data, but left the important issue of culture in abeyance. Deloitte (2009) makes the point that culture surveys and assessment tools could have been used at this stage to assess the risks of clashing corporate cultures affecting results, but that pressures to finalise the merger ruled out such lengthy efforts. Instead, both sides agreed that the issue of culture would have to be addressed by launching a rigorous integration programme immediately after the merger came into effect.

Integration process

Burgelman & McKinney (2006) identify critical components that capture the dynamics of the integration process following a merger:

1. The *integration logic* is formulated by top management and consultants. Long-term strategic and financial goals are set together with the product-market position of the merged company.
2. *Operational integration,* a 6- to 12-month process, is carefully planned by management. Short-term synergies are identified. Redundant products are phased out, and new organisation structures activated. Urgent short-term goals are addressed, for example, holding onto customers.
3. *Strategic integration* involves scanning the rapidly evolving competitive environment, and communicating and achieving long-term performance goals.

When the HP-Compaq negotiations concluded, an integration planning team was formed to guide the integration process, and 1,500 senior people eventually became involved full-time in integration planning (Burgelman & McKinney, 2006). The planning team's role – with help of the two companies' legal and HR staffs – was to define and communicate exactly how the new organisation and related decision-making processes would work. To drive home the importance of managing cultural differences in the new company, the topic was placed on the agenda of meetings of the integration steering committee. The committee comprised a small group of senior executives who could rapidly make decisions and have those decisions be completely unquestioned during execution.

The integration programme had clearly defined synergy targets with short deadlines, set by top-level management, which had the effect of forcing immediate cooperation between managers from each company in order to achieve the desired goals. Integration was promoted by retaining *separate core capabilities*. For instance, the integration team chose the better of what was currently used by HP and Compaq and made that the winner as fast as possible. In effect, each company's functional strengths were identified and allowed to dominate in the new company. Thus, the new company kept HP's strong Printer Division. HP's sales force, on the other hand, was integrated into the highly effective Compaq model. The underlying thinking was that the faster two merged companies can come together, the sooner they will reap the synergies and other benefits of the merger.

Decision-making

Achieving the integration programme's goals would require changes. Consequently, teams of managers were asked to identify operational areas that might benefit from integration planning – areas such as logistics, compensation systems, financial reporting and decision-making. Multinational firms often find it difficult to make decisions quickly and correctly after a merger, and HP and Compaq were no exception. For instance, engineers from both firms would, in the new company, carefully analyse large bodies of data and only then make a decision. Worse, they seemed to regard a desire for more data as a legitimate reason to delay a decision. Such an approach to decision-making, if unchecked, could delay an effective integration. So management intervened by requiring technical units throughout the combined company to emphasise action, and to limit analysis activities to currently available data and options.

Procurement savings

As part of the integration process, management workshops were organised to discuss specific practices in the new company which might have a negative impact on business results and which therefore needed to be changed. One workshop, for instance, came up with proposals for substantial cost savings by implementing a procurement savings plan. The plan was implemented rapidly. It allowed the company to capitalise on its new scale and greater bargaining power and the comparative price information it now had as a result of being able to compare HP and Compaq vendor prices, by submitting to suppliers specific requests for reduced pricing. As a result, $1.1 billion was saved in procurement in the first six months following the merger.

Questions:

1. What integration and performance problems could the IJV eventually experience as a result of cultural and other differences? What actions by management might help to reduce these problems?
2. Explain the main differences between operational integration and strategic integration.
3. What are the advantages and disadvantages of negotiators' discussing initial integration plans while merger negotiations are ongoing?

Importance of cultural compatibility

According to Cartwright & Cooper's (1996) model of culture compatibility, the cultures of the companies must be similar in order for integration to be fully successful. The success of the merged company depends on the ability of the partners to create a coherent "third culture," containing elements of both pre-merger cultures. If the companies have dissimilar national and corporate cultures, major integration problems will result. For instance, employees may actively resist making the many changes needed for a third culture to take root.

When Meritor Automotive bought Volvo's heavy-vehicle axle plant in Sweden in 1998, the integration challenge was as much psychological and cultural as it was operational. The Volvo plant produced all its own axle components, but when it was taken over, it became part of Meritor's global manufacturing system and needed to outsource the production of noncore components that it used to make itself. The changes required a huge shift in mindset. Ashkenas & Francis (2000) describe how this was achieved by means of an integration workshop for Swedish and Meritor managers at which several projects were identified and launched that could achieve business results in 100 days or less and that would demonstrate the benefits of being part of the Meritor global supply system.

Control issues in acquired companies

Acquirers with different country origins tend to implement different *control systems* in acquired firms. French acquirers exercise greater formal control over targets than do British or US acquirers (Calori et al., 1994). US acquirers rely more on informal communication and cooperation than the French, and use formal control mechanisms more than British acquirers. According to Schein (1986), the culturally sensitive exporting of an acquiring company's corporate culture to an overseas acquisition usually allows control to be exercised in an acceptable and effective manner.

Cross-border acquisitions often lead to some convergence in HR approaches to best accepted practice, for example, performance-related pay. After studying several successful acquisitions, Bower (2001) concludes that most acquisitions seem to follow a sequence of steps:

1. The acquirer's accounting and control systems are installed.
2. Non-essential processes are rationalised.
3. Businesses that do not fit the acquirer's strategic objectives are sold off.
4. Organisation structure may be changed, and senior management posts in the new structure are filled.

Sometimes an acquired company is allowed to operate independently. It retains the CEO and other senior executives, for instance, and they have the same power and authority as before the acquisition. Kale et al. (2009) note that Tata Group in India used this light-handed approach when it acquired South Korea's Daewoo Commercial Vehicle Company. Daewoo continued to be managed by Korean managers, while working as part of a global alliance with its Indian counterpart.

KEY POINTS

1. International business alliances are partnerships between firms based in different countries that may result in IJVs, joint R&D programmes, co-production agreements, licensing arrangements, multinational franchising deals and so forth. Negotiating an alliance can be a lengthy process. Often the partner is a potential competitor, leading to inhibited information sharing. Each firm fears that the other firm will use the information to gain competitive advantage.

2. In alliance negotiations, partner selection criteria include superior technology, managerial capability, international experience and the network position of potential partners. In the global liner shipping industry, alliance membership boosts a company's position in interorganisational networks. This, in turn, leads to higher innovation rates and lower financing costs.

3. Exploration alliances focus their efforts on searching for something novel, on developing new technologies that will enhance the value creation potential of the partnership. The outcomes and paybacks are distant in time. Exploitation alliances, on the other hand, involve the partner firms in sharing their complementary assets to maximise joint value creation.

4. Strategic alliances enable firms to gain competitive advantage in the international marketplace. Reasons which motivate companies to form alliances are to enable them to carry out joint R&D programmes, to optimise production, to improve quality standards or to increase international marketing effectiveness. Negotiators must be willing to change their negotiating positions to avoid conflict and keep the negotiations moving towards agreement.

5. IJVs have a high potential for gain but also a high potential for loss. Many agreements to establish an IJV are never implemented – more than half in China. IJVs that are implemented may underperform because of underinvestment. One or more partners may delay full investment until they are sure that market conditions are favourable.

6. Little is known from the research about the dynamics of *multiparty* negotiations to establish alliances. The increasing number of multiparty alliance agreements among airlines and among companies in diverse sectors make it essential for managers to gain a better understanding of the factors involved.

7. International companies negotiate joint ventures with companies in the developing world to gain access to local and regional markets. Usually the international company contributes equity capital and technology, while the local company provides human resources and specialised market knowledge. Negotiators need to be realistic about the possibility of future disputes occurring between the partners and should specify in the contract the national law to be used in case litigation becomes necessary.

8. Interpersonal conflict may occur among IJV due to different work routines but also to conflicting cultural values, beliefs, languages and social conventions.

Cultural and linguistic challenges lead to emotional conflict that reduces overall performance. Conflict may erupt if one of the partners tries to change the terms of the contract or attempts to take control of the decision-making.

9. In some IJVs, the knowledge and experience of local managers are inadequate compared to international standards and lead to poor bottom-line results.

10. Arrangements for training local managers should be agreed at the negotiation stage and specified in the contract. In many cases, expatriate managers will be given the responsibility for training local staff.

11. Trust is the critical factor that determines the partners' commitment to an IJV. Even at the negotiation stage, trustworthy behaviour is more likely if there are prior ties among alliance members which give partners knowledge of how the other partner reacts to problems and conflicts. Long-term trustworthy behaviour by IJV partners largely depends on the quality of governance in the country where the venture is located. Partners may stray from ethical behaviour if laws and regulations in the country are seen as unenforceable.

QUESTIONS FOR DISCUSSION AND WRITTEN ASSIGNMENTS

1. What are the major *negotiating issues* that typically need to be addressed in IJV negotiations?

2. In negotiations between an international company and a small company in a developing country to set up an IJV, what might be each company's *negotiating interests*? What actions might be taken by a negotiating team to identify or clarify the other side's negotiating interests?

3. "In IJVs, dominant foreign ownership structure minimises opportunistic behaviours of local partners and reduces potential partner conflict." Develop this argument.

BIBLIOGRAPHY

Aiello, R. J. & Watkins, M. D. The fine art of friendly acquisition. *HBR*, 78 (6), 2000, 100–107.

Arif, H. & Butt, A. N. Packages and Mitsubishi – international joint venture negotiations. *Asian Case Research Journal*, 10 (1), 2006, 55–76.

Ashkenas, R. N. & Francis, S. C. Integration managers: special leaders for special times. *Harvard Business Review*, 78 (6), 2000, 108–116.

Bazerman, M. H. & Neale, M. A. Negotiating rationally: the power and impact of the negotiator's frame. *Academy of Management Executive*, 6 (3), 1992, 42–51.

Beamish, P. W., Morrison, A. J., Rosenzweig, P. M. & Inkpen, A. *International Management*. McGraw-Hill, 2000.

Bjorkman, I., Stahl, G. & Vaara, E. Impact of cultural differences on capability transfer in acquisitions. *Journal of International Business Studies*, 38, 2007, 658–672.

Boone, A. L. et al. The determinants of corporate board size and composition: an empirical analysis. *Journal of Financial Economics*, 85, 2007, 66–101.

Bower, C. L. Not all M&As are alike – and that matters. *HBR*, 79 (3), 2001, 92–101.

Brett, J. M. & Okumura, T. Inter- and intracultural negotiation: U.S. and Japanese negotiators. *Academy of Management Journal*, 41 (5), 1998, 495–510.

Burgelman, R. A. & McKinney, W. Managing strategic dynamics OT acquisition integration: lessons from HP and Compaq. *California Management Review*, 48, 2006, 6–12.

Calori, R., Lubatkin, M. & Very, P. Control mechanisms in cross-border acquisitions: an international comparison. *Organisational Studies*, 15, 1994, 361–379.

Carter, M. W., Mahoney, J. T. & Northcraft, G. B. Testing the waters: using collective real options to manage the social dilemma of strategic alliances. *Academy of Management Review*, 36 (4), 2011, 621–640.

Cartwright, S. & Cooper, C. L. *Managing Mergers, Acquisitions, and Strategic Alliances: Integrating People and Cultures*. Butterworth-Heinemann, 2nd ed., 1996.

Child J. & Yan Y. Investment and control in inter-national joint ventures: the case of China. *Journal of World Business*, 34, 1999, 3–15.

Dai, C. & Lahiri, S. International business alliance under asymmetric information: technology vis-à-vis information advantage. *Southern Economic Journal*, 77 (3), 2011, 599–622

Das, T. K. & Kumar, R. Interpartner negotiations in alliances: a strategic framework. *Management Decision*, 49 (8), 2011, 1235–1256.

Das, T. K. & Teng, B. Managing risks in strategic alliances. *Academy of Management Executive* 13, 1999, 50–62.

Deloitte Consulting. *Cultural Issues in Mergers and Acquisitions*, Deloitte Consulting LLP, 2009.

Demirbaga, M. & Mirzab, H. Factors affecting international joint venture success: an empirical analysis of foreign–local partner relationships and performance in joint ventures in Turkey. *International Business Review*, 9 (1), 2000, 1–35.

Ding, D. Exploring Chinese conflict management styles in joint venture in the People's Republic of China. *Management Research News*, 19 (9), 1996, 45–55.

Dupont, C. International business negotiations. In V. A. Kremenyuk (ed.) *International Negotiation: Analysis, Approaches, Issues*. Jossey-Bass, 1991, 331–342.

Dyer, J. H., Kale, P. & Singh, H. How to make strategic alliances work. *MIT Sloan Management Review*, 42, 2001, 37–43.

Faems, D., Janssens, M. & Madhok, A. Toward an integrative perspective on alliance governance: connecting contract design, trust dynamics, and contract application. *Academy of Management Journal*, 51 (6), 2008, 1053–1076.

Faure, G. O. Negotiations to set up joint ventures in China. *International Negotiation*, 5, 2000, 157–189.

Fehr, B. *Friendship Processes*. Sage, 1996.

Gillman, A. The link between valuations and due diligence. *Academy of Accounting and Financial Studies Journal*, 6 (2), 2002, 10–13.

Greve, H. R., Baum, J. A. C., Mitsuhashi, H. & Rowley, T. J. Built to last but falling apart: cohesion, friction, and withdrawal from interfirm alliances. *Academy of Management Journal*, 53 (2), 2010, 302–322.

Gulati, R. Does familiarity breed trust? *Academy of Management Journal*, 38, 1995, 85–112.

Hofstede, G. *Culture's Consequences: International Differences in Work-related Values*. Sage, 1980.

Hoskisson, R. A., Hitt, M. A., Ireland, A. & Duane, R. *Competing for Advantage*. Thomson Learning, 2004.

Inkpen, A. C. & Ross, J. Why do some strategic alliances persist beyond their useful life? *California Management Review*, 44 (1), 2001, 132–148.

Kale, P., Singh H. & Ramans, A. P. Don't integrate your acquisition, partner with them. *HBR*, 2009, 109–115.

Kanter, R. M. Mergers that stick. *HBR*, 2009, 87 (10), 121–125.

Klijn, E. et al. Performance implications of IJV Boards: a contingency perspective. *Journal of Management Studies*, 50 (7), 2013, 1245–1266.

Kogut, B. & Singh, H. The effect of national culture on the choice of entry mode. *Journal of International Business Studies*, 19, 1988, 411–432.

Koza, M. P. & Lewin, A. Y. The coevolution of strategic alliances. *Organization Science*, 9, 1998, 225–264.

Kulshreshtha, A. K. How to carry out international business negotiations for industrial globalization overseas. *Chemical Business*, 2009, 17–19.

Kumar, R. & Nti, K. O. National cultural values and the evolution of process and outcome discrepancies in international strategic alliances. *Journal of Applied Behavioral Science*, 40, 2004, 344–361

Kumar, R. & Patriotta, G. Culture and international alliance negotiations: a sensemaking perspective. *International Negotiation*, 16, 2011, 511–533.

Lander, M. W. & Kooning, L. Boarding the aircraft: trust development amongst negotiators of a complex merger. *Journal of Management Studies*, 50 (1), 2013, 1–30.

Lasserre, P. *Global Strategic Management*. New York: Palgrave Macmillan, 2007.

Lewicki, R. J., Saunders, D. M. & Minton, J. W. *Negotiation*. McGraw-Hill, 3rd ed., 1999.

Li, J., Zhou, C. & Zajac, E. Control, collaboration, and productivity in international joint ventures: theory and evidence. *Strategic Management Journal*, 30, 2009, 865–884.

Liu, Z. Foreign direct investment and technology spillovers: theory and evidence. *Journal of Development Economics*, 85 (1/2), 2008, 176–193.

March, J. G. Exploration and exploitation in organizational learning. *Organization Science*, 2, 1991, 71–87.

Meyer, K. E. et al. Doing business in Vietnam. *Thunderbird International Business Review*, 48 (2), 2006, 263–290.

Miller, R. R., Glen, J. D., Jaspersen, F. Z. & Karmokolias, Y. International joint venture in developing countries: happy marriage? IFC Discussion Paper 29, 1997.

Mitchell, J. & Hohl, B. Fiat's strategic alliance with Tata (Case # SM-1528-E). Center for Globalization and Strategy, IESE Business School, University of Navarra, Barcelona, 2008.

Park, G. & Kang, J. Alliance addiction: do alliances create real benefits? *Creativity and Innovation Management*, 22 (1), 2013, 53–66.

Pfeffer, J. A resource dependence perspective on intercorporate relations. In M. Mizruchi & M. Schwartz (eds) *Intercorporate Relations*. Cambridge University Press, 1988, 25–55.

Rao, A., Asha, D. & Schmidt, S. A behavioral perspective on negotiating international alliances. *Journal of International Business Studies*, 29 (4), 1999, 665–694.

Reus, T. H. & Ritchie III, W. J. Interpartner, parent, and environmental factors influencing the operation of international joint ventures: 15 years of research. *Management International Review*, 44 (4), 2004, 369–395.

Ricks, D. *Blunders in International Business*. Blackwell, 3rd ed., 1999.

Robins, J. A., Tallam, S. & Fladmoe-Lindquist, K. Autonomy and dependence of international cooperative ventures: an exploration of the strategic performance of U.S. ventures in Mexico. *Strategic Management Journal*, 23 (10), 2002, 881–901.

Rothaermel, F. T. & Deeds, D. L. Exploration and exploitation alliances in biotechnology: a system of new product development. *Strategic Management Journal*, 25 (3), 2004, 201–221.

Schein, E. Culture: the missing concept in organisational studies. *Administrative Science Quarterly*, 41 (2), 1986, 229–240.

Schweiger, D. M. *M&A Integration: A Framework for Executives and Managers*. McGraw-Hill, 2002.

Schweiger, D. M. & Goulet, P. K. Integrating mergers and acquisitions: an international research review. In C. L. Cooper & A. Gregory (eds) *Advances in Mergers and Acquisitions*, Vol. 1, JAI Press, 2000, 61–91.

Segil, L. *Measuring the Value of Partnering: How to Use Metrics to Plan, Develop, and Implement Successful Alliances*. Amacom, 2004.

Shankarmahesh, M. N., Ford, J. B. & LaTour, M. S. Determinants of satisfaction in sales negotiations with foreign buyers: perceptions of US export executives. *International Marketing Review*, 21 (4/5), 2004, 423–446.

Shi, W., Sun, S. L. & Peng, M. W. Sub-national institutional contingencies, network positions, and IJV partner selection. *Journal of Management Studies*, 49 (7), 2012, 1221–1245.

Urban, S. Negotiating international joint ventures. In P. Ghauri & J-C. Usunier (eds) *International Business Negotiations.* Pergamon, 1996, 231–251.

Vaara, E., Sarala, R., Stahl, G. K. & Bjorkman, I. The impact of organisational and national cultural differences on social conflict and knowledge transfer in international acquisitions. *Journal of Management Studies,* 49 (1), 2012, 1–27.

Vanpouckeab, E. & Vereecke, A. The predictive value of behavioural characteristics on the success of strategic alliances. *International Journal of Production Research,* 48 (22), 2010, 6715–6738.

Weiss, S. The IBM-Mexico microcomputer investment negotiations. In P. Ghauri & J-C. Usunier (eds) *International Business Negotiations.* Pergamon, 1996, 305–334.

Williamson, P. J. & Raman, A. P. How China reset its global acquisition agenda. *HBR,* 89 (4), April 2011, 109–114.

Wittmann, C., Hunt, S. & Arnett, D. Explaining alliance success. *Industrial Marketing Management,* 38, 2009, 743–756.

Yan, A. & Gray, B. Bargaining power, management control, and performance in United States-China joint ventures. *Academy of Management Journal,* 37, 1994, 1478–1518.

Zhao, J. J. The Chinese approach to international business negotiation. *The Journal of Business Communication,* 37 (3), 2000, 209–237.

Zweifel, T. D. *Culture Clash.* Swiss Consulting Group, 2003.

Dispute Resolution

11

INTRODUCTION

As the number of international business transactions increases, so too does the number of potential disputes between the parties. Disputes are a natural part of the dynamics of international business negotiation, and many can be resolved by the parties themselves during the course of a negotiation. For instance, a negotiator can make a small concession to demonstrate good will, hoping the other side will reciprocate or suggest a deadline for reaching agreement on a divisive issue. When negotiators are angry, they may find it difficult to express their feelings coherently since violent emotions overcome their analytical verbal facility. So asking an angry negotiator to explain his or her reasons for being violently opposed to a proposal or an offer, and then listening carefully while he or she explains, may be all that is needed to reduce the level of conflict. Disputes which are complex and deep rooted can sometimes be resolved by using an incremental approach, such as Lowi & Rothman's (1993) 3-phase conflict-resolution model, which consists of adversarial, reflexive and integrative phases. The reflexive phase can have the effect of "unfreezing" the intransigent, adversarial feelings of the disputants, thus enabling them to move towards a more positive and cooperative approach.

Firms which are locked in serious post-contractual disputes often resort to formal dispute-resolution remedies, that is, litigation, arbitration, mediation. Litigation tends to be expensive and lengthy, and many firms prefer to settle out of court rather than go to trial. In arbitration, the arbitrator gives both sides an equal opportunity to present their arguments, but in the end the arbitrator decides the outcome. In mediation, a neutral third party, the mediator, helps the parties come to an agreement on their own. According to PricewaterhouseCoopers (2006), however, the speed and sophistication of international business transactions does not tolerate dispute resolution through long drawn-out formal procedures. In international business, quicker, simpler methods are needed to resolve disputes. An example of a simple method is providing clarifications or additional information when one of the parties strongly objects during negotiations to the other side's proposals for dealing with an issue.

In international business negotiations, different types of conflict are associated with different types of negotiation strategies (Harinck et al., 2000). *Principled negotiation* requires the parties to make a real effort to understand each other's interests, and to think of the other party as a negotiating partner rather than as a negotiating opponent. Bazerman et al. (2000) argue that a principled negotiation approach depends on each side's developing a realistic mental model of the other side, including the other side's goals, interests and strategies. Adopting a principled approach leads the parties to seek ways of resolving a conflict in such a way that joint gains are made.

When a company acts to resolve a serious dispute with a foreign government, commercial considerations are usually the company's main concern, but in many cases these are not the government's main concern. The government, unlike the company, has no shareholders applying commercial pressures. In dispute-resolution talks, a government's stance is more likely to be influenced by policy issues and political goals.

Resolving *multiparty* business disputes mainly depends on building consensus among the parties. A mediator may help build consensus by holding joint discussions with all disputants, as well as by having separate one-to-one conversations with each party. Ideas and suggestions gained from this kind of shuttle diplomacy help the mediator develop a settlement framework that is acceptable to all parties.

Traditional conflict management approaches have, according to some authors, a Western cultural bias. Cameron (2000) argues that Asians express feelings about a serious conflict in *indirect* ways. They use words that are less explicit than those used in Western countries during conflict-resolution negotiations. For Asian negotiators, it might not be appropriate or effective to talk candidly about the feelings underlying a serious conflict that damaged an international business partnership.

INTERNATIONAL BUSINESS CONFLICT

Concept and definitions

Conflict is a natural part of the dynamics of international business negotiation (Brett & Crotty, 2008). Indeed, conflict is inherent in and is part of any negotiated business deal. If there is no conflict, then there is no need to negotiate.

As the number of international business transactions increases, so too does the number of potential disputes between the parties. Many potential areas of conflict in international business have been identified by authors and managers. They include

- opportunism by alliance and international joint venture (IJV) partners;
- disputed ownership of trademarks and copyrights;
- late delivery of goods; late payments;
- project management or royalty fees;
- disputed funding arrangements;
- standards of performance in joint venture companies.

Negotiation is a process by which people with conflicting interests determine how they are going to allocate resources or work together, and conflict results when they disagree – or when they see the other party as an obstacle preventing them from achieving their goals (Brett & Crotty, 2008).

International business negotiations may break down altogether if there is conflict and disagreement about most of the major negotiating issues. Ghauri (1996) describes negotiations between a Swedish machinery manufacturer and an Indian company to try to draw up a cooperation agreement. The draft agreement produced by the Swedish firm was discussed but eventually thrown out as there was strong disagreement about most of the issues discussed. These included sales conditions, prices, working hours of Swedish expatriates and the governing law of the contract.

Positive effects of conflict

However, conflict in negotiations can have positive results. For example, conflict generated by a proposal to repatriate a proportion of an IJV's net profits may motivate the parties to construct new and creative rules and clearer guidelines to prevent similar conflicts occurring in the future. Another example of the positive effect of conflict is when strong disagreements about, say, budgets or cost allocations or profit distribution, rise through different levels of the company until they are settled. In this case, the conflict has the unintended positive effect of keeping top-level management informed. Researchers have pointed to other positive consequences of conflict at the level of the company. Thomas (1976), for instance, points out that conflict can

- contribute to a healthy level of stimulation and activity in the organisation;
- produce ideas of a quality superior to those produced without conflict;
- encourage internal cohesiveness among disputing groups;
- lead to improved relationships in the organisation.

Different types of conflict are associated with different kinds of negotiation strategies. In international business negotiations conflict is often managed crudely through domination strategies, which usually lead to victory for the dominating party. Compromise strategies, on the other hand, involve mutual give and take in which each party loses something in the interests of suppressing the conflict and reaching an agreement.

Types of conflict in negotiations

Task conflict

Two important kinds of conflict that occur during international business negotiations as well as in post-contractual disputes are task conflict and emotional conflict. In task conflict, individual negotiators or negotiating teams disagree about task-related issues such as goals, procedures, decision areas, actions that should be taken, timing details and so on. Task conflict is often positive in terms of its effect on performance since it leads to a deeper understanding of task issues and an exchange of views and information that facilitate problem-solving and decision-making by the parties (Guirdham, 2005).

Emotional conflict

Emotional conflict in negotiations usually takes the form of interpersonal clashes between members of the negotiating teams. The clashes are characterised by anger, frustration and other negative feelings. In international business negotiations in which the negotiators come from diverse cultures, emotional conflict may be based more on stereotyping and less on social comparison than is the case with domestic business negotiations (Pelled et al., 1999). In international business negotiations, dissimilarity in ethnicity and behaviour increases emotional conflict and may cause heated exchanges between negotiating teams.

Importance of speed

Having to operate in conditions of persistent conflict with foreign clients or international business partners exposes a company to risks and unnecessary costs that affect its ability to maximise profits. Thus, every effort must be made by companies to resolve international business disputes as early as possible – while they are still manageable. If the parties are unable to resolve a dispute on their own, they may need to seek expert assistance from a neutral third party, but in many cases help from a third party is not needed. Negotiators often prove capable of resolving disputes on their own, by listening to each other and by being willing compromise.

On the other hand, some international business disputes are serious and lasting. They persist long after the original negotiations between the parties have ended. To find a solution, the parties may have no choice but to use the formal dispute-resolution procedures of litigation, arbitration or mediation. But in international business, speed is important. Thus PricewaterhouseCoopers (2006) points out that the speed and sophistication of international business transactions does not tolerate dispute resolution through formal legal procedures developed by and for the convenience of the legal and accounting professions. In international business, quicker, less formal methods of dispute resolution are often needed.

Many of the disputes that disrupt international business negotiations are capable of being resolved there and then by negotiators' being motivated to take simple, self-help actions. An easy way of reducing the risk of disputes disrupting a negotiation is to deal with the less difficult and less controversial agenda items first. In this way, a number of positive outcomes can be obtained before disagreements occur about more contentious issues such as terms of payment, fees, starting and finishing dates, and other issues on which neither side will give way.

Self-help actions

Other self-help actions that international business negotiators can take to avoid or reduce conflict are the following:

- *Make a concession.* Sometimes conflict in an international business negotiation can be resolved and deadlock avoided by one of the parties making a small concession to demonstrate good will.

- *Suggest a deadline.* One of the parties could suggest imposing a deadline for reaching agreement on a difficult, controversial issue, such as a deadline for completing an international project and consultancy fees to be paid. Deadlines put pressure on negotiators not to use stalling tactics and other types of time wasting. They encourage concession-making and therefore faster progress towards agreement.

- *Take a break.* If negotiations are adjourned to the next day, for instance, this gives both sides a chance to assess what has been achieved so far and, if necessary, to re-evaluate and adjust their goals and strategies.

When deadlock is caused by a particular issue such as a price or a deadline, a breakthrough can sometimes be found by the parties *restating and clarifying their negotiating positions* regarding the issue. When this happens, the weakness of a negotiating position may be exposed, leading the party concerned to adjust and strengthen their position and break the deadlock.

Impact of emotion

Two groups of management trainees are brought into a conference room. They sit on opposite sides of the table in confrontation position. Red nametags and pens are given to one group, green to the other. The groups then complete questionnaires in sight of each other. There is no communication between them. Yet within minutes each group is feeling strong aggressive feelings and fear of the rival group. Violent emotional reactions like these may be triggered in an international business negotiation by such trivia as the other team's hairstyles or pronunciation or skin colour. Fear, suspicion, insecurity and rivalry are the basic raw materials from which these aggressive feelings are made. They can prevent international business negotiators learning each other's viewpoints or truly "hearing" what is being proposed. The interior static can turn a negotiation into a dialogue of the deaf, with conflict just below the surface waiting to erupt.

As the example suggests, conflict in negotiations involves the expression of strong emotions, and people who are emotionally engaged or upset often find it difficult to explain what they are thinking and feeling since violent emotions tend to overcome people's analytical verbal ability (Benish-Weisman, 2009). Under these circumstances, negotiators may be unable to resolve the conflict without the help of an independent third party or some other form of external intervention.

Role of third parties

In the context of international business, mediation is an important form of external intervention since it can modify the stereotypes that conflicting parties may hold of each other. The mediator's starting point is to understand each party's perceptions of the opposing party and of the conflict situation. The mediator ensures that the parties understand each other through listening and paraphrasing skills. However, the parties must solve their own problems. The role of the mediator is to be a facilitator of communication, to ensure that the parties listen to each other on a deeper level than previous hostile feelings allowed.

Members of collectivist cultures usually prefer to settle post-negotiation disputes through further negotiation between the parties and mediation. The assumption is that trusted intermediaries will help both sides confront the issues more effectively. The Chinese assume that compromise and mediation will reduce animosity between the disputants and preserve the business relationship that has been established (Chen, 1996). In many other collectivist countries, trust precedes business, and managers often spend much time and effort at the pre-negotiation stage building trusting relationships with counterparts so that the risk of potential conflict is reduced. Trust in negotiations is sometimes linked to the size of company with which negotiations are held. Thus, Arab negotiators interviewed by Khakhar & Rammal (2013) said they would trust a large foreign multinational enterprise (MNE) more than they would a smaller foreign company looking to enter the Arab region.

Dispute-resolution methods based on further negotiations between the parties do not work well when the parties negotiating have extremely unequal power, as when a serious dispute occurs between a large international firm and a smaller foreign company. Bowen (2005) makes the point that in such cases, the help of a third party might be sought to undertake empowerment of the low-power party in order to alleviate this situation. An outside consultant, for instance, might provide insight into different options open to the low-power disputant.

Advocacy advisors intervene in a conflict on behalf of one of the parties and not as neutral intermediaries. Their aim is to apply their knowledge of conflict-resolution processes to the party's effort to find a solution. Differing types of advocacy advisers specialise in different approaches to disputes. Lawyers specialise in litigation-based strategies, for instance.

Cultural factors

In low-context cultures, dispute-resolution methods that are used usually break disputes down into their component parts and deal with each part in turn. According to Salacuse (1998), for instance, Americans prefer to resolve international business disputes by settling a series of little problems one at a time. High-context cultures, by contrast, attempt to achieve dispute resolution through adaptation and to avoid dichotomous either/or possibilities (Guirdham, 2005). Latin Americans and Chinese negotiators, for instance, prefer to agree to a few general dispute-resolution principles that can be used to resolve particular facets of the dispute.

According to Cameron (2000), conflict-resolution methods that rely on open communication and on inducing the parties to candidly talk to each other have a distinctly Western (low-context) cultural bias. Asian business people, for instance, generally use indirect and implicit communication as opposed to open communication to express their feelings about a business conflict and the people from other cultures who are involved in it. To the extent that they discuss the conflict, they tend to use words that are less explicit and blunt than those used by negotiators in Western countries. In China, Japan and some other Asian countries, *face negotiation* has implications for how people manage conflict. Thus, Ting-Toomey & Kurogi (1998) argue that culturally competent facework is an important aspect of dispute management.

A difficulty that impedes some dispute-resolution approaches that rely on talking is finding word equivalents for emotions across cultures. Russian negotiators, for instance, would find it difficult to explain to a third party how strongly they felt that the behaviour of their Japanese counterparts in a negotiation was *unfair* since there is no word for "fair" in Japanese or Russian.

Case Study

MINI-CASE: Conflict between Canadian and Venezuelan partners

A Canadian engineering company and a Venezuelan firm are holding negotiations to set up a joint venture in Venezuela to produce and market a range of domestic electrical products. The Canadian negotiating team points out that their patents, know-how and trademark are very well known internationally and would help the IJV market its products throughout South America.

The Venezuelan team responds positively to this argument and on this basis agrees to the Canadian negotiators' proposal that the IJV should pay a fee to the Canadian company to use the trademark. After several more rounds of negotiation, the two firms sign an agreement to establish a 50/50 joint venture. But the IJV starts to experience problems almost immediately.

Within a few months of the IJV company's becoming operational, Canadian managers in the IJV are becoming embroiled in culturally loaded disputes with their Venezuelan counterparts. The two sides start to blame each other for poor marketing and procurement decisions and for unrealistic production scheduling. A more basic problem is how the IJV managers can achieve a better understanding of a market that is becoming more complex by the day. Some of the complexity arises from a trickle of new government regulations, and also from intense competitive pressures as other local and foreign manufacturers jostle for a piece of the market,

Matters are brought to a head when the Venezuelan parent company learns that many of the Canadian company's patents have in fact expired so that their value is considerably less than was assumed during the negotiations to establish the venture. Moreover, the Venezuelan parent company will be selling at least three-quarters of the IJV's products inside Venezuela, and so will not need to use the Canadian company's trademark. There is no reason, therefore, why the IJV should pay the trademark licence fee as specified in the agreement. The agreement will have to be renegotiated. Do the Canadians agree?

The Canadian parent company in Toronto is unsure how to respond to this suggestion.

Questions:

1. How should the Canadian company respond to the Venezuelan proposal for a renegotiation?
2. What ways other than renegotiation could be found to deal with the patent and trademark problems identified by the Venezuelans? How might these alternative approaches help resolve the conflict?
3. What arguments might be used to support the point of view that renegotiation would be damaging for the IJV and for the partnership between the two parent companies?

Intergroup dialogue

A mechanism which has been successfully used to resolve serious cases of conflict between parties from different cultures in a controlled, constructive way is *intergroup dialogue*. In intergroup dialogue, the parties engage in meaningful conversations for the purpose of developing a better understanding of their opponents. According to Williams (1994), intergroup dialogue proceeds through a sequence of distinct stages:

1. The parties describe what they find offensive in each other's behaviour.
2. By carefully listening to each other, they get an understanding of each other's cultural perceptions.
3. By listening, each side learns how the problem would be handled in the opponent's culture.

At the end of the discussion, the parties have a much better understanding of each other's position, and are often able to agree on a method of reaching a conflict resolution.

Other ways of resolving serious post-negotiation disputes include those described by Tinsley (1998), who identifies differences in the way in which Japanese, German and US managers handle disputes. Japanese managers prefer the dispute to be resolved by higher authority, German managers prefer to use pre-existing procedures, rules and regulations to settle the dispute, while US managers focus on addressing the underlying issue.

FORMAL DISPUTE RESOLUTION

Post-contractual disputes

Many international business partnerships experience disputes long after the initial negotiations have been concluded, that is, during the implementation period of the contact. Some of these disputes are serious and long lasting. Common reasons for post-contractual disputes to occur have been identified by researchers, including Wilkenfeld et al. (2003) and Tinsley (1999). Common reasons include

- disputes about costs and prices,
- conflicting objectives of the partners,
- lack of contract or commercial management expertise,
- lack of transparency between supplier and client,
- mismatch of expectations between the client and the supplier,
- poor definition in the contract of the scope of service,
- disagreement about exit management arrangements.

Examples of post-contractual disputes are the following:

- A European equipment supplier to overseas development programmes wishes to cancel a distribution agreement made with a business partner in Brazil. The Brazilian partner insists on keeping to the terms of the original contract and threatens litigation.
- An African government makes a reassessment of its terms of business with a foreign investor because the country's need for investor capital and technology is less than it was a few years ago at the time of the original contract. The government calls for the original contract to be renegotiated.
- A Pakistani company wishes to renegotiate a Pakistani-Japanese joint venture contract in order to increase its representation on the new company's board, but the Japanese company refuses to consider the proposal.

To find a solution to disputes such as these, the parties may have to resort to using formal dispute-resolution procedures, notably mediation, arbitration and litigation.

To reduce the potential negative impact of future disputes, negotiators should ensure at the negotiation stage that appropriate clauses are inserted in the contract, specifying actions to be taken if future disputes occur. Such clauses often state, for instance, the dispute-resolution procedure to be used – litigation, arbitration or mediation – and the geographical location of any dispute-resolution hearing. Location is important. In China, for instance, it is unwise for parties to select a non-Chinese location since, as Wang (2009) explains, Chinese courts will usually not enforce a foreign court judgment.

Disputes with a foreign government

When an international company experiences a serious post-contractual dispute with a foreign government and negotiates to resolve the problem, the main concern of the company is commercial, but the government is more likely to be influenced by policy and political considerations, or even by conditions laid down by international lending institutions such as the World Bank or the International Monetary Fund (IMF). Moreover, protocol may rule out an *informal* settlement of the dispute since within a government there is usually a strict hierarchy that dictates who speaks to whom, topics that can be discussed, observance of hierarchy and so on. Such constraints can make progress towards dispute settlement with a foreign government extremely slow – particularly during an election year, when the government will be reluctant to take any actions that could be criticised and lose it votes.

Cost is another factor that companies need to take into account when considering how a serious dispute with a foreign government might be resolved. The cost of prosecuting a government – for maladministration, say, or for withholding payments – is generally much higher and the likelihood of winning much lower than when a private-sector company is being prosecuted. That is why, to improve the chances of the dispute's being quickly resolved, the company's solicitors might have to develop one or more face-saving ways in which the government can settle without having to make a cash payment. An example of such a settlement method is when a government in a developing country agreed to provide rent-free office accommodation in a government building for a company's expatriate staff for the remaining two years of a technical assistance contract.

Renegotiation

Serious disputes between a government and a foreign investor sometimes occur because of a shift in the power balance away from the foreign company and towards the government. When alternative providers of foreign direct investment (FDI) become available, for instance, the government's reliance on the foreign company diminishes, and the government's relative power vis-à-vis the company increases. This increase in relative power may lead the government to repudiate the terms of the original agreement and to call for renegotiation.

In a post-contractual dispute with a foreign company, the government has a decisive advantage – its ability to renegotiate the original contract. Even if the company threatens to arbitrate the dispute, the move could backfire since the government could retaliate by blacklisting the company from future projects. Salacuse (1999) gives the example of a large foreign investment project in a developing country which, at the time of the original contract, was granted exemption by the government from all taxes and duties. But within months it became clear that these terms were having a negative impact on the economy. This prompted the government to call for the contract to be renegotiated.

In cases like these, renegotiation is likely to go ahead, in spite of demands by foreign investors that penalties should be imposed on the party (usually the government) which breaks the original contract.

Danone-Wahaha dispute

As an example of the kind of conflict that foreign companies may experience in an emerging economy, consider the long-running dispute between Group Danone, a giant in dairy product and bottled water markets around the world, and Wahaha, China's largest bottled water company. Danone and Wahaha formed their first joint venture (JV) in 1996, but over the next ten years, the number of JVs grew to 39, with annual sales totalling $2 billion.

Tao & Hillier (2008) describe how, in 2005, Wahaha breached the JV agreement, establishing mirror companies that produced and sold products almost identical to those of the Danone-Wahaha JVs. This led to a serious dispute between the partners. The conflict seemed to be resolved in 2006 when the two sides agreed to integrate the mirror companies into the JVs in return for a payment of $566 million by Danone. The agreement eventually fell through because Zong, Wahaha's founder and chief executive, thought the mirror companies were worth far more than Danone's offer.

Subsequently, Danone requested arbitration in Stockholm and filed lawsuits in Los Angeles and other cities, mainly over trademark infringement. Zong requested arbitration in China to confirm that Wahaha Group owned the Wahaha trademark. Some 12 lawsuits and arbitration cases were initiated within China and six other jurisdictions, and the dispute became one of the biggest IJV disputes in China's history.

In 2009, Danone agreed to sell its 51 percent stake in the joint ventures to Wahaha, putting an end to all legal proceedings. In the end, Danone left China, surrendering its stake in the joint ventures in exchange for an estimated $500 million.

FORMAL DISPUTE-RESOLUTION METHODS

The Danone-Wahaha case illustrates how, when serious disputes arise between international business partners and hostility makes them refuse to talk to each other, some means must be found to resolve the conflict. In such cases, the parties usually resort to formal conflict-resolution procedures. The main formal dispute-resolution remedies available to firms which become embroiled in serious post-contractual disputes are

- litigation,
- arbitration,
- mediation.

Choice of method

When a company is embroiled in a damaging dispute with an international business associate, which dispute-resolution method should be considered? At this stage, an independent adviser should be able to explain the pros and cons of each option. Different types of adviser tend to give different types of advice. Lawyers, for instance, specialise in litigation-based approaches and advice. There are also general conflict-resolution advisers whose advice may vary according to the outcome desired by the parties.

When Lumineau & Malhotra (2011) studied documents relating to 102 interfirm business disputes, they found that the three formal dispute-resolution methods are associated with different costs. The high-cost method is litigation. Yet in spite of the high costs, companies often resort to litigation to resolve complicated, high-stake international business disputes. Some of the reasons for *avoiding* litigation wherever possible are discussed below.

MNEs' PREFERENCES

Seventy-three percent of 143 MNEs surveyed by PricewaterhouseCoopers (2006) preferred to use international arbitration rather than mediation or litigation in national courts to resolve serious international business disputes. Three-quarters of the MNEs surveyed used *administered arbitration* under the auspices of an established arbitration institution for the following reasons:

- convenience
- reputation of the arbitration institution
- familiarity with the proceedings
- prior understanding of the costs and fees involved

Although the possibility of being embroiled in a legal dispute in a foreign country is intimidating for most companies, a minority of the MNEs surveyed preferred litigation to arbitration. These companies were carrying out business mainly in developed countries, and they had confidence in the national courts of the developed countries in which they operated.

The survey uncovered major concerns by the MNEs about structures and mechanisms that are used to resolve international business disputes. The concerns included

- the need to improve the framework for resolving multiparty, multicontract and multiclaim disputes;
- the need for a mechanism to reduce arbitration costs;
- the need to establish an appeals procedure for arbitral awards;
- the need for more countries to become members of the UN Convention on the Recognition and Enforcement of Foreign Arbitral Awards.

Litigation

Western firms often adopt an adversarial, legalistic stance when serious disputes arise in international business and choose litigation as the default method of resolving the problem, even though national legal systems are rarely constructed with a special view to dealing with international business issues (Baxter, 1990). Litigation is an expensive and slow method of settling a complex international business dispute, especially as the original contract may be governed by two or more legal systems. As Long (1994) notes, the possibility of facing the opponent in a court in the opponent's own country is a strong incentive to avoid litigation, bearing in mind that most courts are biased in favour of local firms.

Information that is needed to prepare a party for litigation can be expensive to acquire. Heavy costs are also incurred in paying lawyers' and court fees. Such considerations help explain why most firms settle out of court rather than go to trial. In the US, for instance, only a very small proportion of domestic and international business disputes actually go to trial (Cheit & Gersen, 2000).

Agreeing to an out of court settlement rather than going to trial has important advantages for international business disputants:

- Litigation usually damages any pre-existing business relationship which has been built up and which is integral to a company's international expansion plans.
- Heavy legal fees and time costs contrast with the certainty of a pre-trial settlement. Many firms settle out of court because of their reluctance to risk an unfavourable decision.
- Transnational distribution of assets is common in international business.
- If litigation is pursued and a judgment made, the successful party may find it difficult or impossible to reach the foreign assets.

Litigation may be quicker and less expensive in countries where there are special commercial courts with judges experienced in dealing with commercial cases.

International commercial arbitration is used extensively as an alternative to litigation. But some States are unwilling to arbitrate, and bank creditors and their lawyers tend to prefer litigation for disputes arising out of international loan agreements (Baxter, 1990). Asian companies generally try to avoid litigation when involved in international business disputes. According to Long (1994), law courts in China and other Asian societies are more concerned with serving the interests of society in general than with protecting the rights of individual parties in international business disputes. In some legal systems in the Middle East and North Africa, international business disputes are decided according to principles of sharia law.

Arbitration

Companies around the world use international arbitration in preference to litigation to resolve serious disputes with international business partners. The 1958 United Nations Convention on the Recognition and Enforcement of Foreign Arbitral Awards has 134 signatory countries, including the US, the UK, Japan, Germany, China, Russia and all other industrialised countries (Tractenberg, 2012). China's arbitration commissions handled more than 1,000 disputes involving foreign partners in 2005 (Business China, 24 April 2006).

In arbitration, the parties can choose their own person or persons to adjudicate the dispute between them. This has the consequence that the parties have to pay the arbitrators' fees and the administration costs of the arbitration. According to

Long (1994), disputants from developing countries usually prefer arbitrators of their own nationality, while Westerners are more concerned with the arbitrators' legal and technical expertise. In some developing countries, the inadequacy of arbitration institutions and lack of enforcement of arbitration awards are serious problems. For instance, understaffed and underfunded courts may be incapable of collecting money and assets following an arbitration award.

Arbitration is not necessarily a speedy way of resolving international business disputes. In arbitration between Intel Corporation and Advanced Micro Devices, involving over $1 billion in alleged damages, the parties spent the first six months arguing over the arbitration rules. However, in most cases international arbitration can be concluded within nine months from the filing of the request to the rendering of an award (Tractenberg, 2012). In *ad hoc arbitration*, the parties draft their own rules and procedures. In *administered arbitration*, rules and procedures are provided by an established arbitration institution, such as the American Arbitration Association or the International Chamber of Commerce.

Binding decision

When arbitration is the chosen dispute-resolution method, the disputants present their sides of the conflict to the arbitrator in whatever form and manner they please. The parties can decide whether lawyers should be present at the hearing and what standards of evidence will be used (Sander & Rozdeiczer, 2005). The arbitrator gives both sides an equal opportunity to present their arguments, but in the end it is the arbitrator who decides the outcome. Usually the arbitrator resolves the dispute by issuing an award which is confidential and cannot be appealed.

Choosing to resolve a conflict situation in international business depends on the disputants' attitude to risk. If both parties are risk averse, a *negotiated settlement* would probably be the best option – as opposed to the riskier option of giving an arbitrator the power to determine a settlement.

Hot tubbing

Variations of the arbitration framework include hot tubbing, multiple versus single arbitrators, and binding versus nonbinding arbitration decisions. Hot tubbing is a new procedure used in some arbitration cases in which opposing experts sit side by side and testify simultaneously on behalf of the disputants. The arbitrator questions and tests the experts, as opposed to the parties' counsel doing the questioning. The arbitrator questions the experts to determine where they differ, putting the same questions to each expert in turn. The result, according to Tractenberg (2012), is a less adversarial procedure and greater efficiency in collecting all the information needed to reach the right arbitral decision.

MINI-CASE: Arbitration or mediation?

Working in small groups, study the following situation and answer the questions that follow. Each group may then make a brief presentation of its answer to the other groups for their comments.

An international hotel company is awarded a contract to manage two hotels in a former Soviet republic. The contract specifies the fees and terms of payment for the management services to be provided by the company. But within a few months of the international company's taking over, a dispute arises over the international company's expenses and the calculation of management fees.

The hotel owners, a property company, decide to take action. They inform the hotel company by letter that, with immediate effect, they have decided to withhold payment of fees until the dispute has been settled. The hotel company responds by threatening to terminate the contract, pointing out that if it does so, the owners will immediately have to stop using the name and logos of the international brand.

Both parties decide at this point that arbitration would be a better way than litigation to resolve the dispute, and accordingly, a few weeks later the dispute goes to an arbitration tribunal in the capital city. The owners claim compensation for early termination of contract. The international company counter-claims for failure to pay proper fees. The hearing begins with examining evidence. However, after two days the tribunal asks the disputants if they are willing to go into mediation, explaining that this is a simpler and much less costly process. After taking the advice of legal counsel, both sides agree to this suggestion.

Subsequently, the tribunal, acting as mediator, caucuses with each side privately, sounding out their particular grievances and how they might be willing to compromise. This process continues until, after two days, a compromise is agreed. The hotel company will continue to manage the two hotels as specified under the terms and conditions of the original contract. The owners will pay the management fees previously withheld, together with modest compensation to cover loss of interest earnings on fees not received.

Questions:

1. What would have been the likely outcome for each of the parties if arbitration had been used to resolve the dispute?
2. What would have been the disadvantage to each of the parties of using litigation to resolve the dispute?
3. Was the dispute capable of being resolved by the parties on their own, without the help of a neutral third party?

Mediation

Mediation is a form of third-party intervention in which the mediator helps the parties negotiate an agreement. Mediation is highly appropriate in situations in which parties need to cooperate in the future and therefore do not wish to damage the business relationship that already exists. Where this is the case, mediation is preferable to *arbitration*, which relies on coercion.

The goal of mediation is for a neutral third party to help disputants come to an agreement on their own, as opposed to making a judgment about which party is in the right. Historical data reveal that disputes that are mediated are typically characterised by *compromise* among the disputants, and so are more likely to end in agreement (Wilkenfeld et al., 2003).

In disputes between companies based in different countries and with different languages, misunderstandings are common. Thus, one of the mediator's tasks is to make sure that the messages from each side are correctly interpreted and fully understood by the other side. A mediator is essentially a third party trusted by both sides, and ideally will be fluent in both of the disputants' first languages so that professional interpreters are not needed. Another possibility is to have co-mediators, one fluent in each of the languages. Dominguez-Urban (1997) makes the point that having co-mediators who are culturally similar to the parties reduces the effect of cultural differences and helps build trust in the mediation process.

A mediator helps parties resolve acrimonious business disputes by deflating unreasonable claims, suggesting compromises and encouraging the disputants to search for a solution. Sometimes a mediator will prepare a single negotiating text, then modify it after receiving feedback from the parties. An important advantage of mediation is that it allows the disputing parties to resolve the problem by taking a "business" approach, using business language and arguments, rather than a legal approach. Another advantage is that mediation entails the parties themselves controlling the process and outcome. Mediators use various strategies to facilitate interactions between disputants, but leave it to the disputants themselves to resolve the dispute. The dispute is resolved when the settlement agreement is put in writing and signed by both parties.

Mediators play a more dominant role in collectivistic than in individualistic cultures (Hofstede and Usunier, 1996). Companies in collectivist countries usually prefer to settle international business disputes through mediation. This is because collectivistic societies emphasise harmony, and mediators are able to discuss sensitive issues and help reconcile differences without direct confrontation. Leung (1988) found that managers from Hong Kong preferred mediation as a conflict-resolution method because they judged that mediation reduces animosity and preserves the business relationship. In China, when there is conflict between Chinese and foreign business partners, provincial authorities often play the role of informal mediator. According to Faure (2000), their intervention usually resolves the conflict.

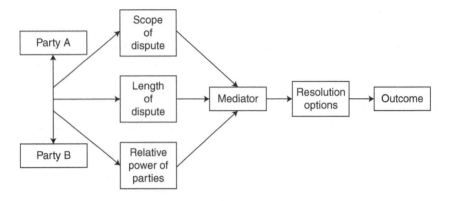

Figure 11.1 Using mediation to resolve international business disputes

Note: A mediator can help resolve acrimonious business disputes by deflating unreasonable claims and suggesting compromises. Mediation is often used as a conflict-resolution method by companies in collectivist countries because it reduces animosity and preserves the business relationship.

Multiparty business disputes

Multiple parties can participate in mediation and work out an agreement that is acceptable to all sides. When there are three or five or ten disputing firms from diverse countries, the mediator has to try to *build consensus* among the parties by holding joint discussions as well as private conversations with each party. Ideas and suggestions gained from this shuttle diplomacy may help the mediator develop a settlement framework that is acceptable to all disputants (Kovach, 2005). Sometimes the negotiator will draw up a detailed draft agreement for all parties to approve.

A skilled mediator can help bring about an agreement by privately asking each negotiating party whether it would accept a particular package if the other parties would also accept the package. If each agrees to accept the package if the other parties will do so, the mediator will usually assemble all the parties and ask them to sign an agreement which incorporates the agreed package.

On the other hand, an incompetent mediator can easily exacerbate the conflict between the parties and put an agreement beyond their reach. The mediator might, for instance, share information which has been given in confidence by one party with the other party or parties, thereby losing trust and damaging the prospects of a negotiated settlement being reached.

KEY POINTS

1. The speed and sophistication of international business transactions does not tolerate dispute resolution through long, drawn-out formal procedures developed by and for the convenience of the legal and accounting professions. Quicker, more informal methods are usually needed to resolve

disputes. Sometimes conflict can be resolved and deadlock avoided by one of the parties making a small concession to demonstrate good will.

2. Some conflicts are too complex or too deep rooted to be resolved in their entirety during a negotiation. Such conflicts can sometimes be resolved incrementally. Lowi & Rothman's (1993) 3-phase model is an example of an incremental approach to conflict resolution, consisting of an adversarial phase, a reflexive phase and an integrative phase. The reflexive phase unfreezes negotiators from their adversarial feelings and helps them to move towards a more positive and cooperative approach to the other side.

3. Negotiators from "extremity" cultures are more likely than those from "moderate" cultures to become involved in conflict situations. In extremity cultures, both strong agreements and strong disagreements occur in many social situations, including negotiations. Within subcultural groups in extremity cultures, strong agreements are expressed towards favoured viewpoints, but equally strong antipathies or hostility are expressed towards opposing viewpoints. Many countries in the Middle East and Latin America have been identified as extremity cultures.

4. The formal dispute-resolution remedies of litigation, arbitration and mediation are available to firms which become locked in post-contractual disputes. Litigation tends to be expensive and lengthy, and many firms prefer to settle out of court rather than go to trial. In arbitration, an arbitrator gives both sides an equal opportunity to present their arguments, but in the end it is the arbitrator who decides the outcome. The goal of mediation is for a neutral third party to help disputants come to an agreement on their own.

5. The method preferred by most MNEs to resolve international business disputes is *administered arbitration* under the auspices of an established arbitration institution. Advantages of the method include convenience, reputation of the arbitration institution, familiarity with the proceedings, and prior understanding of the costs and fees involved. However, a mechanism to reduce arbitration costs is needed. MNEs also point to the lack of an appeals procedure for arbitral awards.

6. The possibility of facing the opponent in a court in the opponent's own country is a strong incentive to avoid litigation as a way of resolving disputes in international business, especially since many courts are biased in favour of local firms. Preparation for litigation information is needed, and information can be expensive to acquire. Heavy costs are also incurred in paying lawyers' and court fees.

7. When an international company wishes to resolve a serious dispute with a foreign government, commercial considerations are the company's main concern, but they are not necessarily the government's main concern. In dispute-resolution negotiations, a government's actions and decisions are more likely to be influenced by policy issues, political goals or even by conditions laid down by international lending institutions such as the World Bank or the IMF.

8. Principled negotiation requires each partner to think of the other side as a negotiating partner, not a negotiating opponent, and to make an effort to understand the other party's interests. This important first step makes it possible for the parties to seek solutions to the conflict that maximise joint gain. A principled negotiation approach depends on each side's developing a realistic mental model of the other side's goals, interests and strategies.

9. Expressions of anger in a negotiation may make negotiators fear that their outcomes will be reduced, leading them to make unnecessary concessions aimed at satisfying the angry party's needs. Anger can trigger a reciprocal response and cause an escalation of the conflict. Negotiators experiencing fear in negotiations may become less effective negotiators, becoming risk averse and more likely to avoid conflict by making higher offers as a way of appeasing the other party.

10. Conflict can have a positive effect on negotiations. For instance, it can energise the discussion and lead to higher-quality options and solutions being produced. In international business negotiations, different types of conflict are associated with different types of negotiation strategies. Conflict can be managed crudely through a strategy of domination, leading to victory for the dominating party. Compromise strategies, on the other hand, involve mutual give and take in which each party loses something in the interests of reaching an agreement.

11. In multiparty business disputes, a mediator will often try to build consensus among the parties in order to resolve the dispute. Mediators promote consensus building by holding private conversations and then joint discussions with all disputants. Ideas and suggestions gained from this kind of shuttle diplomacy help the mediator develop a settlement framework that is acceptable to all parties.

QUESTIONS FOR DISCUSSION AND WRITTEN ASSIGNMENTS

1. A serious post-contractual dispute has arisen between a foreign mining company and the host government. Assess the main options that are open to each side to resolve the conflict.

2. a) Arbitration is the dispute-resolution method preferred by most MNEs. Explain why.
   b) Under what circumstances would arbitration be a better way than litigation of resolving a long-standing dispute between a Western-based manufacturer of women's fashion accessories and a retailer in Japan.

3. The three partners of an IJV, located in the Asian country of one of the partners, are locked in a profit-distribution dispute that repeated negotiations between the partners have failed to resolve. They are beginning to think about formal dispute-resolution methods. In this context, what are the options? What are the advantages and disadvantages of each option?

4. Two international alliance partners agree that the partnership should be dissolved, but strongly disagree about the best way to dissolve it. The parties have exhausted their attempts to negotiate a resolution on their own. They are ready for outside help. What advice might an external third party give them?

BIBLIOGRAPHY

Bardi, A. & Goodwin, R. The dual route to value change: individual processes and cultural moderators. *Journal of Cross-Cultural Psychology*, 42 (2), 2011, 271–287.

Baxter, I. F. International business disputes. *International and Comparative Law Quarterly*, 39 (2), 1990, 288–299.

Bazerman, M. H., Curhan, J. R., Moore, D. A. & K. L. Valley. Negotiation. *Annual Review of Psychology*, 51 (1), 2000, 279–314.

Benish-Weisman, M. Between trauma and redemption: story form differences in immigrant narratives of successful and nonsuccessful immigration. *Journal of Cross-cultural Psychology*, 40 (6), 2009, 953–968.

Bowen, A. A. The power of mediation to resolve international commercial disputes and repair business relationships. *Dispute Resolution Journal*, 60, 2005, 58–65.

Brett, J. M. & Crotty, S. Culture and negotiation. In P. B. Smith, M. F. Peterson & D. C. Thomas (eds) *The Handbook of Cross-cultural Management Research*. Sage, 2008, 269–283.

Brett, J. F., Northcraft, G. B. & Pinkley, R. L. Stairways to heaven: an interlocking self-regulation model of negotiation. *Academy of Management Review*, 24 (3), 1999, 435–451.

Business China. No dispute about it. 24 April 2006, 2–4.

Cameron, D. *Good to Talk: Living and Working in a Communication Culture*. Sage, 2000.

Cheit, R. & Gersen, J. When businesses sue each other: an empirical study of state court litigation. *Law and Social Inquiry*, 25, 2000, 798–816.

Chen, G. O. H. *Negotiating with the Chinese*. Dartmouth, 1996.

Dominguez-Urban, I. The messenger as the medium of communication: the use of interpreters in mediation. *Journal of Dispute Resolution*, 1, 1997, 1–281.

Faure, G. O. Negotiations to set up joint ventures in China. *International Negotiation*, 5, 2000, 157–189.

Fisher, R., Ury, W. & Patton, B. *Getting To Yes: Negotiating Agreement without Giving In*. Penguin Books, 2nd ed., 1991.

Ghauri, P. Introduction. In Ghauri, P. N. & J. Usunier (eds) *International Business Negotiations*. Pergamon, 1996, 3–20.

Harinck, F., De Dreu, C. K. W. & Van Vianen, A. E. M. The impact of conflict issues on fixed-pie perceptions, problem solving, and integrative outcomes in negotiation. *Organizational Behaviour and Human Decision Processes*, 81 (2), 2000, 329–358.

Hofstede, G. & Usunier, J. C. (1996). Hofstede's dimensions of culture and their influence on international business negotiations. In P. N. Ghauri, P. N. & J. C. Usunier (eds) *International Business Negotiations*. Pergamon, 119–129.

Khakhar, P. & Rammal, H. G. Culture and business networks: international business negotiations with Arab managers. *International Business Review*, 22, 2013, 578–590.

Kovach, K. K. *The Handbook of Dispute Resolution*. Jossey-Bass, 2005.

Lerner, J. S. & Keltner, D. Fear, anger and risk. *Journal of Personality and Social Psychology*, 81, 2001, 146–159.

Leung, K. Some determinants of conflict avoidance. *Journal of Cross-cultural Psychology*, 19, 1988, 125–136.

Lewin, K. *Resolving Social Conflicts*, Oxford: Harper & Row, 1948.

Long, A. Dispute resolution in international trade. *International Trade Journal*, 8 (3), 1994, 367–387.

Lowi, M. & Rothman, J. Arabs and Israelis: the Jordan River. In G. O. Faure & J. Z. Rubin (eds) *Culture and Negotiation: The Resolution of Water Disputes*. SAGE, 1993.

Lumineau, F. & Malhotra, D. Trust and collaboration in the aftermath of conflict: the effects of contract structure. *Academy of Management Journal*, 54 (5), 2011, 981–998.

Osgood, C. E. Reciprocal initiative. In J. Roosevelt (ed.) *The Liberal Papers*. Anchor, 1962.

PricewaterhouseCoopers. *International Arbitration: Corporate Attitudes and Practices*, 2006.

Pelled, L. H. et al. Exploring the black box: an analysis of work group diversity, conflict and performance. *Administrative Science Quarterly*, 44, 1999, 1–28.

Pruitt, D. G. & Carnevale, P. J. *Negotiation in Social Conflict*. Brooks/Cole Publishing, 1993.

Salacuse, J. W. Making deals in strange places. In J. W. Breslin & J. X. Z. Rubin (eds) *Negotiation Theory and Practice: Programme on Negotiation*. Harvard Law School, 1999, 251–259.

Sander, F. E. A. & Rozdeiczer, L. Dispute resolution handled by outside parties. In M. Moffitt & R. Bordone (eds) *Handbook of Dispute Resolution*. Jossey-Bass, 2005.

Smith, P. B. Communication styles as dimensions of national culture. *Journal of Cross-cultural Psychology*, 42 (2), 2011, 216–233.

Tao, J. & Hillier, E. A tale of two companies. *China Business Review*, May–June 2008, 44–47.

Thomas, K. W. Conflict and conflict management. In Dunnette, M. (ed.) *Handbook of Industrial and Organizational Psychology*. Rand McNally, 1976, 889–935.

Ting-Toomey, S. & Kurogi, A. Facework competence in intercultural conflict. *International Journal of Intercultural Relations*, 22, 1998, 187–225.

Tinsley, C. Models of conflict resolution in Japanese, German, and American cultures. *Journal of Applied Psychology*, 83 (6), 1998, 316–323.

Tractenberg, C. International arbitration – what's in it for your franchise? *Franchising World*, February 2012, 73–76.

Wilkenfeld, J., Young, K., Asal, V. & Quinn, D. Mediating international crises: cross-national and experimental perspectives. *Journal of Conflict Resolution*, 47 (3), 2003, 279–301.

Williams, A. Resolving conflict in a multicultural environment. *MCS Conciliation Quarterly*, 1994, 2–6.

Bibliography – Books for further study

Brett, J. M. *Negotiating Globally*. Jossey-Bass, 2001.

Cellich, C. & Jain, S. *Practical Solutions to Global Business Negotiations*. Business Expert Press, 2012.

Earley C. & Ang S. *Cultural Intelligence: Individual Interactions across Cultures*. Stanford University Press, 2003.

Ghauri, P. & Usunier, J-C. (eds) *International Business Negotiations*. Pergamon, 2nd ed., 2003.

Graham, J. & Requejo, W. H. *Global Negotiation: The New Rules*. Palgrave Macmillan, 2008.

Kremenyuk, V. *International Negotiation: Analysis, Approaches*. Jossey-Bass, 2nd ed., 2002.

Lewicki, R. L., Saunders, D. M. & Barry, B. *Negotiation*. 6th ed., McGraw-Hill, 2009.

Maude, B. *Managing Cross-cultural Communication*. Palgrave Macmillan, 2011.

Salacuse, J. *The Global Negotiator*. Palgrave Macmillan, 2003.

Saner, R. *The Expert Negotiator*. Martinus Nijhoff Publishers, 3rd ed., 2008.

Solomon, R. H. & Quinney, N. *American Negotiating Behaviour: Wheeler-dealers, Legal Eagles, Bullies and Preachers*. US Institute of Peace Press, 2010.

Thomas, D. C. *Cross-cultural Management: Cross-cultural Concepts*. Sage, 2nd ed., 2008.

Zweifel, T. D. *Culture Clash: Managing the Global High-performance Team*. Swiss Consulting Group, 2003.

SEMINAL WORKS FOR BACKGROUND READING

Bazerman, M. H. & Lewicki, R. J. *Negotiating in Organisations.* Sage, 1983.

Fisher, R. & Ury, W. *Getting to Yes.* Penguin Books, 1983.

Lax, D. A. & Sebenius, J. K. *The Manager as Negotiator: Bargaining for Cooperation and Competitive Gain.* Free Press, 1986.

Raiffa, H. *The Art and Science of Negotiation.* Harvard University Press, 1982.

Zartman, I. W. *The Negotiation Process: Theories and Applications.* Sage, 1978

Index